The Feature Structure
of Functional Categories

OXFORD STUDIES IN COMPARATIVE SYNTAX
Richard Kayne, General Editor

The Feature Structure
of Functional Categories

A Comparative Study
of Arabic Dialects

ELABBAS BENMAMOUN

NEW YORK   OXFORD
OXFORD UNIVERSITY PRESS
2000

For Liang-Wei and Zachary

Oxford University Press

Oxford   New York
Athens   Auckland   Bangkok   Bogotá   Buenos Aires   Calcutta
Cape Town   Chennai   Dar es Salaam   Delhi   Florence   Hong Kong   Istanbul
Karachi   Kuala Lumpur   Madrid   Melbourne   Mexico City   Mumbai
Nairobi   Paris   São Paulo   Singapore   Taipei   Tokyo   Toronto   Warsaw

and associated companies in
Berlin   Ibadan

Copyright © 2000 by Elabbas Benmamoun

Published by Oxford University Press, Inc.
198 Madison Avenue, New York, New York 10016

Oxford is a registered trademark of Oxford University Press

All rights reserved. No part of this publication may be reproduced,
stored in a retrieval system, or transmitted, in any form or by any means,
electronic, mechanical, photocopying, recording, or otherwise,
without the prior permission of Oxford University Press.

Library of Congress Cataloging-in-Publication Data
Benmamoun, Elabbas.
The feature structure of functional categories :
a comparative study of Arabic dialects / Elabbas Benmamoun.
p.   cm. — (Oxford studies in comparative syntax)
Includes bibliographical references and index.
ISBN 0-19-511994-0; ISBN 0-19-511995-9 (pbk.)
1. Arabic language—Dialects—Syntax.   2. Minimalist theory
(Linguistics)   I. Title.   II. Series.
PJ6723.B36 1999
492.7'7—dc21   98-52404

1 3 5 7 9 8 6 4 2

Printed in the United States of America
on acid-free paper

Acknowledgments

The ideas in this book developed over the last few years. I have greatly benefited from presentations of parts of this work at various places. In particular, I am grateful to the students and colleagues at the University of Illinois and audiences at the University Mohammed Ben Abdellah in Fes, the University of Oxford, the University of Paris X, the School of Oriental and African Studies, UCLA, USC, and the University of York. I owe special thanks to David Adger, Joseph Aoun, Hagit Borer, Edit Doron, Mushira Eid, Moha Ennaji, Jacqueline Gueron, Richard Kayne, Ruth Kempson, Shalom Lappin, Mohammad Mohammad, Jamal Ouhalla, David Pesetsky, Francisco Ordóñez, Fatima Sadiqi, Jean-Roger Vergnaud, James Yoon, and Maria-Luisa Zubizarreta. I also wish to thank Steve Peter for his invaluable help in preparing the manuscipt for publication. Thanks are also due to Mustafa Mughazy and Mouna Sari for their help with the index. I would also like to express my appreciation to Cynthia L. Garver and Peter Ohlin of Oxford University Press for their support and patience throughout the editing and production process.

Contents

Abbreviations

Acc	Accusative		Q	Question morpheme
Agr	Agreement		S	Singular
Adv	Adverb		Spec	Specifier
A(dj)	Adjective		Subj	Subjunctive
Asp	Aspect		SVO	Subject verb object
AspP	Aspectual phrase		T	Tense
C	Complementizer		TP	Tense phrase
CP	Complementizer Phrase		V	Verb
CS	Construct State		VSO	Verb subject object
D	Dual		1	First person
DP	Determiner Phrase		2	Second person
EPP	Extended Projection Principle		3	Third person
F	Feminine			
Fut	Future		**Languages**	
Gen	Genitive		EA	Egyptian Arabic
Hab	Habitual		MA	Moroccan Arabic
Imp	Imperative		SA	Standard Arabic
Ind	Indicative		SanA	Sanʕaanii Arabic
Indef	Indefinite			
LF	Logical Form		**Phonetic Transcription**	
Loc	Locative		ð	Voiced interdental fricative
M	Masculine		š̌	Voiceless palatal fricative
N	Noun		ž̌	Voiced palatal fricative
Neg	Negation		x	Voiceless velar fricative
Nom	Nominative		ħ	Voiceless pharyngeal fricative
Num	Number			
O	Object		ɣ	Voiced velar fricative
NPI	Negative polarity item		q	Voiceless uvular stop
P	Plural		ʕ	Voiced pharyngeal fricative
Part	Participle			
Pass	Passive		ʔ	Glottal stop
PF	Phonetic form		ə	Schwa
PRED	Predicate			
Prog	Progressive			

Letters with a dot underneath represent pharyngalized (emphatic) consonants.

The Feature Structure
of Functional Categories

1

Comparative Arabic Syntax

This chapter introduces key empirical issues that arise in the context of tense, negation, and agreement in Arabic dialects (Moroccan Arabic, MA; Standard Arabic, SA; Egyptian Arabic, EA) and their theoretical implications for current conceptions of the syntax of functional categories. In section 1.1, I lay out the main empirical generalizations that any analysis, regardless of its theoretical assumptions, must deal with. In section 1.2, I discuss the theoretical issues that arise within the minimalist framework as we try to deal with these empirical generalizations.

1.1 Main Empirical Generalizations

1.1.1 The Syntax of Tense in Arabic

Previous analyses of verbless sentences in Arabic have focused exclusively on one single issue—namely, the absence of an overt verbal copula in the present tense (1a) and its obligatory presence in the past tense (1b).[1]

(1) a. Omar muʕəllim   MA
       Omar teacher
       'Omar is a teacher.'

    b. Omar kan   muʕəllim
       Omar be.past.3ms teacher
       'Omar was a teacher.'

Thus, when verbless sentences are contrasted with sentences in the past tense, two types of analyses have been suggested. Under one analysis, the difference between (1a) and (1b) has to do with the presence of an overt copula in the past tense and a null copula in the present tense. This amounts to saying that both sentences contain a VP. Under another analysis, the difference between (1a) and (1b) is that verbless sentences are small clauses with no functional projection or a VP (verb phrase) projection that contains tense, while past tense sentences contain a functional projection specified for tense.

What is significant about the previous analyses is that the contrast between verbless sentences and sentences with verbal copulas is not attributed to any fundamental difference between the present and past tenses. In this book, I argue that to understand the syntax of verbless sentences we must understand the Arabic tense system and particularly the differences between the present and past tenses. In fact, when we look closely at the Arabic tense system we find systematic differences between present tense sentences with verbal predicates and their past tense counterparts. The relevant generalizations are given in (2) and (3).

(2)   In the present tense, the verb:

    a.   may not merge with negation (4a)[2]

    b.   prefers (for some speakers) to follow the subject in sentences (4b) and idioms (4c)

    c.   has person agreement as a prefix (4d)

    d.   can co-occur with the morphological independent negative *laysa* in Standard Arabic (4e).

(3)   In the past tense, the verb:

    a.   must merge with negation (5a)

    b.   prefers (for some speakers) to precede the subject in sentences (5b) and idioms (5c)

    c.   has person agreement as a suffix (5d)

    d.   cannot co-occur with the morphological independent negative *laysa* in Standard Arabic (5e).

(4)   a.   miš bi-yi-ktib   EA
       neg asp-3m-write
       'He isn't writing.'

    b.   lə-wlad   ta-y-ləʕb-u   MA
       the-children asp-3m-play-p
       'The children are playing.'

    c.   llah y-barik   fii-k
       God 3m-bless in-you
       'May God bless you.'

    d.   ta-ktub-u   SA
       2-write-ind
       'You write or you are writing.'

    e.   laysa   ṭ-ṭaalibu   ya-ktubu
       neg.3ms the-student 3m-write-ind
       'The student does not write.'

(5)   a.   Omar ma-katab-š   ig-gawaab   EA
       Omar neg-write.past.3ms-neg the-letter
       'Omar didn't write the letter.'

    b.   nəʕs-u   l-wlad   MA
       sleep.past-p the-children
       'The children slept.'

   c.   barak   llahu fii-k
        bless.past.3ms God in-you
        'May God bless you.'

   d.   ʔanta katab-ta   SA
        you   write.past-2ms
        'You wrote.'

   e. * laysa   ṭ-ṭaalibu   kataba
        neg.3ms the-student write.past.3ms

The differences between the present tense and past tense noted above go beyond the distribution of the verbal copula, which has so far been the focus of most analyses. What the generalizations in (2) and (3) show is that there are systematic syntactic differences between the present tense and past tense even in sentences with verbal predicates. Therefore, I will contend that the key to understanding verbless sentences resides in an analysis of the nature of the syntax of the various tenses in Arabic.

From the generalizations in (2) and (3) it is clear that tense determines the syntax of verbs. The task, then, is to uncover the reasons that the different tenses interact differently with verbs. With respect to the contrast between the present and past tense, I argue that the generalizations in (2) and (3) can all be accounted for if the verbs are in different positions. In the present tense the verb is in a position lower than the position of negation, while in the past tense it is in a position higher than negation. I will propose that the same feature that forces the presence of the verbal copula in the past tense forces the verb to be in a position higher than negation. The question then is: what feature of the past tense forces the verb to be in a position higher than negation?

Let us assume with most current theories of functional categories that tense and negation occupy different projections, with the tense projection dominating the negative projection.

(6)   TP
            ⟋‾‾⟍
      T   NegP
          ⟋‾‾⟍
     Neg   VP
               |
               V

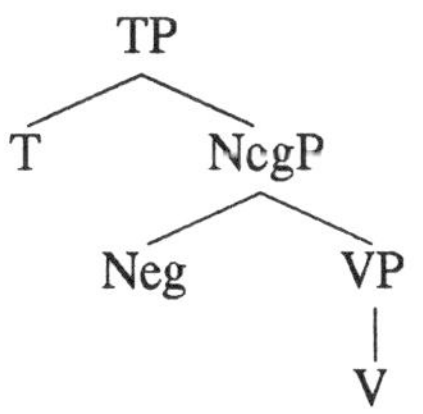

Suppose further that the past tense must be paired with a verbal element (to be made precise in the following discussion). Given this assumption, we can explain why it requires the presence of the verbal copula and why it displays the generalizations in (3). The verbal copula is present so that it can be paired with the past tense. The generalizations in (3) follow as consequences of this pairing, as will be shown.

Turning to verbless sentences (1a) and the generalizations in (2), I argue that the feature that requires pairing with a verbal element is absent in the present tense (1a). This explains why the verb stays lower than negation and why the verbal copula is absent.

Our investigation of the syntax of tense in Arabic thus must start with an in-depth analysis of its morphology. This topic is taken up in chapter 2, which specifically deals with the question of whether the two verbal paradigms, the perfective (7a) and imperfective (7b), carry tense information and, if they do, how that tense information is expressed.

(7)   a.   katab-tu   SA
          write.past-1s
          'I wrote.'

      b.   ʔa-ktub-u
          1s-write-ind
          'I write or I am writing.'

With respect to the perfective on the one hand, the answer is positive. I will show that it carries past tense information. However, contra the prevalent view in the literature that tense (or aspect) is an autosegmental feature, I will propose that it is an abstract tense feature. The autosegmental vocalic features carry voice only. With respect to the imperfective, on the other hand, I will show that it does not carry any tense information, particularly the present tense. This implies that the present tense is not instantiated on any lexical head in Arabic. Building on these conclusions, in chapter 3, I discuss in detail the feature structure of the elements in tense, particularly the present and past tense (as well as the future and imperative). I will argue that the present tense lacks the feature that forces it to be paired with a verbal element, while the past tense (and future and imperative) is specified for this feature. In chapter 4, I will build on this conclusion to derive the generalizations in (2) and (3).

1.1.2   The Syntax of Sentential Negation in Arabic

The second part of the book takes up similar issues that arise in the context of sentential negation. Most recent analyses assume that negation interacts with lexical heads and maximal projections (XPs) in two ways. With respect to lexical heads, negation may block the merger of tense and the verb (8), an analysis that has its origins in Chomsky (1957).

(8)   a. * John ate not
      b. * John not ate

With respect to XPs, negation may interact with phrases by licensing them. This is the case of Negative Polarity Items (NPIs) and negative quantifiers.

(9)   ma-šəf-t   ħətta wafiəd   MA
      neg-see.past-1s any   one
      'I didn't see anyone.'

However, another facet of the syntax of sentential negation that has been ignored is its interaction with nominal elements even when they are not NPIs or negative quantifiers. This interaction is evident in the modern Arabic dialects and Standard Arabic. In both, sentential negation can either merge with a verb that carries verb subject agreement (10a) or a pronominal subject (10b) or carry subject agreement (10c).

(10) a. ma-ktab-š   MA
          neg-write.past.3ms-neg
          'He didn't write.'

      b. ma-nii-š   EA
          neg-I-neg
          'I am not.'

      c. lays-at ṭ-ṭaalibat-u   mariiḍatan   SA
          neg-3fs the-student-nom sick
          'The student is not sick.'

Thus, any account of sentential negation must also deal with the relation between negation and the subject. I will argue that, on a par with tense, negation has a feature that requires that it be paired with a nominal element. This pairing could be achieved by merging with a head that carries a nominal element such as agreement (10a) or an inherently nominal element (10b) or entering into specifier head (Spec-head) relation with an inherently nominal element (10c).

In addition to accounting for these facts, allowing negation to interact with nominal elements will open up the possibility to account for long-standing but still unresolved problems about the inventory of sentential negatives and their distribution in Arabic. In many dialects, such as Moroccan Arabic, sentential negation can be expressed as a single complex form, *ma-ši* (11a) or as a discontinuous element, *ma-X-š* (11b). In Standard Arabic, the negative *laa* (12a) has three variants: two variants that inflect for tense but no agreement (12b, c) and one variant that inflects for agreement but no tense (12d).

(11) a. Omar ma-ši   mṛid   MA
          Omar neg-neg sick
          'Omar is not sick'

      b. Omar ma-ktəb-š   lə-bra
          Omar neg-write.past.3ms-neg the-letter
          'Omar did not write the letter.'

(12) a. **laa** ya-drus-uu-n   SA
          neg 3m-study-mp-ind
          'They do not study.'

      b. **lam**   ya-ðhab-uu
          neg.past 3m-go-mp
          'They did not go.'

      c. **lan**   ya-ðhab-uu
          neg.fut 3m-go-mp
          'They will not go.'

   d. laysa   ya-ktubu š-šiʕr
       neg.3ms 3m-write the-poetry
       'He does not write poetry.'

In addition, the negatives that do not inflect for agreement (*laa*, *lam*, *lan*) must be adjacent to the verb (13a), as shown by the fact that the subject cannot intervene between them, while the one that inflects for agreement does not have to be adjacent to the verb (13b).

(13) a. ***lam**   ṭ-ṭaalibu   ya-ðhab
           neg.past the-student 3m-go

      b. laysa   ṭ-ṭaalib-u   ya-ktubu š-šiʕr
           neg.3ms the-student-nom 3m-write the-poetry
           'The student does not write poetry.'

I will argue that in both the modern Arabic dialects (chapter 5) and Standard Arabic (chapter 6) there is one single negative, which must be paired with a nominal element in two ways. On the one hand, if it is paired with a head (carrying subject agreement), we get the discontinuous form in the modern dialects and the forms that lack agreement and must be adjacent to the verb in Standard Arabic. On the other hand, if it is paired with the subject we get the nondiscontinuous form in the modern dialects and the negative that inflects for agreement and does not have to be adjacent to the verb in Standard Arabic. The two different realizations interact in crucial ways with predicates, as will be discussed in greater detail. To the extent that this analysis is correct, it brings us closer to a unified analysis of tense and negation as two functional categories whose interaction with lexical heads and XPs is to a large degree driven by their requirements to be paired with nominal and verbal elements.

Finally, the theory that sentential negation must be paired with a nominal element will help provide an analysis for a yet unaccounted for generalization about imperatives in Arabic.

(14) An imperative verb must carry person agreement in negative imperatives but not in positive imperatives.

As is well known, in many languages there is a morphological asymmetry between positive imperatives and negative imperatives. In Arabic, the asymmetry consists of the absence of person agreement in the former (15) and its obligatory presence in the latter (16).

(15) ktəb   kətb-i   kətb-u   MA
      write.ms   write.fs   write-p
      'Write.'   'Write.'   'Write.'

(16) ma-tə-ktəb-š   ma-t-kətb-i-š   ma-t-kətb-u-š   MA
      neg-2-write.ms-neg neg-2-write.fs-neg neg-2-write-p-neg
      'Do not write.'   'Do not write.'   'Do not write.'

I will argue in chapter 7 that as a nominal element the person feature is obligatory in negative imperatives due to the requirement that sentential negation be paired with a nominal element.

1.1.3 Agreement Asymmetries

The last functional category I will explore is agreement. The focus of the last two chapters, which make up part III of the book, will be on two types of agreement asymmetries. The first well-known agreement asymmetry obtains in the context of the subject verb object (SVO) and verb subject object (VSO) orders in Standard Arabic. The asymmetry concerns the fact that number agreement is realized by an affix only in the SVO orders (18a).

(17) a. ʔakal-**at**   ṭ-ṭaalibaat-u   SA
            eat.past-3fs the-students.fp-nom
            'The students ate.'

      b. * ʔakal-**na**   ṭ-ṭaalibaat-u
            eat.past-3fp the-student.fp-nom

(18) a. ṭ-ṭaalibaat-u   ʔakal-**na**
            the-student.fp-nom eat.past-3fp
            'The student ate.'

      b. * ṭ-ṭaalibaat-u   ʔakal-**at**
            the-student.fp-nom eat.past-3fs

In addition, when the subject is null (such as a Wh-gap [19] or null subject[3] [20]) number agreement is obligatory.

(19) a. žaaʔa   l-ʔawlaadu llaðiina nažafi-**uu**
            come.past.3ms the children that   pass.past .3mp
            'The children who passed came.'

      b. * žaaʔa   l-ʔawlaadu llaðiina nažafia
            come.past.3ms the-children that   pass.past.3ms
            'The children who passed came.'

(20) a. kun-**na**   ya-ʔkul-**na**   SA
            be.past-3fp 3-seat-fp
            'They were eating.'

      b. * kaan-**at**   ya-ʔkul-**na**
            be.past-3fs 3-eat.fp

Taking all these facts together the main generalization about the distribution of number agreement is given in (21).

(21)   Number agreement must be realized by an affix on the verb if the latter is not
       followed by an overt lexical subject.

Interestingly, in the modern dialects such as Moroccan Arabic, this agreement asymmetry does not arise.

(22)   a.   kla-w   lə-wlad   MA
            eat.past-3p the-children
            'The children ate.'

       b.   lə-wlad   kla-w
            the-children eat.past-3p

       c. * kla   lə-wlad
            eat.past.3s the-children
            'The children ate.'

    The second agreement asymmetry arises in the context of NPs. When an NP
occurs by itself (23a) or in the so-called free state (23b), it must carry the (in)definite
marker.

(23)   a.   l-wəld
            the-boy
            'the boy'

       b.   lə-ktab   dyal l-wəld
            the-book of   the-boy
            'the boy's book'

However, if the NP occurs in the so-called Construct State only the last rightmost
member can carry the (in)definite marker.

(24)   a.   ktab l-wəld   MA
            book the-boy
            'the boy's book'

       b. * l-ktab l-wəld
            book   the-boy
            'the boy's book'

That the second member of the CS in (24a) is definite is evident from the fact that
adjectives, which must agree in the definiteness with the nouns they modify (25a), must
do so in the CS as well (25b).

(25)   a.   lə-ktab   ž-ždid[4]
            the-book the-new

       b.   ktab l-wəld ž-ždid
            book the-boy the-new
            'the boy's new book'

Following Borer (1988) and Siloni (1997) that (in)definiteness is an agreement feature (given that it is part of the agreement relation that involves nouns and adjectives), the generalization in (26) summarizes the distribution of the (in)definiteness feature.

(26)   The (in)definiteness feature must be realized by an affix on the noun when the noun is not in Construct with a genitive NP.

The generalization in (26) seems to parallel the generalization in (21). The (in)definiteness agreement asymmetry that arises in the context of NPs is similar to the agreement asymmetry that arises in the context of the VSO order in Standard Arabic.

Previous accounts for the generalizations in (21) and (26) share two fundamental assumptions. First, they consider the two asymmetries as different phenomena that should be handled by different mechanisms. Second, they treat the two asymmetries as syntactic in nature. That is, the absence of number agreement and the marker of (in)definiteness are due to some syntactic properties that obtain exclusively in the context of the VSO order and the CS.

I will propose a unified account that explains the two generalizations in morphological terms. I will argue that the asymmetries are not due to syntactic factors but to how agreement features are spelled-out in the morphology. In the VSO order and CS, merger between the verb and the subject, on one hand, and between the members of the CS, on the other, is one mechanism that the morphological component uses to spell-out agreement features. The merger of the verb and the subject amounts to spelling-out the number feature, making the presence of the number affix redundant. Similarly, the merger of the members of the CS (Borer 1988, 1996) effectively enables the rightmost member to spell-out the (in)-definiteness feature of the preceding member, thus making the (in)definiteness marker redundant. In short, in VSO and CS affixes and NPs are in a paradigmatic relation.

Several arguments will be given to show that this merger is neither lexical nor syntactic. Rather, it will be suggested that this merger takes place in the component where morphosyntactic features are spelled out. The main conclusion of the two chapters that make up this part is that the syntactic component does not need to be enriched (with diacritics features) or devices (such as overt vs. covert agreement checking) to account for the agreement asymmetries in question. The postsyntactic morphological component that spells out the morphosyntactic features of the phrase marker has at its disposal various ways to accomplish that task. In addition to affixation and feature percolation, merger is another option. Therefore, in the syntax the verb in both the VSO and SVO order and the head noun in both the CS and the free state are specified for all the features that may be spelled-out differently depending on the mechanisms available within the morphology of the individual language.

1.2   Theoretical Assumptions and Implications

Having presented the main empirical generalizations that obtain in the context of tense, negation, and agreement in Arabic that any analysis must contend with, I now turn to the theoretical issues that arise in this context. I will start with a brief survey of the current views regarding functional categories and then discuss the modifications that are necessary to account for the empirical problems briefly introduced here.

1.2.1   The Syntax of Functional Categories

Recently, functional categories have figured prominently in syntactic debates (see in particular Pollock 1989; Ouhalla 1990; and Cinque 1999). The interaction between these categories and lexical categories has been invoked to account for empirical generalizations about word order, unbounded dependencies, polarity relations, case, agreement, among others. One particular aspect of the syntax of functional categories that is directly relevant to this book concerns the features that drive the displacement of heads, particularly verbs, and maximal projections, particularly NPs.

The idea that functional categories such as tense, agreement, and negation head functional projections that conform to the basic X′-schema (Spec, head and complement) has allowed Pollock (1989) to account for Emonds's (1978) original insight that word order differences between English and French in the distribution of their verbal heads, negation, quantifiers, and adverbs can be dealt with in terms of absence or presence of overt verb movement.

(27) a.   John embrasse souvent Marie
           John kisses   often   Mary
           'John often kisses Mary.'

      b. * John kisses often Mary

(28) a.   John n'aime   pas Marie
           John neg loves neg Mary
           'John does not love Mary.'

      b. * John loves not Mary

(29) a.   Mes amis   aiment tous Marie
           my friends love   all Mary
           'All my friends love Mary.'

      b. * My friends love all Mary

(30) French: NP T+V (Neg, Q, Adv) NP
      English: NP T (Neg, Q, Adv) V NP

Pollock's analysis relied on one crucial assumption—namely, that inflectional categories are generated separately from their host. How languages combine the inflections with their lexical hosts is expected to account for language variation. If a language, such as French, resorts to overt verb raising to the inflection, we get the order where the adverb, negation, and the quantifier occur between the verb and the direct object. If a language has lowering, we get the order where these elements should not intervene between the verb and the direct object. Ignoring other irrelevant details, the main point is that language variation has to do with the choice of options available for bringing together the bare verb and its inflection (lowering or raising).

However, one immediate problem that arose was that lowering rules leave unbounded traces. The problem is inevitable because of the assumption that the relation between the inflectional head and the lexical head is a morpho-phonological one, the lexical head provides support to the inflectional head. The lexical head enters the derivation as a bare stem, and the inflectional head enters the derivation as a bound morpheme (sometimes with no phonological matrix). The job of head movement or lowering rules is to provide a host for the phonologically dependent inflectional head. Given this view of the relation between functional categories and the lexical host, the options are quite limited. In particular, one cannot opt for an abstract covert movement to get around the problems of lowering rules. The reason is that notions such as bound and free are not relevant to covert syntax (Logical Form). These are morphological notions that are relevant to the overt part of the grammar that directly interacts with the articulatory perceptual interface.

To resolve this problem, Chomsky (1995) suggested that the tense morpheme may be lexically generated on the verb, thus removing word formation, in the sense of merging elements that make up words, from the domain of syntax. In this respect, this was a strong lexicalist position. However, there is still an abstract projection headed by tense that triggers verb movement (and NP movement), albeit for different reasons.

Thus, verb movement to the abstract Tense Phrase (TP) is no longer a word formation process that combines a bare stem and a morpheme. TP, as a functional category, is specified for some features that attract verbs and NPs (subjects). These features are [+D] and [+V]: [+D] expresses the generalization that tense interacts with the subject (Extended Projection Principle [EPP]), and [+V] expresses the generalization that tense merges with verbs in most languages.[5]

The difference between functional categories and lexical categories is that categorial features on the former must be eliminated by being checked by the categorial features of the latter, particularly nouns and verbs. This is probably due to the assumption that the categorial features [+V] and [+N] on lexical categories are interpretable, while those on functional categories are non-intrepretable. The job of the checking operation, then, is to eliminate the noninterpretable categorial features. In French the [+V] feature of tense is eliminated overtly, while in English it is eliminated overtly in the context of auxiliary verbs and covertly in the context of lexical verbs.

One diagnostic in English for the presence of these features is Do-support and NP movement. Do-support is an indicator of the [+V] feature of tense, and the raising of the subject from the Spec of VP to the Spec of TP is an indicator of its [+D] feature. Do-support applies in the past tense, present tense, and imperatives (among other context).

(31) a.   Mary does not like Bill.

      b.   Mary did not like Bill.

      c.   Do not go there.

The standard explanation for Do-support is that the verb and the head of TP must merge at some point in the derivation. This generalization applies to the T head whether the feature is [+past], [+present], or [+Imp] (Lasnik 1981). If this merger does not apply, for example when the head of TP moves to Comp (as is the case in questions) or when negation intervenes between the verb and tense, the dummy verb *do* is inserted to fulfill the function that would have been fulfilled by the verb. Within the Minimalist Program the function that the verb fulfills is checking the [+V] feature of tense. With respect to the [+D] feature, all the tenses in English seem to be [+D], as shown by the fact that the subject must be in the Spec of TP overtly.

1.2.2   Theoretical Implications

Assuming that the theory in the preceding discussion is correct in spirit, we can now give content to the statement that past tense and negation in Arabic must be paired with verbal and nominal elements. Given the theory that functional categories are specified for categorial features, this can be reformulated by saying that past tense is [+V] and [+D] and thus attracts the verb and the NP subject, respectively. Negation is also [+D] and thus attracts the NP subject or subject agreement.

However, to adequately extend this analysis to all the functional categories discussed in this book, I will propose that this theory of the feature structure of functional categories and how they are paired with lexical elements needs to be modified. The main modifications I will introduce are briefly summarized here.

First, I will argue that functional categories may not be specified for both categorial features [+V, +D]. Thus, a particular functional head may have one categorial feature in one language and may totally lack it in another. In the same vein, functional categories within the same language may have different categorial feature specifications. This is the case of the present tense in English and Arabic. In the former it is [+V] and [+D], while it is only [+D] in the latter. The past tense, by contrast, is [+V] and [+D] in both languages, while the imperative is [+V] only.

(32)   Feature Structure of Tense

	Arabic	French	English
Present	+D	+V, +D	+V, +D
Past	+V, +D	+V, +D	+V, +D
Imperative	+V	+V	+V

Since the present tense in Arabic lacks the [+V] categorial features, we account for absence of the verbal copula in verbless sentences and for the possibility that in sentences with verbal predicates the verb may remain lower than negation (cf. the generalizations in 2).

Second, as already indicated, I will argue that the sentential negative head is also specified for categorial features, particularly the feature [+D]. This implies that maybe all functional categories are specified for categorial features. For negation, at least, substantial evidence will be given from Arabic that this is indeed the case.

The idea that all functional categories are specified for categorial features opens up the possibility of reducing most cases of syntactic displacement to the interaction between lexical categories and the categorial features of functional categories. Thus, the fact that negation in Moroccan Arabic attracts nominal and adjectival predicates

(33) follows from the categorial [+D] feature of negation plus the assumption that, on a par with the NP subject, nominal predicates can be attracted by the [+D] feature of negation.

(33) a.   Omar ma-mṛiḍ-š   MA
             Omar neg-sick-neg
             'Omar is not sick.'

       b.   Omar ma-muʕəllim-š
             Omar neg-teacher-neg
             'Omar is not a teacher.'

Third, I will depart from most recent analyses and argue that to be paired with categorial features on a functional head an element does not need to be inherently specified for those features. More specifically, I will argue that a head that carries a noninherent categorial feature can be paired with that feature on another head. Thus, a verb that carries agreement features, which are nominal in character, can check the [+D] feature of tense or negation. This situation obtains particularly in the context of checking the categorial features of negation and tense.

The book is organized as follows. The first part, chapters 2, 3, and 4, deals with the syntax of tense. The second part, chapters 5, 6, and 7, focuses on negation. The third part, chapters 8 and 9, takes up the issue of agreement in number and (in)definiteness, respectively. The focus will be mainly on three Arabic dialects: Moroccan Arabic, Standard Arabic, and Egyptian Arabic.

I

THE FEATURE STRUCTURE OF TENSE

2

The Tense Systems of Egyptian Arabic, Moroccan Arabic, and Standard Arabic

This chapter introduces the morphology of verbs in matrix clauses in Egyptian Arabic, Moroccan Arabic, and Standard Arabic. I will describe in sufficient detail the morphology of the past, present, and future tenses and the imperatives in the three dialects. The aim is to identify the different elements that can occupy the tense projection and their morpho-syntactic properties. In the course of the description, I discuss some of the prevailing assumptions about the morphology of tense and aspect in Arabic, particularly the autosegmental account, and suggest alternative analyses where necessary. The detailed description of tense in the three dialects will set the scene for the next two chapters, 3 and 4, which explore the formal features and the syntactic distribution of the various elements in the tense projection (TP).[1]

2.1 Verb Morphology in Standard Arabic, Moroccan Arabic, and Egyptian Arabic

In Standard Arabic, Moroccan Arabic, and Egyptian Arabic, verbs occur in two main morphological forms, the imperfective and the perfective. Morphologically, the main difference between the two forms is in the realization of their agreement features. In the imperfective, agreement features are realized by both prefixes and suffixes.[2] The prefixes carry mainly person, except in the first person plural in Standard Arabic, where number is also realized on the prefix, while the suffixes carry mainly number (Benmamoun 1992, 1993; Noyer 1992). By contrast, gender is carried by number if the latter is phonologically realized as is the case in the plural; otherwise it is realized on the person prefix, except in the second person singular feminine, where it is realized by a suffix. In the perfective, by contrast, all the agreement morphology is realized by suffixes.

2.1.1 Standard Arabic

As already pointed out, the perfective form is exclusively suffixal. The verb consists of the stem (the root and its vowel melody) and an agreement suffix. The complete paradigm is given in the table in (1). [3]

(1)　Standard Arabic Perfective

Person	Number	Gender	Affix	Verb+Affix
1	Singular	F/M	-tu	daras-tu
2	"	M	-ta	daras-ta
2	"	F	-ti	daras-ti
3	"	M	-a	daras-a
3	"	F	-at	daras-at
2	Dual	M/F	-tumaa	daras-tumaa
3	"	M	-aa	daras-aa
3	"	F	-ataa	daras-ataa
1	Plural	M/F	-naa	daras-naa
2	"	M	-tum	daras-tum
2	"	F	-tunna	daras-tunna
3	"	M	-uu	daras-uu
3	"	F	-na	daras-na

The imperfective in Standard Arabic occurs in different morphological forms, usually referred to as moods distinguished by their endings (Wright 1889: 57–60, Hassan 1973, vol. 4: 277–440; Fleisch 1979: 122–136). In the so-called indicative form, the ending is *u* if the verb ends in a consonant and *na/ni* if the verb ends in a long vowel. In the so-called subjunctive, the ending is *a* if the verb ends in a consonant and there is no ending if the verb ends in a long vowel. In the so-called jussive form, there is no ending. The table in (2) presents the bare imperfective with no mood endings.[4] The tables (4), (6), and (8) present the indicative, subjunctive, and jussive moods, respectively.

(2)　Standard Arabic Imperfective

Person	Number	Gender	Affix	Affix+verb
1	Singular	M/F	ʔa-	ʔa-drus
2	"	M	ta-	ta-drus
2	"	F	ta-ii	ta-drus-ii
3	"	M	ya-	ya-drus
3	"	F	ta-	ta-drus
2	Dual	M/F	ta-—aa	ta-drus-aa
3	"	M/F	ya-—aa	ya-drus-aa
1	Plural	M/F	na-	na-drus
2	"	M	ta-—uu	ta-drus-u
2	"	F	ta—na	ta-drus-na
3	"	M	ya—uu	ya-drus-uu
3	"	F	ta—na	ta-drus-na

The indicative is used in sentences with present tense interpretation (3a, b), with the future morpheme (3c), with modal particles (3d), with the auxiliary verb *kaana* (3e), and with circumstantial adjuncts (3f).

(3) a. ya-drus-u   SA
         3m-study-ind
         'He studies./He is studying.'

     b. laa ya-drus-u
         neg 3m-study-ind
         'He does not study.'

     c. sa-ya-drus-u
         fut-3m-study-ind
         'He will study.'

     d. qad   ya-drus-u
         might 3m-study-ind
         'He might study.'

     e. kaana ya-drus-u
         be.past 3m-study-ind
         'He was studying./He used to study.'

     f. xaraža/sa-yaxružu   ya-fiḍ ak-u
         leave.past.3ms/fut-3m-leave 3m-laugh-ind
         'He left laughing./He will leave laughing.'

The full indicative paradigm is given in the table in (4).

(4)   Standard Arabic Indicative

	Singular	Dual	Plural
1	ʔadrus-u	nadrus-u	nadrus-u
2M	tadrus-u	tadrusaa-ni	tadrusuu-na
2F	tadrusii-na	tadrusaa-ni	tadrusna
3M	yadrus-u	yadrusaa-ni	yadrusuu-na
3F	tadrus-u	tadrusaa-ni	yadrusna

The subjunctive is used with the tensed negative that expresses future, *lan*, (5a) and in embedded nonfinite clauses after the subjunctive complementizer *ʔan* (5b) and some other subordinating particles such as *li/kay* (for, in order) and *ħattaa,* (until, so that). (5c) illustrates this property with *li* (in order).

(5) a. lan   ya-drus-a   SA
         neg.fut 3m-study-subj
         'He will not study.'

     b. yu-riid-u   ʔan ya-drus-a
         3m-want-ind to   3m-study-subj
         'He wants to study.'

     c. qaama li-ya-naam-a
         get.past.3ms up.3ms to-3m-sleep-subj
         'He got up to go to the bed.'

The full subjunctive paradigm is given in the table in (6).

(6)   Standard Arabic Subjunctive

	Singular	Dual	Plural
1	ʔadrusa	nadrusa	nadrusa
2M	tadrusa	tadrusaa	tadrusuu
2F	tadrusii	tadrusaa	tadrusna
3M	yadrusa	yadrusaa	yadrusuu
3F	tadrusa	tadrusaa	yadrusna

The jussive is mainly used after the negative that expresses past tense *lam* (7a) and negative imperatives or prohibitives (7b).

(7)   a.   lam   ya-drus
             neg.past 3m-study
             'He didn't study.'

       b.   laa ta-drus
             neg 2-study
             'Don't study.'

The full jussive paradigm is given in the table in (8).

(8)   Standard Arabic Jussive

	Singular	Dual	Plural
1	ʔadrus	nadrus	nadrus
2M	tadrus	tadrusa	tadrusuu
2F	tadrusii	tadrusaa	tadrusna
3M	yadrusa	yadrusaa	yadrusuu
3F	tadrusa	tadrusaa	yadrusna

As these paradigms illustrate, all the so-called moods use the same template and vowel melody. The only difference between them has to do with the presence or absence of an ending after the agreement suffix.

2.1.2   Moroccan Arabic and Egyptian Arabic

Moroccan Arabic and Egyptian Arabic pattern with Standard Arabic as far as the distribution of agreement features in the imperfective and the perfective. However, in Moroccan Arabic and Egyptian Arabic the paradigms are smaller than in Standard Arabic. In particular, there are no mood distinctions, at least morphologically, in these two dialects. Also, in Moroccan Arabic and Egyptian Arabic there is no dual or gender distinctions in the plural forms. Moreover, in Moroccan Arabic, in the imperfective, person agreement is realized by the same prefix in the singular and plural, while number is realized by a suffix.[5]

(9)   a.   ta-n-ktəb
           asp-1-write
           'I am writing.'

      b.   ta-n-kətb-u
           asp-1-write-p
           'We are writing.'

The two paradigms from Moroccan Arabic are illustrated by tables (10) and (11).

(10) Moroccan Arabic Perfective

Person	Number	Gender	Affix	Verb+Affix
1	Singular	F/M	-t	ktəbt
2	"	F/M	-ti	ktəbti
3	"	M	-Ø	ktəb
3	"	F	-at	kətbat
1	Plural	M/F	-na	ktəbna
2	"	M/F	-tu	ktəbtu
3	"	M/F	-u	kətbu

(11) Moroccan Arabic Imperfective

Person	Number	Gender	Affix	Affix+Verb
1	Singular	M/F	n-	nəktəb
2	"	M	t-	təktəb
2	"	F	t—I	tkətbi
3	"	M	y-	yəktəb
	"	F	t-	təktəb
1	Plural	M/F	n-—u	nkətbu
2	"	M/F	t-—u	tkətbu
3	"	M/F	y-—u	ykətbu

As already noted, Egyptian Arabic (tables 12 and 13) patterns with Moroccan Arabic with respect to the absence of the dual and gender distinctions in the plural.

(12) Egyptian Arabic Perfective

Person	Number	Gender	Affix	Verb+Affix
1	Singular	F/M	-t	katabt
2	"	M	-t	katabt
2	"	F	-ti	katabti
3	"	M	-Ø	katab
3	"	F	-it	katabit
1	Plural	M/F	-na	katabna
2	"	M/F	-tu	katabtu
3	"	M/F	-u	katabu

(13) Egyptian Arabic Imperfective

Person	Number	Gender	Affix	Affix+Verb
1	Singular	M/F	ʔa-	ʔaktib
2	"	M	ti-	tiktib
2	"	F	ti—i	tiktibi
3	"	M	yi-	yiktib
3	"	F	ti-	tiktib
1	Plural	M/F	ni-—u	nikətb
2	"	M/F	ti-—u	tiktibu
3	"	M/F	yi-—u	yiktibu

To sum up, the perfective and imperfective are essentially the two morphological forms of verbs in Arabic. A long debated and still unresolved issue within Arabic linguistics has revolved around the information (features) that these two forms carry. The specific question is whether, in addition to agreement, these two forms carry temporal and aspectual features. The next section deals with this issue.[6]

2.2   The Typology of Tense in Arabic

2.2.1   The Past Tense

The perfective form usually occurs in the past tense. I will take this to mean that there is a category tense with a past tense feature as part of the syntactic representation of these sentences.

(14) a.   žaaʔa   ʔams   SA
        come.past.3ms   yesterday
        'He came yesterday.'

     b.   ža   l-barəfi   MA
        come.past.3ms   the-yesterday
        'He came yesterday.'

     c.   ga   m-barifi   EA
        come.past.3ms   the-yesterday
        'He came yesterday.'

One of the controversial issues that arise in the context of the past tense concerns its morphological realization. There are two candidates to consider: (1) the agreement morphology suffixed to the verb realizes both tense and agreement and (2) the vocalic melody realizes the past tense; the suffix is just a realization of the agreement morphology.

2.2.1.1 *Agreement as a Realization of Past Tense*

One fact that argues against the first hypothesis—namely, that agreement is a realization of both past tense and agreement, comes from the Standard Arabic negative *laysa*

(Benmamoun 1992: 217). This negative carries the same inflection as the verb in the past tense but is restricted to sentences in the present tense (Moutaouakil 1987: 77–80).[7]

(15) a.   lays-a   fii l-bayt-i
           neg-3ms in   the-house
           'He is not in the house.'

      b.   lays-uu   fii l-bayt-i
           neg-3mp in   the house-gen
           'They are not in the house.'

(16)

Person	Number	Gender	Affix	Neg+Affix
1	Singular	F/M	-tu	las-tu
2	"	M	-ta	las-ta
2	"	F	-ti	las-ti
3	"	M	-a	lays-a
3	"	F	-at	lays-at
2	Dual	M/F	-tumaa	las-tumaa
3	"	M	-aa	lays-aa
3	"	F	-ataa	lays-ataa
1	Plural	M/F	-naa	las-naa
2	"	M	-tum	las-tum
2	"	F	-tunna	las-tunna
3	"	M	-uu	lays-uu
3	"	F	-na	las-na

Notice the identical suffixes on the verb *kataba* in the past tense in (1) and on the negative *laysa* in (16). This shows clearly that the suffix on the perfective verb carries agreement only. However, it is also clear that the exclusively suffixal agreement pattern on verbs always indicates that the verb is in the past tense. Therefore, even if the agreement suffix does not carry tense, it does signal that the tense is past.

2.2.1.2   *The Vocalic Melody as Realization of Past Tense*

The second hypothesis claims that, in the spirit of McCarthy's (1979, 1981) groundbreaking autosegmental account of Arabic morphology, tense information is carried by the vocalic melody, which occupies a different tier or plane separate from the consonantal tier.[8] The representation of the verb *kataba* (write) consists of three grammatical elements: the consonantal root, which ranges over the semantic field of the predicate; the vocalic melody, which expresses tense/aspect; and the CV tier, which represents the morphological template on which the other two tiers are mapped.[9]

(17)   Semantic Field: KTB
       Tense/Aspect: a—a
       CV Tier: CVCVCV

This generalization stems from the fact that the vocalic melodies of the verb in the perfective and the imperfective are different. Therefore, according to this hypothesis, in a form such as *katab* the vocalic melody carries tense/aspect information that gets attached to the verbal CV tier via left to right autosegmental mapping.

(18)

$$
\begin{array}{c}
A \\
\diagup\diagdown \\
C\ V\ C\ V\ C\ V \\
\diagdown\ \vert\ \diagup \\
KTB
\end{array}
$$

This analysis does not fare any better. First, the vocalic melody in (17) is restricted to active verbs, a well-established generalization within Arabic linguistics, traditional and modern. Passive verbs, by contrast, have a different vocalic melody. This contrast is illustrated in (19).

(19) a.   **katab**-at   ṭ-ṭaalib-u   r-risaalat-a   SA
           write.past-3fs the-student-nom the-letter
           'The student wrote the letter.'

      b.   **kutib**-at   r-risaalat-u
           write.pass.past-3fs the-letter-nom
           'The letter was written.'

The same generalization extends to the imperfective verb. The active and passive imperfective verbs vary in their vocalic melodies.[10]

(20) a.   ya-**ktub**   r-risaalat-a   SA
           3ms.writes the-letter-acc
           'He is writing the letter.'

      b.   tu-**ktab**   r-risaalat-u
           3fs.write.pass the-letter-nom
           'The letter is being written.'

The view that the vocalic melody in the perfective and imperfective forms carries voice is widely held within Arabic linguistics, traditional and modern. Once we accept this view, the theory that the vocalic melody carries tense or aspect in addition to voice becomes questionable, because voice is a derivational category, as is evident from the fact that different voices have different valences (e.g., passive voice vs. active voice). Given that tense is an inflectional category and voice a derivational category, it is extremely unlikely that they can be expressed by the same grammatical morpheme, in this case the vocalic melody. Most cases of cumulative exponence (one morpheme realizing more than one feature) discussed in the literature deal with inflectional features (see Mathews 1974; Carstairs-McCarthy 1987; and Noyer 1992).

This is even clearer in Moroccan Arabic, where there is no elaborate vocalic melody. In Moroccan Arabic there is only one short vowel—namely, the schwa /ə/—whose distribution is phonologically predictable in the context of both the perfective and the imperfective verbs.[11]

(21) a.   yə-ktəb   vs.   ktəb
           3m-write   wrote

     b.   y-kətb-u   vs.   kətb-u
           3-write-p   wrote-p

To express voice, Moroccan Arabic relies on a different strategy, namely, prefixation of a passive/reflexive/middle morpheme to the perfective and imperfective verbs.

(22) ta-y-t-kətb-u   vs.   t-kətb-u
      asp-3-pass-write-p   pass-wrote-p
      'They are being written.'   'They were written.'

Significantly, the loss of the vocalic melody has meant loss of expressing voice by vowels in Moroccan Arabic. It did not lead to the loss of expressing tense/aspect, as incorrectly predicted by the theory that the vocalic melodies carry tense.[12]

In fact, the only morpho-phonological clue as to whether the verb is in the perfective or imperfective in Moroccan Arabic comes from the agreement system. In the perfective the agreement system is exclusively suffixal, while in the imperfective it is suffixal and prefixal. In short, the vowel melody plays no role in realizing tense or aspect.

2.2.1.3 Past Tense as an Abstract Morpheme

Thus, contrary to previous analyses, neither the agreement morphology on the perfective verb nor the vocalic melody realizes past tense. This leads to the following question: how is the past tense expressed? I would like to argue that the past tense is an abstract morpheme that does not have any specific phonological realization. The only indicator is suffixal agreement. In this respect, the past tense is similar to the present tense in English which is also phonologically null. The only morphological reflex it has is third person singular agreement on lexical verbs (*eat* vs. *eats*) and suppletive forms of the copula (*am, are, is*). However, like the English present tense, the abstract past tense in Arabic is syntactically active in that it has features that need to be checked by the subject and the verb. Anticipating the discussion in chapter 6, a slightly similar situation to that of Do-support in English which has usually been taken as an argument for a present tense projection, arises in Standard Arabic. In the context of the past tense and the negative *laa*, the past tense is realized on the suppletive negative *lam* rather than the verb.

(23) a.   darasa   SA
           study.past3ms
           'He studies.'

     b.   lam   ya-drus
           neg.past 3m-study
           'He didn't study.'

I will take this to indicate that there is a past tense feature that heads an independent projection. When the verb merges with the past tense, the complex is realized as in (23a). When the past tense merges with negation, the complex is realized as in (23b). Notice that the agreement on the verb in (23b) is not the same as the agreement it carries in (23a). This is another argument that the agreement suffix on the verb does not realize past tense. When the verb carries abstract past tense features it carries suffixal agreement; when it does not it carries the prefixal and suffixal agreement associated with the imperfective form.

In brief, the perfective verb carries past tense features. However, these features are not realized by an overt affix. The only morphological reflection is the suffixal agreement pattern that the past tense verb selects. However, it is clear that suffixal agreement by itself does not realize past tense because the negative *laysa* carries exactly the same type of agreement but is restricted to sentences in the present tense. In the next section, I will turn to the imperfective form and argue that the so-called imperfective morphology also does not carry any temporal or aspectual information. However, unlike the perfective verb, which carries abstract past tense features, the imperfective does not carry any abstract features; it is simply the realization of a nonfinite verb.

2.3   The Syntactic Status of the Imperfective

2.3.1   Distribution of the Imperfective Verb

Putting aside the mood endings in Standard Arabic, in all dialects, the imperfective form occurs in the following contexts.

First, in the context of verbs with present tense interpretation (progressive and habitual):

(24) a.   ya-drusu   SA
           3m-study
           'He studies.'

      b.   ta-yə-qra   MA
           hab-3m-study
           'He studies.'

      c.   bi-yi-drus   EA
           hab-3m-study
           'He studies.'

Second, in the context of the future tense:

(25) a.   sa-ya-drusu   SA
           fut-3m-study
           'He will study.'

      b.   ɣadi yə-qra   MA
           going 3m-study
           'He will study.'

   c.   fia-y-saafir   EA
       going 3m-travel
       'He will travel.'

Third, in the context of auxiliaries and modals:

(26) a.   kaana   ya-drusu   SA
       be.past.3ms 3m-study
       'He was studying./He used to study.'

      b.   kan   ta-yə-qra   MA
       be.past.3ms prog/hab-3m-study
       'He was studying./He used to study.'

      c.   kan   b-i-drus   EA
       be.past.3ms prog-3m-study
       'He was studying./He used to study.'

(27) a.   qad   ya-drusu   SA
       probable 3m-study
       'He might study.'

      b.   xəṣṣ-u   yə-qra   MA
       must-his 3m-study
       'He must study.'

      c.   laazim yi-drus   EA
       must   3m-study
       'He must study.'

Fourth, when the negative carries tense in Standard Arabic:

(28) a.   lam   ya-drus
       neg.past 3m-study
       'He did not study.'

      b.   lan   ya-drusa
       neg.fut 3m-study
       'He will not study.'

Fifth, in embedded nonfinite clauses:

(29) a.   ʔaraada   ʔan yu-saafira   SA
       want.3ms to   3m-travel
       'He wants to travel.'

      b.   bɣa   y-ṣafər   MA
       want.3m 3-travel
       'He wants to travel.'

c.   ʕaawiz   y-safir   EA
     wanting   3-travel
     'He wants to travel.'

Sixth, in negative imperatives:

(30) a.   laa ta-drus   SA
          neg 2-study
          'Don't study.'

     b.   ma-tə-qra-š   MA
          neg-2-study-neg
          'Don't study.'

     c.   ma-ti-ʔra-š   EA
          neg-2-read-neg
          'Don't read.'

Seventh, in circumstantial adjuncts:

(31) a.   xaraža/sa-ya-xružu   ya-ḍħ ak-u   SA
          leave.past.3ms/fut-3m-leave 3m-laugh-ind
          'He left laughing./He will leave laughing.'

     b.   xrəž   ta-y-ḍħək   MA
          leave.past.3ms asp-3m-laugh
          'He left laughing.'

     c.   xarag   bi-ḍħak   EA
          leave.past.3ms asp-3m.laugh
          'He left laughing.'

The fact that the imperfective form occurs in the context of the present tense, future tense, past tense, imperatives, and non-finite clauses shows clearly that it does not morphologically carry any temporal or aspectual information, contrary to what has been previously claimed. It is difficult to come up with a temporal or aspectual feature that is shared by all these constructions. This inevitably leads to the conclusion that the prefix and the suffix on the imperfective are agreement morphemes only.

2.3.2   The Imperfective Verb as Default Form of the Verb

The most plausible characterization of the imperfective is that it is the default form of the verb (the nonfinite form). Apart from the present tense sentences, in all the contexts already listed, the main temporal information is carried either by a clitic, an auxiliary, the negative, or a matrix verb. Thus, the imperfective is resorted to whenever the relevant verb does not carry the main tense information.[13]

This idea is independently motivated by the fact that some nominalization processes seem to take as input the imperfective form (see McCarthy 1979 for a detailed analysis of the verbal and nominal morphology of Arabic).

(32) a.   ya-ktub   SA
           3m-write
           'He writes.'

      b.   ma-ktab
           loc-write
           'office'

(33) a.   yu-ʕallim-u
           3m-teach
           'He teaches.'

      b.   mu-ʕallim
           n-teach
           'teacher'

As is evident from (32) and (33), the imperfective verb (32a, 33a) and the nominal (32b, 33b) have exactly the same vocalic melody, which clearly indicates that the two forms are related (perhaps derivationally). This in turn suggests that the imperfective does not carry any temporal information, given that in most languages nominals are derived from or are related to nontensed verbs.

Returning to the mood endings in Standard Arabic, it is not clear at this point what their semantic interpretations are.[14] Each mood ending seems to comprise a heterogenous class of temporal and syntactic contexts. For example, the jussive occurs in the context of imperatives and past tense negatives. Yet there does not seem to be any semantic feature these two constructions share that forces the selection of the jussive rather than the subjunctive or the indicative.[15] Similarly, the subjunctive occurs in the context of embedded nonfinite clauses, which cross-linguistically is the context where it is usually found.[16] However, the subjunctive occurs also in matrix future tense clauses negated by *lan* (28b). One could argue that the two constructions have something in common—namely, reference to a subsequent event or state.[17] However, this does not extend to the affirmative future verb (25a) or modals such as *qad* (27a) which co-occur with the indicative form of the verb rather than the subjunctive.[18] For these reasons, I will assume that the mood markers are morphological elements that mark a syntactic dependency relation between a matrix verb and its complement, as is the case with subjunctives or between a tensed negative and imperative and their VP complements, which is the case of subjunctive and jussives.[19] Crucially, these mood markers do not translate into formal features that head projections in the syntactic representations of their sentences. However, where morphologically relevant I will continue to use the traditional terminology to refer to the various classes within the imperfective verb.

2.4   The Present Tense

As already mentioned, the imperfective (indicative) form occurs also in the context of sentences with present tense interpretation. The difference between Standard Arabic on the one hand and Moroccan Arabic and Egyptian Arabic on the other hand, is

that the former uses the bare imperfective form while the latter prefixes an aspectual
morpheme, *ta/ka/bi*, to the imperfective verb. The *ta/ka/bi* prefixes have progressive
and habitual interpretations.

(34) a.   ?al-?awlaadu ya-lʕab-uu-n   SA
           the-children   3m-play-mp-ind
           'The children are playing.'

      b.   lə-wlaad   ta-y-ləʕb-u   MA
           the-children asp-3-play-p
           'The children are playing.'

      c.   bi-yi-dris   hina dilwaʔt   EA
           asp-3m-study here now
           'He is studying now.'

(35) a.   ṭ-ṭaalib-u   ya-skunu huna   SA
           the-student-nom 3m-live   here
           'The student lives here.'

      b.   lə-wlad   ta-y-qra-w   hna   MA
           the-children asp-3m-study-p here
           'The children study here.'

      c.   ʕaadatan bi-yi-dris   hina   EA
           usually   asp-3m-study here
           'He usually studies here.'

I will assume that there is an aspectual projection immediately above the VP.
This projection is headed by the clitic *ta/ka* in Moroccan Arabic, by *bi* in Egyptian
Arabic, and by an abstract morpheme in Standard Arabic. Independent evidence that
these are clitics that head their own projection in the syntax and are subsequently
merged with the verb comes from the fact that one clitic can have scope over conjoined
verbs, as shown by the sentence in (36) from Egyptian Arabic (Eisele 1988, 130) and
(37) from Moroccan Arabic.

(36) ṭuul il-waʔt bi-y-liff   w yi-suuf w y-laaiz ...   EA
      all   the-time asp-3m-go-around and 3m-look and 3m-notice ...
      'All the time he is going around and looking, noticing . . .'

(37) Omar ta-y-ktəb   w yə-qra buḥdu   MA
      Omar asp-3m-writes and 3m-read alone
      'Omar writes and reads on his own.'

That the aspectual morpheme has scope over both verbs in (36) and (37) is supported
by the fact that in Moroccan Arabic the presence of the aspectual prefix is obligatory
in present tense sentences.

(38) * (ta)-y-qra budu
       (asp)-3m-read alone

Such a contrast between (37) and (38) can be explained by taking *ta* to be a syntactically independent element that heads its own projection, which dominates conjoined VPs. The aspectual morpheme cliticizes onto the verb immediately to its right.

(39)

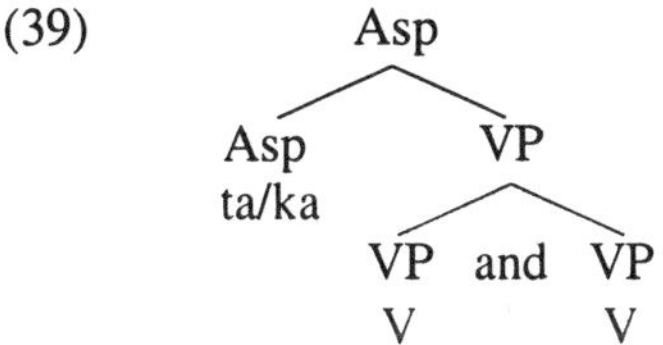

We thus have strong arguments that, like the past tense, the present tense is an abstract morpheme, in the sense that it is not expressed by an independent morpheme on the predicate. However, unlike the past tense, the present tense does not have an agreement morpheme that is exclusive to its verbs, nor does it have a suppletive form of negation. The same agreement morpheme is used in the future tense, nonfinite clauses, and negative imperatives. So in this respect, the two tenses are very different. This fundamental difference between the two tenses will be crucial in determining how they interact with verb movement (chapters 3 and 4).

2.5   The Future Tense

The future tense in Standard Arabic is realized by the particle *sawfa* and the clitic *sa*.[20] As already pointed out, the form of the verb used in this context is the imperfective (more precisely, the indicative).

(40) a.   sawfa ?u-saafiru   SA
            will   1s-travel
            'I will travel.'

      b.   sa-u-saafiru
            fut-1s-travel
            'I will travel.'

In Moroccan Arabic future time reference is expressed by using the participial predicate ɣadi (going) or its reduced form, ɣa, while in Egyptian Arabic it is expressed by the proclitic *ha*, which is derived from the motion participial predicate *raayih* (going).

(41) a.   Omar ɣadi lə-d-dar   MA
            Omar going to-the-house
            'Omar is going home.'

      b.   Omar raayifi li-l-bit   EA
            Omar going   to-the-house
            'Omar went home.'

In this respect, the use of these two predicates is equivalent to the use of *aller* and *go* in English and French, respectively.

(42) a.   I am going to travel tomorrow.

      b.   Je vais voyager demain
            I go   travel   tomorrow
            'I will travel tomorrow.'

Thus, unlike Standard Arabic, Moroccan Arabic and Egyptian Arabic do not seem to have morphemes that are used exclusively in the future tense.[21] Future time reference is expressed by the present tense and the participle form of a motion predicate. I will refer to this realization of future time reference as the prospective, adopting the label that Comrie (1976: 64) gives to these constructions (see also Eisele 1988).[22] However, I will argue in chapter 5 that the ɣa(di) in Moroccan Arabic is evolving into a pure marker of future tense. Egyptian Arabic, by contrast, seems to display a pure prospective present.

This fundamental difference between Standard Arabic on the one hand and Moroccan Arabic and Egyptian Arabic on the other hand correlates with another fact: Standard Arabic has a suppletive form of the negative *laa* that is used exclusively in the future tense.

(43) lan   yu-saafira   SA
      neg.fut 3m-travel
      'He will not travel.'

The presence of a negative that carries future tense in Standard Arabic is not surprising since future as a feature of TP exists in this language. Whatever process accounts for the relation between the verb and future tense will carry over to the tensed negative *lan*. In chapter 6, I develop an analysis whereby the negative element *laa* and its tensed variants occupy a projection between TP and VP. The negative will then be able to merge with the head of TP. In Moroccan Arabic and Egyptian Arabic, we predict the prospective present to have the same syntax as the regular present. This prediction is to a large extent correct, as I will show in chapter 5.

2.6   Imperatives

The imperative in Arabic is also related to the imperfective form used in the present and future tenses (ignoring mood endings).[23] However, there is one important difference between positive imperatives and negative imperatives. Positive imperatives lack the person prefix, while negative imperatives must have it. This situation is illustrated here.

(44) a.   ktub   laa ta-ktub   SA
            write   neg 2-write
            'Write.'   'Do not write.'

    b.   ktub-ii   laa ta-ktub-ii
         write-fs   neg 2-write-fs
         'Write.'   'Do not write.'

    c.   ktub-uu   laa ta-ktub-uu
        write-mp   neg 2-write-mp
        'Write.'   'Do not write.'

    d.   ktub-na   ta-ktub-na
        write-fp   2-write-fp
        'Write.'   'Do not write.'

(45) a.   ktəb   ma-tə-kteb-š   MA
        write   neg-2-write-neg
        'Write.'   'Do not write.'

    b.   kətb-i   ma-t-kətb-i-š
        write-fs   neg-2-write-fs-neg
        'Write.'   'Do not write.'

    c.   kətb-u   ma-t-kətb-u-š
        write-p   neg-2-write-p-neg
        'Write.'   'Do not write.'

Egyptian Arabic (Eisele 1988: 133):

(46) a.   iktib   ma-ti-ktib-š   EA
        write   neg-2-write-neg
        'Write.'   'Do not write.'

    b.   iktib-i   ma-ti-ktib-ii-š
        write-f   neg-2-write-fs-neg
        'Write.'   'Do not write.'

    c.   iktib-u   ma-ti-ktib-uu-š
        write-p   neg-2-write-p-neg
        'Write.'   'Do not write.'

Thus, the difference between positive imperatives and negative imperatives is the presence of person agreement in the latter. This important contrast will be the focus of chapter 7, which deals with the features structure of imperatives and negation.

2.7   Conclusion

In this chapter, I have explored the morphology of the two main verbal paradigms in Arabic, the perfective and imperfective. The main conclusion that emerged is that the perfective verb carries abstract past tense while the bare imperfective is not specified for any temporal or aspectual features. I have also discussed the imperative verb where we observed an important asymmetry: positive imperatives, unlike negative imperatives, do not carry person agreement features. Having described verbal morphology in this chapter, in the next chapter I turn to the feature content of the elements that head the TP projection. It will turn out that the morphological difference between the past tense and the present tense reflects the different categorial feature specifications that characterize the elements that head TP. The differences between positive and negative imperatives with respect to person agreement will be taken up in chapter 7 and will be shown to follow from the feature structures of the imperative verb and negation.

<h1 style="text-align:center">3</h1>

The Categorial Features of Tense

In the previous chapter, I focused on the morphology of tense in Arabic. I explored the temporal properties of the perfective and imperfective verbs and concluded that only the former carries temporal features—namely, abstract past tense features. The imperfective verb, by contrast, is not specified for any temporal features. In this chapter, I turn to the syntax of verbs in the three dialects studied in the previous chapter. I will explore the formal features of the elements that occupy the tense projection and argue that the catgeorial feature matrices of these elements are not uniform. In particular, I argue that the categorial features of the past tense and the present tense are not the same. This, in turn, will help account for key syntactic differences between the present tense and the past tense to be discussed in chapter 4.

3.1   Typology of the Categorial Features of Tense

As discussed in chapter 1, Chomsky (1995) proposes that tense in English is specified for two categorial features, the feature [+V] and the feature [+D]. The feature [+V] determines the interaction between tense and the verb, while the feature [+D] determines its interaction with the subject (EPP). Thus, in the sentence in (1) the auxiliary verb moves to tense (T) to check its [+V], while the subject raises from the Spec of VP to Spec of T to check its [+D] feature.[1] The two stages of the derivation are given in (2) and (3).

(1)   John had left.

(2)

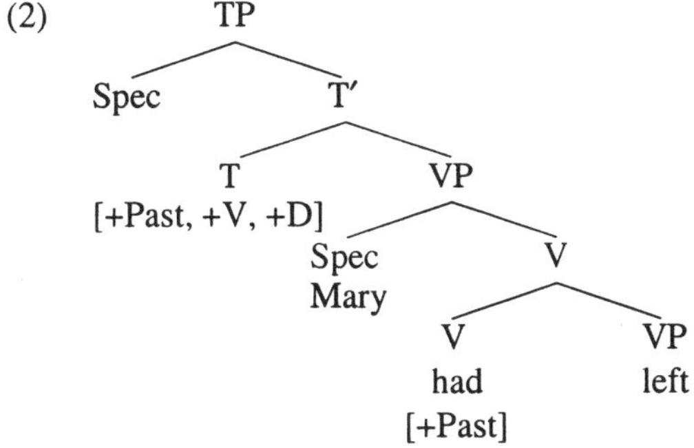

(3)

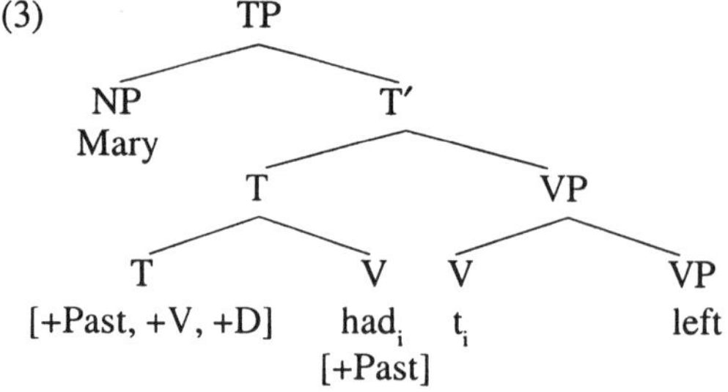

However, it is conceivable that in some languages the head of TP could be specified for only one of these two categorial features. This is more so because the categorial features in question are considered unintrepretable. Therefore, their absence is not crucial for any of the two interfaces (LF and PF). Thus, assuming that the features of the functional categories are privative, we expect the following three possibilities.[2]

(4)   a.   T → [+D, +V]
       b.   T → [+D]
       c.   T → [+V]

I will propose that this is exactly the situation in Arabic. In the next sections, I will argue that the entry in (4a) characterizes the past tense while the entry in (4b) characterizes the present tense. In chapter 7, I will show that the entry in (4c) is found in imperatives.

3.2   The Feature Structure of the Arabic Tense System

With this background in mind, let us consider the feature composition of the tense system of Arabic, starting with a comparison between the present tense and the past tense. One major difference between the present tense and past tense in Arabic is that the latter always requires a verbal predicate while the former does not. Consider the following contrast.

(5)   a.   Omar muʕəllim   MA
             Omar teacher
             'Omar is a teacher.'

       b.   Omar kan   muʕəllim
             Omar be.past.3ms teacher
             'Omar was a teacher.'

Assuming that the present tense heads a tense projection, the fact that a verbal head is obligatory in the past tense but not in the present tense remains a mystery if we assume that tense in general is universally specified as [+V] and [+D]. In (5a), there is no verbal head to check the putative [+V] feature of the present tense regardless of the level of representation or the point in the derivation where checking takes place. At this point, it could be argued that the present tense in Arabic is also [+V] but that the verbal copula that realizes it is phonologically null. This is a long-running issue in generative Arabic linguistics.[3] Three positions have been advanced over the last thirty years.[4]

1. Verbless sentences are essentially small clauses with no functional projection (Mouchaweh 1986: 134–203).

2. Verbless sentences contain a copula (Bakir 1980: 173–176; Fassi Fehri 1982: 71–76, 1993: 155–156). The copula is either null/zero (Fassi Fehri) or subsequently erased (Bakir).

3. Verbless sentences contain a functional projection specified for present tense but no copula (Steel 1981: 73–97; Jelinek 1981: 7–29).

These analyses are taken up in the next two sections.

3.2.1   Verbless Sentences as Small Clauses

The small clause analysis of verbless sentences has been suggested by Mouchaweh (1986) and adopted by Rapapport (1987) for Hebrew. The central claim is that there is no functional projection above the lexical projection in verbless sentences. Both the subject and the nonverbal predicate are contained within the small clause which can be an AP as in (6a), an NP as in (6b), or a PP as in (6c).

(6)   a.   al-žawwu   žamiilun   SA
             the-weather nice
             'The weather is nice.'

       b.   Omar muʕəllim   MA
             Omar teacher
             'Omar is a teacher.'

       c.   Omar f-d-dar
             Omar in-the-house
             'Omar is in the house.'

According to this approach, there is no temporal projection in the structure that corresponds to the sentences in (6).

(7)   A/N/PP

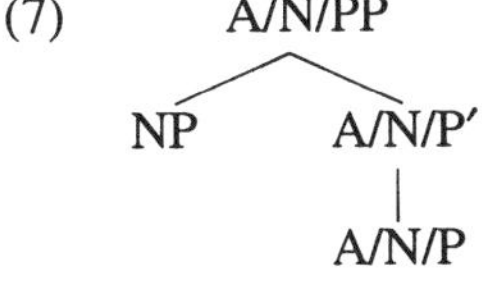

In this respect, these sentences are not different from the embedded genuine English small clauses in (8).

(8)   a.   I found [John angry]

       b.   I consider [John a good teacher]

First, the sentence in (6c) can contain temporal adverbs, which arguably must be anchored by tense (Eisele 1988).

(9) Omar f-d-dar daba   MA
   Omar in-the-house now
   'Omar is in the house now.'

Second, a verbless sentence embedded under a tensed matrix clause does not necessarily have the same temporal reference as the matrix tense. Rather, it has its own present tense interpretation. This is shown in (10), where the matrix sentence has a past tense interpretation while the embedded verbless sentence has a present tense interpretation.

(10) a. qal   bəlli Omar f-d-dar
     say.past.3ms that Omar in-the-house
     'He said that Omar is in the house.'

   b. qul-ti   bəlli Omar naʕəs
     say.past-2s that Omar sleeping
     'You said that Omar is sleeping.'

The fact that the embedded verbless sentence can have independent temporal reference strongly suggests that it cannot be treated on a par with small clauses, which depend for their temporal reference on the matrix clause, as shown in (11).

(11) šəf-t   Omar naʕəs
   see.past-1s Omar sleeping
   'I saw him and he was sleeping.' (not 'I saw him and he is sleeping.')

Third, as illustrated in (10), the verbless sentence is dominated by the complementizer *bəlli*, which selects tensed clauses. This complementizer is not allowed in nontensed clauses (12a) or in the context of genuine small clauses (12b).

(12) a. sʕib   baš y-ži
     difficult that 3m-come
     'It is difficult for him to come.'

   b. *šəf-t   bəlli Omar naʕəs
     see.past-1s that Omar sleeping

Fourth, the subject is assigned nominative Case. This is clearly the case in Standard Arabic, where Case is morphologically realized.

(13) ṭ-ṭaalib-u   fii l-maktabati   SA
   the-student-nom in the-library
   'The student is in the library.'

Assuming that nominative Case on argument NPs is assigned or checked by tense, the fact that the subject in (13) is nominative follows if there is a T head that assigns or checks nominative Case.

Fifth, both the subject and the predicate can be Wh-moved in questions and relatives, which suggests that these clauses are CPs.

(14) a. škun f-d-dar   MA
         who in-the-house
         'Who is in the house?'

     b. fin   Omar
         where Omar
         'Where is Omar?'

     c. l-wəld lli   f-d-dar
         the-boy who in-the-house
         'The boy who is in the house'

Sixth, the subject of the verbless sentence can be an expletive pronominal.

(15) pro lazəm   tə-mši ltəmma
     3ms necessary 2-go   there
     'It is necessary for you to go there.'

Since expletives are not thematic they are presumably not generated within the lexical projection. In fact, expletive subjects are assumed to be generated purely for the purpose of checking the [+D] feature of tense (Chomsky 1995).

That there is an expletive subject in (15) is confirmed by the fact that when the copula is overt, as is the case in the past tense, it carries agreement that is usually associated with the expletive, namely, third masculine singular.

(16) kan   lazəm   tə-mši l-təmma
     be.past.3ms necessary 2-go   to-there
     'It was necessary for you to go there.'

Seventh, the distribution of NPIs also suggests that there is a functional projection headed by tense. For example, the distribution of NPIs in Moroccan Arabic (Benmamoun 1997) crucially interacts with finiteness. Thus, an NPI in an embedded finite clause cannot be licensed by a negative in the matrix clause, as shown in (17).

(17)* ma-ta-y-ḍənn   bəlli Nadia tlaq-at   ħətta waħəd
      neg-asp-3m-think that Nadia meet.past.3fs any   one

Interestingly, the same facts obtain in copular constructions with present tense interpretation.

(18)* ma-ta-y-ḍənn   bəlli Nadia mʕa ħətta waħəd
      neg-asp-3ms-think that Nadia with any   one

Notice that NPIs within PPs are fine as long as the licensing negative is clausemate (19) or the NPIs are within a nonfinite clause (20).

(19) Nadia ma mʕa ɦətta wafiəd
      Nadia neg with any   one
      'Nadia is not with anyone.'

(20) ma-bɣa-h   y-tlaqa   ɦətta wafiəd
      neg-want.past.3ms-him 3m-meet any   one
      'He does not want him to meet anyone.'

The fact that NPIs within a copular construction cannot be licensed by a superordinate negative can be straightforwardly explained if these constructions contain a temporal projection that defines a local domain where NPIs must be licensed.[5]

Thus, we have strong arguments that verbless sentences are not small clauses with no functional projections, particularly a tense projection. Rather, they are full-fledged clauses that display the same properties that obtain in tensed clauses.

In short, it is most likely that verbless sentences are clauses with a tense projection. The question is whether they contain a verbal copula (a VP). Some analyses have suggested that there is a copula in verbless sentences, but it is not overt, either because it has been deleted (Bakir 1980) or because it is phonologically null (Fassi Fehri 1993). I discuss these alternatives in the next section.

3.2.2   The Null Copula Analysis

Bakir (1980) tentatively suggests that there is a verbal copula in these clauses. For Bakir (1980: 176), the NP that precedes the copula is a topic and the subject is a pronominal element that occurs after the copula. Two deletion rules apply: one that deletes the copula and one that deletes the pronominal subject under identity with the topic.

(21)

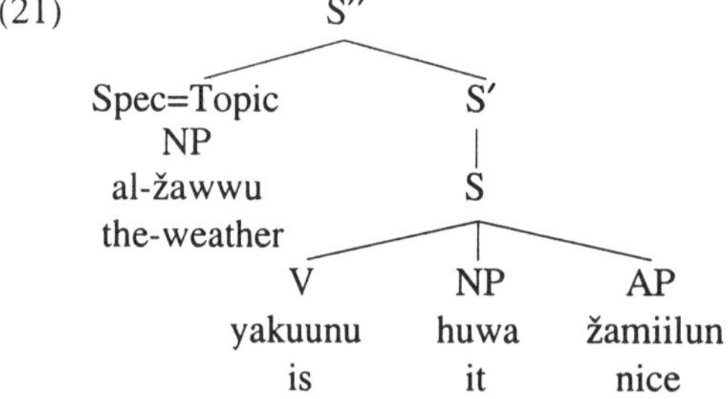

Bakir's analysis was driven mainly by the quest for consistency, namely, that copular constructions have the same structures as sentences that contain verbal predicates.

The null copula hypothesis as advanced in Fassi Fehri (1993) has two facets that are not necessarily related. First, it assumes that there is functional projection that hosts tense. Second, it assumes, somewhat on par with Bakir, that there is a copula. For Bakir, the copula undergoes deletion, but according to Fassi Fehri it is inserted as null (without a phonological matrix).[6] The assumption that there is a functional projection hosting tense accounts for all the six objections against the small clause analysis. However, the assumption that there is a (null) copula is problematic for the following reasons.[7]

First, when the copula is overt in Standard Arabic, it assigns accusative Case to the predicate.

(22) a.   kaana   l-waladu mariiḍ-an
            be.past.3ms the-boy   sick-acc
            'The boy was sick.'

      b.   kaana   ʔibnuh ṭaalib-an
            be.past.3ms son.his student-acc
            'His son was a student.'

By contrast, in verbless sentences the predicate is always nominative.

(23) a.   l-waladu mariiḍ-un
            the-boy   sick-nom
            'The boy is sick.'

      b.   ʔibnuh ṭaalib-un
            son.his student-nom
            'His son is a student.'

For the null copula analysis these facts are difficult to account for, as pointed out in Déchaine (1993). It is not clear why the null copula should assign a different Case from the overt copula. Notice that this has nothing to do with tense per se, for the copula in the future tense also assigns accusative Case.

(24) sa-ya-kuunu ṭaalib-an/*ṭaalib-un
      fut-3m-be   student-acc/*student-nom
      'He will be a student.'

However, if we assume that there is no verbal copula in (23) we can easily account for the absence of Accusative Case in verbless sentences since there is no verb to assign it.

Second, it is not clear under the null/deleted copula hypotheses why this situation obtains only in the present tense. More specifically, the reason that in the context of the past and future tenses the copula is always overt is mysterious. The fact that the copula is null/deleted only in the present does not follow from any property of the present tense.

This problem does not arise if we dispense with the idea that sentences always have a verb, as in the analysis of Bakir (1980), or a VP, as in the analysis of Fassi Fehri (1993). This is exactly the analysis advanced in Jelinek (1981), which I am going to adopt and expand on.

3.2.3 Verbless Sentences Have a Functional Projection but No Verbal Predicate

Jelinek (1981), on the basis of Egyptian Arabic data, argues for an auxiliary (AUX) node that is specified for the present tense feature only.

(25)

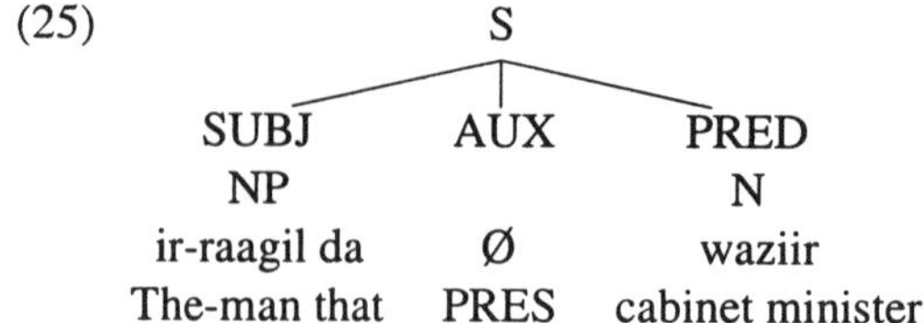

This analysis does not face any of the problems raised in the preceding section. The present tense feature is syntactically projected and therefore can interact with temporal adverbs, assign nominative Case to the subject, and define locality domains for NPIs. Moreover, as clauses, verbless sentences are expected to be as big as CPs. Thus, it is not surprising that they can host questions and can have expletive subjects when the predicate does not take a thematic subject. In addition, Jelinek points out that in sentences with an overt copula the verb and the negative complex it carries can either precede or follow the subject. The same facts can be duplicated in Moroccan Arabic.

(26) a. ma-kan-š   Omar f-d-dar   MA
         neg-be.past.3ms-neg Omar in-the-house
         'Omar was not in the house.'

     b. Omar ma-kan-š   f-d-dar
         Omar neg-past.3ms-neg in-the-house
         'Omar was not in the house.'

Then she rightly argues that under a null copular analysis one would expect the same ordering options to be available; namely, the putative null copula and negation should be able to either precede or follow the subject. This prediction is not borne out. Negation must follow the subject, as shown by the ungrammaticality of (27).

(27) a. *ma-ši   Omar f-d-dar
         neg-neg Omar in-the-house

     b. Omar ma-ši   f-d-dar
         Omar neg-neg in-the-house
         'Omar is not in the house.'

In addition to these arguments against the null copula hypothesis, two more pieces of evidence can be given to support Jelinek's position.

   First, as we will see in greater detail in chapter 5, in Moroccan Arabic sentential negation is realized by the proclitic *ma* and the enclitic *š*. In most Arabic dialects with similar sentential negation, such as Egyptian Arabic, the tensed verb is "sandwiched" between the two negative morphemes, which can be derived by moving the verb negation and then to tense.

(28)

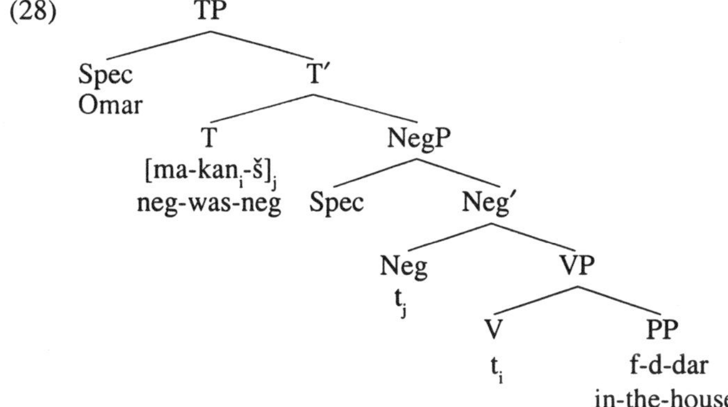

However, Moroccan Arabic diverges from the other dialects in that nonverbal predicates can also host sentential negation.

(29) a. Omar ma-mṛiḍ-š   MA
         Omar neg-sick-neg
         'Omar is not sick.'

     b. Omar ma-muʕəllim-š
         Omar neg-teacher-neg
         'Omar is not a teacher.'

These facts follow if nonverbal predicates can raise in Moroccan Arabic to negation.

(30)

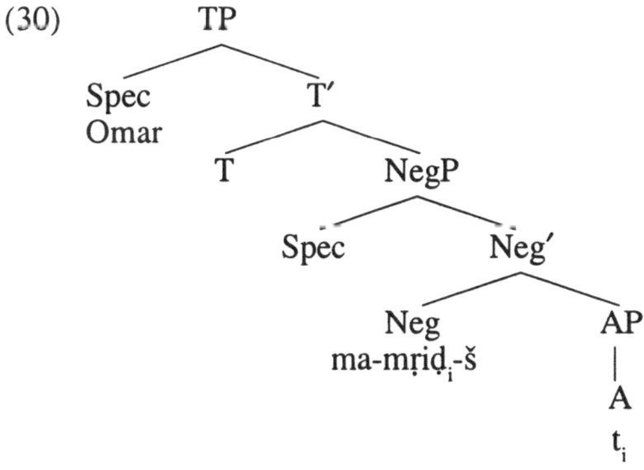

However, this would be difficult to derive under the null copula hypothesis without some auxiliary assumptions. If the null copula is located between the projection of negation and the nonverbal predicate, as seems to be the case in the context of the overt copula, movement of the nonverbal predicate should be blocked in (31), on a par with (32).

(31) a.   Omar ma-kan-š   mṛid
        Omar neg-be.past.3ms-neg sick
        'Omar was not sick.'

      b.   Omar ma-kan-š   muʕəllim
        Omar neg-be.past.3ms-neg teacher
        'Omar was not a teacher.'

(32) a. * Omar ma-mṛid-š   kan
        Omar neg-sick-neg be.past.3ms

      b. * Omar ma-muʕallim-š   kaan
        Omar neg-teacher-neg be.past.3ms

In (31), the copula seems to block the movement of the nonverbal predicate to the negative due to minimality, which prevents the movement of one head across another head (Rizzi 1990). The copula is closer to negation than the adjectival predicate, as illustrated in (33).

(33)

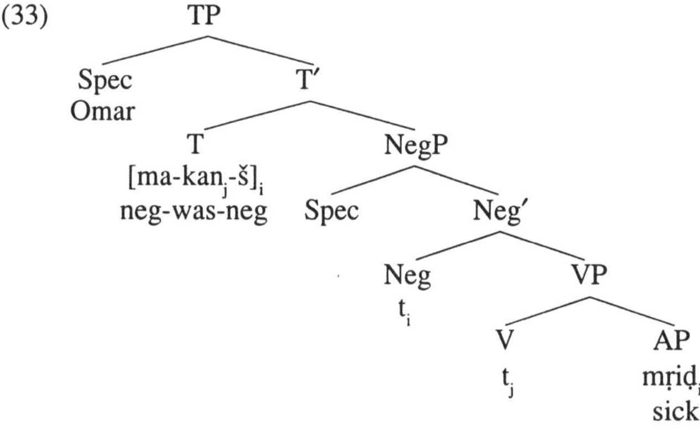

The same facts should obtain in verbless sentences if we posit a null copula. Of course, one could assume that the nonverbal predicate moves and merges with the copula and then the whole complex, copula+Neg, subsequently merges with negation. However, this analysis would predict that in all instances this merger should be obligatory, but in fact, in Moroccan Arabic the merger of negation and nonverbal predicates is not obligatory.[8]

(34) a.   Omar ma-ši   mriḍ
        Omar neg-neg sick
        'Omar is not sick.'

      b.   Omar ma-ši   muʕəllim
        Omar neg-neg teacher
        'Omar is not a teacher.'

Second, there is an imperfective form of the copula, which is morphologically identical to other verbs when they occur in the present tense. However, this form of

the copula occurs only in the context of a specific interpretation of the present tense
that will be explained here. Consider the following example from Moutaouakil (1987:
64).

(35) ya-kuun l-žawwu   ḥaarran fii ṣ-ṣayfi   SA
     3m-be   the-weather hot   in the-summer
     'The weather is usually hot in the summer.'

The same facts can be duplicated in Moroccan Arabic.

(36) a. ta-y-kun   l-žəww   sxun f-ṣ-ṣif   MA
         asp-3m-be the-weather hot   in-the-summer
         'The weather is hot in the summer.'

     b. Omar (ta-y-kun)   dima   waqəf   təmma
         Omar (asp-3m-be) always standing there
         'Omar always stands there.'

However, this form of the copula is not allowed in verbless sentences such as
illustrated in (37).

(37)* Omar (ta-y-kun)   ṭwil
      Omar (*asp-3m-be) tall

Both verbless sentences and the sentences in (35) and (36) have a present (habitual)
tense interpretation, but one allows for the presence of the copula and the other does
not. It is hard to see how a null copula analysis can account for this difference since
there is an overt form of the copula that can occur in the present tense.

The semantic difference between present tense sentences that can contain the
copula and those that cannot is that the former are generic sentences that contain stage-
level predicates describing situations that are usually true in the past, are true in the
present, and are expected to be true in the future (Moutaouakil 1987: 64). Like generic sentences (or characterizing sentences in the sense of Krifka et al. 1995), the
preceding sentences can be modified by an adverbial such as *f-l-ɣalib* (usually).

(38) Omar f-l-ɣalib   ta-y-kun   waqəf   təmma
     Omar in-the-majority asp-3m-be standing there
     'Omar usually stands there.'

By contrast, sentences containing individual-level predicates that describe states
of affairs that are permanent or stage-level predicates that describe situations that are
true in the present moment only, cannot contain the copula. For example, the sentence
in (36a) refers to the weather in the summer, though the moment of speech could be
located in another season. This contrasts sharply with the temporal interpretation of
sentences without the copula, which must refer to a state of affairs that obtains at the
moment of speech only. This becomes clear when we use deictic temporal adverbs
such as *daba* (now) or *lyum* (today) or any element that clearly restricts the reference
to the moment of speech and not the past or the future.

(39) a. l-žəww   sxuun lyum
          the-weather hot   today
          'The weather is hot today.'

      b. * l-žəww   ta-y-kun   sxun lyum
          the-weather asp-3m-be hot today

      c. Omar (*ta-y-kun) ṭwil
          Omar (asp-3m-be) tall
          'Omar is tall.'

Example (39a) refers to the weather as it is today. In this sense, it is deictic and therefore the copula is not allowed as shown by the ungrammaticality of (39b). Example
(39c) describes a property of Omar that is permanent and therefore could be taken as
deictic.[9]

To distinguish between the two types of present tense sentences, I will refer to
the one without the copula as the deictic present tense and the one with the copula as
the generic present tense. I will also assume that the generic present tense that may
take the copula contains a (generic) modal feature. When the modal feature is present,
the copula can be present. In this respect, it behaves like modals with present tense
interpretation, which require a copula.

(40) a. ṭ-ṭaalibu   qad *(ya-kuunu) ṭawiilan   SA
          the-student may   3m-be   tall
          'The student might be tall.'

      b. lazəm   *(y-kun) təmma   MA
          necessary 3m-be   there
          'He must be there.'

In short, the fact that in the deictic present tense the imperfective form of the
copula is not allowed shows clearly that there is no verbal copula in verbless sentences.
For the rest of the book, I will continue to use the term *present tense* with the inten-
tion of referring to the deictic present.

To sum up, we have good evidence for Jelinek's analysis of verbless sentences
in Arabic as constituents with a node that contains tense. Updated to minimalist terms,
verbless sentences are TPs that dominate a nonverbal predicate. But if this is case, as
the evidence seems to suggest, why is the copula absent? I take up this question in the
next section.

3.3 A Theory of the Categorial Features of Tense

3.3.1 The Present Tense

To explain why the copula is absent in the present tense let us reconsider the analyses of verbless sentences. All the analyses that have been advanced have tried to cap-
ture the intuition that tense determines whether a copula should be present. This relation between tense and the copula has been captured by either a condition on the copula
deletion rule (Bakir 1980), a copula support rule (Moutaouakil 1989: 84), a copula

spell-out rule (Fassi Fehri 1993), or a selection process whereby TP requires a VP if it is specified for the appropriate feature, such as past, future, or a modal feature (Bahloul 1994). The VP provides a host that supports the feature in tense. However, none of these analyses explains why the present tense does not force the presence of the copula. Surely the T head in the present tense is specified for a tense feature at least, and therefore it is not clear why the copula insertion rule does not apply to it.[10]

Part of this problem dissolves once we adopt the minimalist idea that movement to tense is not driven by the requirement to provide a host for tense. Since tense does not need a host the distribution of the copula must be found elsewhere. That is, we still need to explain why a verb is not required in verbless sentences.

This problem can be solved if we give up the idea that all tenses are specified as [+V] and [+D]. Suppose that the deictic present tense is [+D] only. Since it is not [+V], there is no need for a verbal copula. However, its [+D] feature must be checked, a role that can be adequately fulfilled by the subject.[11]

(41)

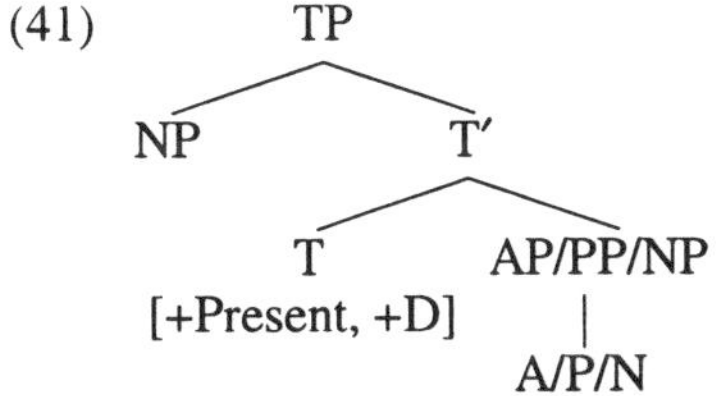

Given this analysis, the ungrammaticality of the sentence in (39b) follows if a verbal copula is not allowed because the deictic present tense is not [+V] and therefore does not require a verbal head to check any of its features. By contrast, the generic present tense may optionally be specified [+V] given its modal nature, in which case the copula is inserted to check its categorial [+V] feature.

Assuming these different feature matrices, we can correctly account for why a verbal head must be present in the context of nonverbal predicates in English and French but not in Arabic. In Arabic, a verb is not necessary in the present tense because the T head does not have a [+V] feature that needs to be checked. The only element that must be present is one that can check the [+D] feature, a role that is usually fulfilled by the subject.[12] In English and French, by contrast, the present tense, deictic and generic, is [+V], and therefore the presence of a verbal head that can check the [+V] feature is obligatory.

(42) (Deictic) Present Tense:

	Arabic	English/French
	[+D]	[+V, +D]
Copula	no	yes

Thus, the present tense in Arabic illustrates one instance where only one categorial feature is used—namely, the [+D] feature.

3.3.2 The Past Tense

As already pointed out, the past tense requires the presence of the copula.

(43) kan   Omar f-d-dar   MA
      be.past.3ms Omar in-the-house
      'Omar was at home.'

I will take this to imply that the past tense is [+V]. The copula then checks the categorial [+V] feature. Recall also that suffixal agreement is used with the past tense. The subject agreement suffix on the verb could be taken to indicate that it is [+D]. This does not entail that agreement is a realization of the past tense. Agreement only reflects a relation between the subject and the [+D] EPP (Extended Projection Principle) feature of the past tense.

3.3.3   The Future Tense

Future tense also seems to be [+V] and [+D]. The presence of [+V] feature is reflected by the fact that it always requires a verbal copula.

(44) sa-ya-kuunu fii l-bayti   MA
      fut-3m-be   in the-house
      'He will be in the house.'

The verb that merges with future tense always requires agreement, which I take to be a reflection of its [+D] feature.

3.4   Conclusion

In this chapter, I have explored the feature structure of the elements that occupy the head of the tense projection. The main conclusion, summarized in (45), is that the elements in tense do not have the same categorial feature specifications.

(45) Present [deictic]   [+D]
      Past   [+D, +V]
      Future   [+D, +V]

Thus, it is clear that the categorial features of the elements in tense are not uniform. The past and future tenses are specified for both features [+D] and [+V], while the present tense is specified only for the former.[13] The obvious question that arises is whether this characterization of the heads of TP has any empirical content. The answer is positive, as I argue in the next chapter.

4

Checking the Categorial Features of Tense

The idea that in verbless sentences tense is [+D] only is essentially an update within the feature system of Chomsky (1995) of previous analyses of verbless sentences as constructions that contain an Infl (Inflection) node that is specified for Agr (agreement) only (Doron 1986) or an AUX node that is specified for tense with no VP complement (Jelinek 1983). However, all the previous analyses implicitly or explicitly assume a fundamental difference between verbless present tense sentences and present tense sentences that contain verbal predicates. The assumption is that the feature composition of each of the two Infl (or TP) projections is different. One interacts with the verb—that is, triggers verb movement—and the other does not. Since verb movement within minimalism is motivated by feature checking, this would imply that the present tense in sentences with verbal predicates is [+V], in addition to being [+D]. In this chapter, I discuss the syntax of tense in light of the conclusions of the previous chapter. Focusing particularly on the contrast between the present tense and past tense, I show that the idea that characterizing the present tense as [+D] only in both sentences with and without verbal predicates will turn out to be crucial to deriving the following generalizations, which, as far as I know, have not been dealt with before, particularly generalizations (2), (3), and (4).

1. In Egyptian Arabic, merger with Negation is optional in the present tense but obligatory in the past tense.
2. Morphologically independent Neg is possible in the present tense but not in the past tense. Also, in the present tense, the morphologically independent negative *laysa* in Standard Arabic can either precede or follow the subject.
3. Idiomatic expressions display the SVO order in the present tense and VSO order in the past tense.
4. Person agreement is realized as a prefix in the present and as a suffix in the past.

I shall argue that these differences between the present tense and the past tense follow if the verb does not need to move to T in the present tense while it must do so in the past tense. This contrast can in turn be attributed to the conclusion of the previous chapter—namely, that the past tense has a [+V] feature, which must be checked by a verb, while the present tense is not specified for a [+V] feature.

4.1   Verb Movement and Negation

In Egyptian Arabic, the verb must merge with negation in the past but does not have to do so in the present tense, a contrast that has been noticed before (Jelinek 1983; Eisele 1988) but, as far as I know, has not received an explanation.

(1)   a.   ma-bi-yi-ktib-š   EA
           neg-asp-3m-write-neg
           'He isn't writing'.

      b.   miš bi-yi-ktib
           neg asp-3m-write
           'He isn't writing.'

(2)   a.   Omar ma-katab-š   ig-gawaab
           Omar neg-write.past.3ms-neg the-letter
           'Omar didn't write the letter.'

      b. * Omar mi-š   katab   ig-gawaab
           Omar neg-neg write.past.3ms the-letter

Given the proposal that the past tense has a [+V] feature and the present tense does not, plus the assumption that negation is located between TP and VP, the contrast can be readily explained. Since the past tense is [+V], the verb must move and merge with it. This forces the verb to first combine with negation (due to relativized minimality) on the way to tense.

(3)

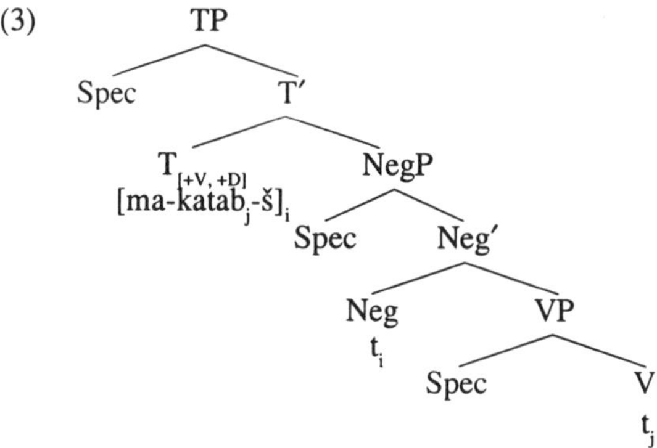

The present tense, by contrast, is not [+V]. Thus, the verb does not need to move to tense as already argued, but can remain in a projection lower than NegP, such as aspect (AspP) or VP. Therefore, it follows that the verb does not have to combine with negation.[1]

(4)

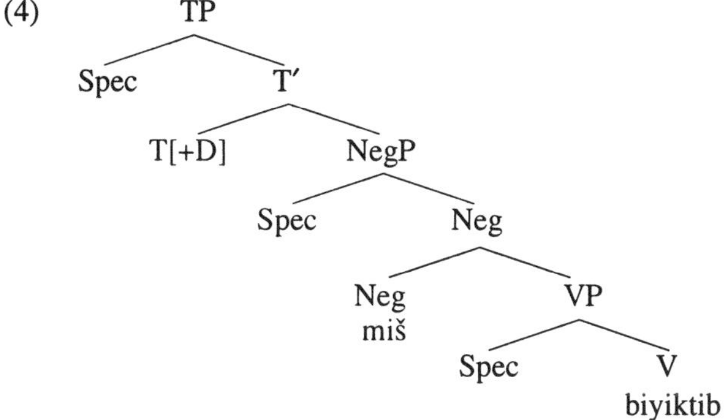

This analysis implies that the merger with negation in the present tense (1a) seems to take place for reasons that do not have to do with the features of tense. In the next chapter, I will argue that the merger with negation is driven by properties of sentential negation.

4.2   Independent Negatives

Another major contrast between sentences in the past tense and their present tense counterparts concerns the distribution of sentential negation in Standard Arabic. Since negation in Standard Arabic will be dealt with in greater detail in chapter 6, I will only focus on the aspects of sentential negation that are relevant to the present chapter. Two negatives are of particular relevance, the negatives *laa* and *laysa*. *laysa* can occur in verbal and verbless sentences (5), but only if they have a present tense interpretation (6).

(5)   a.   laysa   ya-lʕabu   SA
             neg.3ms 3m-play
             'He does not play.'

       b.   laysa   muʕalliman
             neg.3ms teacher
             'He is not a teacher.'

(6) * laysa   laʕiba
        neg.3ms play.past.3ms

However, *laa* and its suppletive past tense counterpart occur only in sentences with verbal predicates.

(7)   a.   laa ya-lʕabu
             neg 3m-play
             'He does not play.'

   b.* laa muʕallimun
       neg teacher

   c. lam   ya-kun muʕalliman
       neg.past 3m-be teacher
       'He was not a teacher.'

Moreover, these two negatives are different in another respect: *laysa* is an independent negative in that it can be separated from the verb by the subject, while *laa* and its suppletive counterparts must be affixed to the verb, which suggests that these negatives are bound elements (Shlonsky 1997).

(8)   a.   laysa   ʔaxii   muʕalliman
           neg.3ms brother.my teacher
           'My brother is not a teacher.'

      b. * laa ʔaxii   ya-drusu
           neg brother.my 3m-study

In chapter 6, I will argue that the negative *laa* and its variants are generated in a negative projection between TP and VP (very much like *ma-š* in Moroccan Arabic). Now suppose that *laysa* also heads a negative projection between TP and VP.

(9)

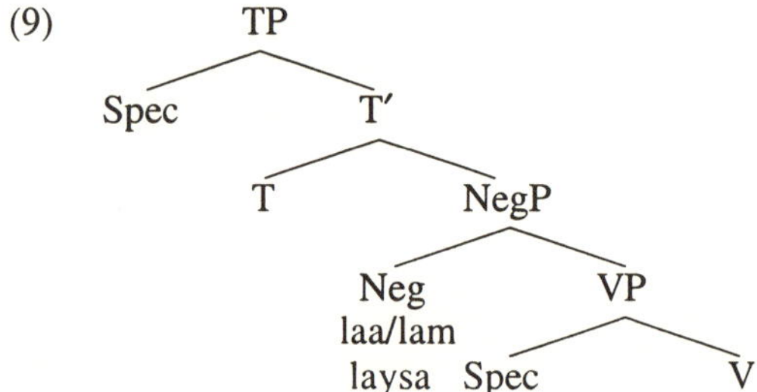

In the past tense, T is [+D] and [+V]. Therefore, the verb must move and merge with tense to check its [+V] feature. When *lam* occupies NegP, the verb merges with it and the whole complex moves to T for reasons that will be discussed in chapter 6.

(10)

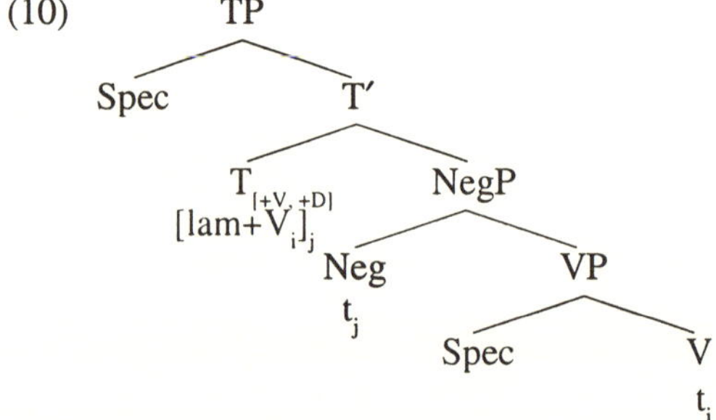

However, if *laysa* occupies NegP, given that it is not a bound morpheme, the verb cannot merge with it and move to tense. The only option is for the verb to move across negation to tense. This derivation, however, violates minimality.[2]

(11)

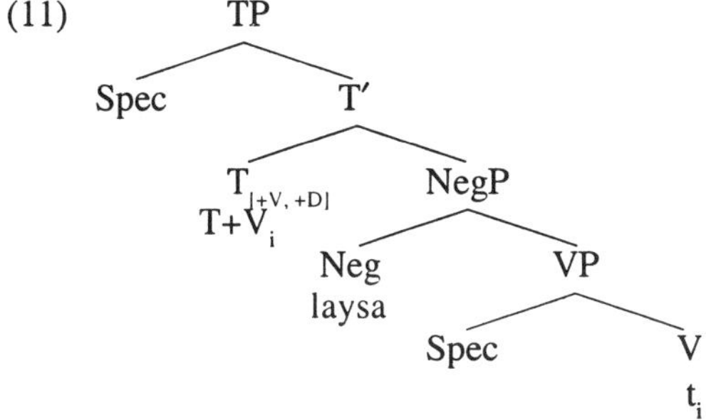

Therefore, *laysa* cannot occur in the context of TP specified for [+V], which is the case in the past tense. In past tense sentences with *laysa* preceding the subject, two derivations are possible and both are ill-formed. In the first derivation illustrated in (12), *laysa* could skip tense and move directly to a projection higher than TP; call it FP. However, this movement violates minimality. In the second derivation, illustrated in (13), *laysa* could move to tense and then to F, but this will result in *laysa* pied-piping tense and its unchecked [+V] feature.

(12)

(13)

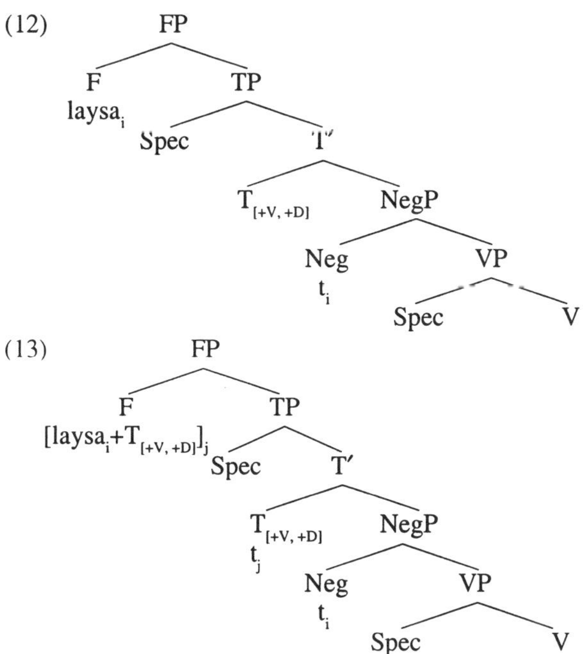

In the present tense, both *laysa* and *laa* are possible. Now recall that T of the present tense is [+D] only. Crucially, it is not [+V] and therefore does not require merger with a verb. If *laa* occupies NegP, the verb will move and merge with it. This is illustrated in (14). If *laysa* occupies NegP, the verb remains in situ. It does not need to move to tense because the latter is not [+V]. Therefore, *laysa* is compatible with present tense because no minimality effects could arise.[3] This is illustrated in (15).

(14)

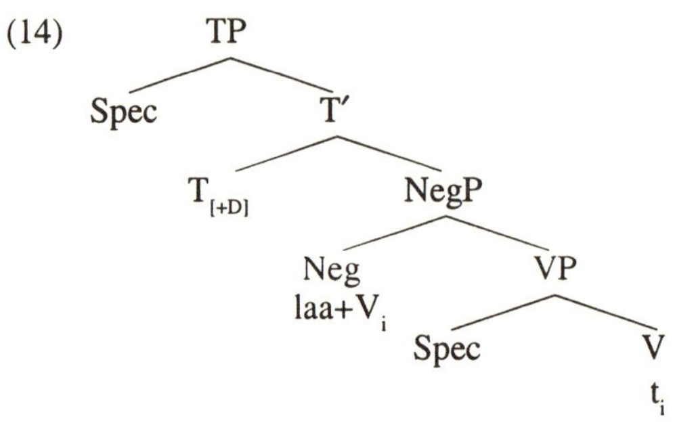

(15)

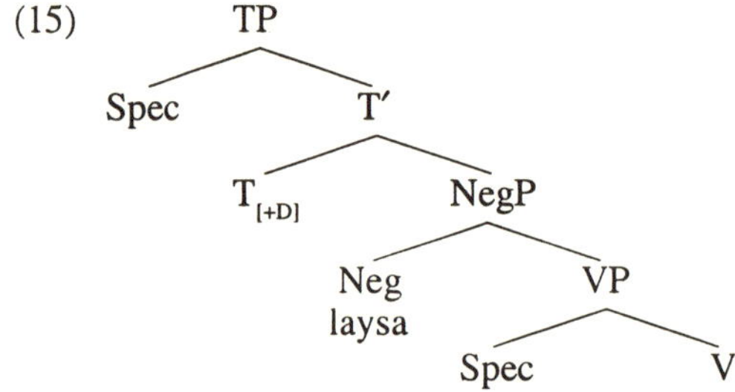

In short, by giving the past tense and present tense different feature specifications we have been able to account for why an independent morpheme can occur in the space between tense and the verb in the present tense but not in the past tense. In the past tense, on the one hand, verb movement to tense is required to check its [+V] feature. Intervening morphologically independent heads will always block this movement due to minimality. In the present tense, on the other hand, morphologically independent elements are tolerated between tense and the verb precisely because the latter does not need to move to tense given that that there is no [+V] feature that would drive this movement.

4.3   Idiomatic Expressions and Word Order Asymmetries

So far we have seen a clear difference between the present tense and the past tense. The present tense does not have a categorial [+V] feature, while the past tense does. This accounts for the asymmetries with respect to word order and merger with negation in the past tense and present tense. In this section, I discuss another context where the same asymmetry arises. This is the context that obtains in expressions that Ferguson (1983: 12–228) calls God-wishes. In the context of these expressions, on the one hand, if the verb is in the past tense, the VSO order is obligatory. On the other hand, if the verb carries the imperfective morphology that usually occurs in the presence tense, the SVO order is strongly preferred.[4] The following examples are all from Moroccan Arabic, but they can be easily duplicated in other dialects.

(16) a. rafim-u llah   MA
        bless.past.3ms-him God
        'May God bless him.'

     b. llah y-rəfim-u
        God 3m-blessed-him
        'May God bless him.'

(17) a. žaza-k llah
        reward.past.3ms-you God
        'May god reward you.'

     b. llah y-žazi-k
        God 3m-reward-you
        'May God reward you.'

(18) a. baraka llahu fii-k
        bless.past.3ms God in-you
        'May God bless you.'

     b. llah y-barik fii-k
        God 3m-bless in-you
        'May God bless you.'

Ferguson cites similar cases in Syrian Arabic, though all of them are in the imperfective form.

(19) a. ʔalla y-sallma-k
        God 3m-keep-you
        'May God keep you.'

     b. ʔalla yə-šfi-k
        God 3m-heal-you
        'May God heal you.'

This asymmetry can be explained if we assume this featural characterization of the present and past tense. Since verb movement to tense is strictly driven by the requirement to check the [+V] feature, we expect the verb to stay in situ or lower than TP in the present tense (20). By contrast, the verb in the past must raise to tense to check its [+V] and [+D] features (21).

(20)

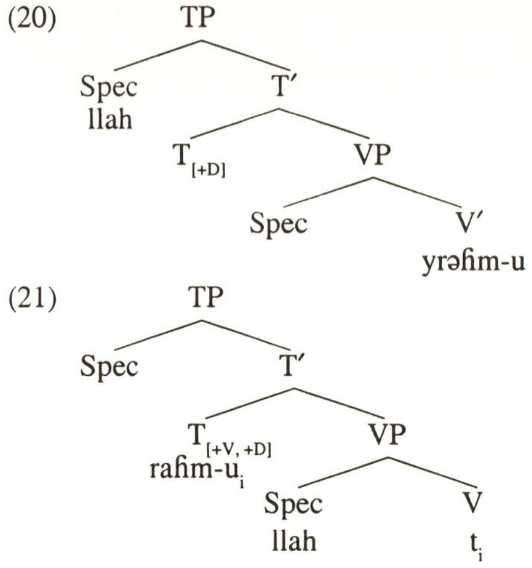

(21)

To summarize, the syntax of idiomatic expressions, which Ferguson calls God-wishes, supports the main thesis in this chapter. In idioms, the SVO order is usually found in present tense sentences while the VSO order is more likely to occur in past tense sentences. This word order asymmetry follows because in the past tense the verb must move to tense to check its [+V] feature, which makes it an eligible checker for the [+D] feature as well. In the present tense, by contrast, the verb does not need to move to tense since the latter lacks a [+V] feature.

4.4   The Morphological Distribution of the Person Prefix

The distribution of agreement features also displays an asymmetry according to tense. As indicated in chapter 2, in the past tense the agreement morphology on the verb is exclusively suffixal. In the present tense, by contrast, the verb has both prefixal and suffixal morphology. Let us look at these paradigms in more detail.

(22)   Past Tense Paradigm in Standard Arabic

Person	Number	Gender	Affix	Verb+Affix
1	Singular	F/M	-tu	katab-tu
2	"	M	-ta	katab-ta
2	"	F	-ti	katab-ti
3	"	M	-a	katab-a
3	"	F	-at	katab-at
2	Dual	M/F	-tumaa	katab-tumaa
3	"	M	-aa	katab-aa
3	"	F	-ataa	katab-ataa
1	Plural	M/F	-naa	katab-naa
2	"	M	-tum	katab-tum
2	"	F	-tunna	katab-tunna
3	"	M	-uu	katab-uu
3	"	F	-na	katab-na

(23) Imperfective Paradigm in Standard Arabic

Person	Number	Gender	Affix	Affix+Verb
1	Sg	M/F	ʔa-	ʔa-ktub
2	"	M	ta-	ta-ktub
2	"	F	ta-ii	ta-ktub-ii
3	"	M	ya-	ya-ktub
3	"	F	ta-	ta-ktub
2	Dual	M/F	ta---aa	ta-ktub-aa
3	"	M/F	ya---aa	ya-ktub-aa
1	Plural	M/F	na-	na-ktub
2	"	M	ta---uu	ta-ktub-u
2	"	F	ta---na	ta-ktub-na
3	"	M	ya---uu	ya-ktub-uu
3	"	F	ta---na	ta-ktub-na

Starting with the perfective/past tense paradigm, notice that the agreement suffix is almost identical to the independent form of the corresponding pronoun, as illustrated by in (24).

(24) Standard Arabic Pronouns and Agreement Affixes

ʔanaa	-tu	katab-tu
ʔanta	-ta	katab-ta
ʔanti	-ti	katab-ti
huwa	-a	katab-a
hiya	-at	katab-at
ʔantumaa	-tumaa	katab-tumaa
humaa	-aa	katab-aa
humaa	-ataa	katab-ataa
naħnu	-naa	katab-naa
ʔantum	-tum	katab-tum
ʔantuna	-tunna	katab-tunna
hum	-uu	katab-uu
hunna	-na	katab-na

The *n* prefix in the first and second person is probably an epenthetic element related to the focus particle *na* in *ʔinna*.[5]

(25) ʔinna l-walada   mariiḍun   SA
      that   the-boy-acc sick
      'The boy is indeed sick.'

The initial glottal stop is the usual epenthetic consonant inserted to provide an onset for the syllable in Semitic in general and Arabic in particular (Brame 1970). Thus, in Moroccan Arabic, where consonantal clusters are permitted, the second person pronoun is realized as *nta*. With respect to the first person singular suffix *tu* in Arabic, apparently the old Semitic one was *ku* (the form in Akkadian), which probably changed to *tu* in Old Arabic and some other Semitic languages. As far as the third person is concerned, the view that is widely accepted within comparative historical semitic is that they all evolved from demonstratives. Taking all these facts into consideration, the picture that emerges is that the independent pronouns and the agreement system in the perfective are relatively identical, with only minor adjustments that may have to do with whether the relevant form is dependent or independent (thus requiring epenthetic segments) and historical change.

The Arabic agreement system thus undoubtedly evolved from a pronominal system that has been incorporated into the verb and became pure agreement (Gray 1934: 65; Fleisch 1979: 5–27). Gray (1934: 65) provides the following table (26) of independent pronouns and agreement affixes in the two paradigms. He takes these forms as representing the Proto-Semitic (or Old Semitic) system. The merits of this assumption need not concern us here. What is significant is the clear correspondence between the pronominal system and the agreement affixes, which no student of comparative Semitic denies.

(26)		Independent	Perfect	Imperfect
	1s	ʔan-aa(ku)	-kuu	ʔa-
	2ms	ʔan-t-a	-t-a	t-
	2fs	ʔan-t-i	-t-ii	t-
	1p	nafi-nu	-na	n-
	2mp	ʔan-t-um-u	-t-um-u	t-
	2fp	ʔan-t-inna-a	-t-inn-a	t-

Now what is intriguing is the fact that this agreement system is suffixal. One possible explanation is that this is a consequence of two properties of the language that have to do with the syntax of verbs and subjects. In the past tense, the verb moves to tense while the subject remains in a lower projection. This yields a configuration where the pronominal is to the right of the verb. Merger between the verb and the pronominal produces a verb with a pronominal enclitic.

(27)

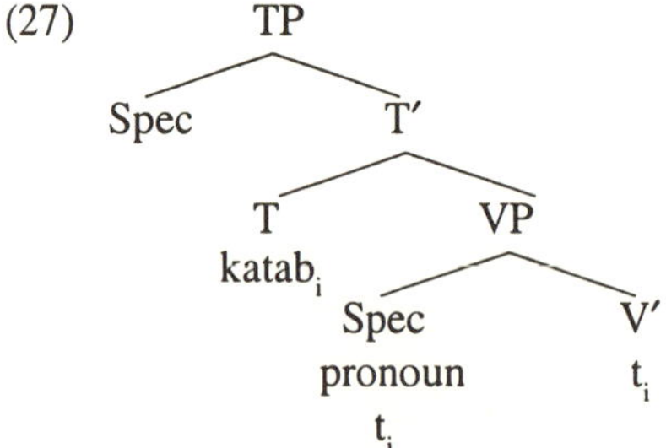

This is exactly the situation we should expect if the verb must move to tense in the past tense to check its [+V] feature.

Now let us turn to the imperfective paradigm. As can be seen from the preceding paradigm, in the imperfective the prefix realizes mostly person (and in some cases gender) while the suffix realizes number and gender (Benmamoun 1992, 1993). Considering what I mentioned earlier about the glottal stop and nasal segments that make up the first part of the first and second person pronouns, one fact that stands out is that the person prefix is almost identical to the person morpheme that is part of the morphological makeup of the pronominal.

(28)   Standard Arabic Independent Pronouns and Agreement Afffixes

ʔanaa	ʔa-
ʔanta	ta-
ʔan-ti	ta-ii
huwa	ya-
hiya	ta-
ʔantumaa	ta-aa
humaa	ya-aa
humaa	ta-aa
naħnu	na-
ʔantum	ta-uu
ʔantuna	ta-na
hum	ya-uu
hunna	ya-na

Another fact that may be significant is that the suffix that carries number and gender in the Standard Arabic imperfective form is identical to the suffix on nouns except in the third person feminine, where plural is realized by lengthening the vowel of the singular feminine.

(29)   Standard Arabic Imperfective Verbs and Nouns

ya-ktub	(he writes)	muʕallim	(one teacher.M)
ta-ktub	(she writes)	muʕallim-at	(one teacher.F)
ya-ktub-**aan**	(they write.D)	muʕallim-**aan**	(two teachers.M)
ta-ktub-**aan**	(you write.D)	muʕallim-at**aan**	(two teachers.F)
ta-ktub-**uun**	(they write.MP)	muʕallim-**uun**	(teachers.M)
ya-ktub-na	(they write.FP)	muʕallim-aat	(teachers.F)

While the correlation between the number suffix on the imperfective verb and its counterpart on nouns is not perfect (we are dealing with a system that has evolved over thousands of years, after all), the fact that four out of six forms show perfect correlation suggests that the two forms are drawing from the same paradigm of number (and gender). This indicates that the number and gender agreement markers are due to later developments. Taking these two sets of facts together—the person prefix, which to a large extent resembles the independent pronominals, and the number and gender suffix, which resembles the number and gender suffix on nouns—the following tentative explanation may go a long away toward accounting for them. The fact that the prefix in the imperfective carries person agreement, which is the defining feature of pronominals could follow if the prefix is a relic of a merged pronominal, which has lost its number (and sometime gender) components. Now this merger is clearly different from the merger we suggested for the past tense verb. The latter merges to the right, while the former merges to the left. This receives a straightforward explanation within the theory suggested in the earlier discussion, namely that the imperfective verb, which is the form found in the present tense, does not move to TP. The order that results has the subject to the left of the verb, hence the proclitic nature of person agreement in the imperfective.

(30)

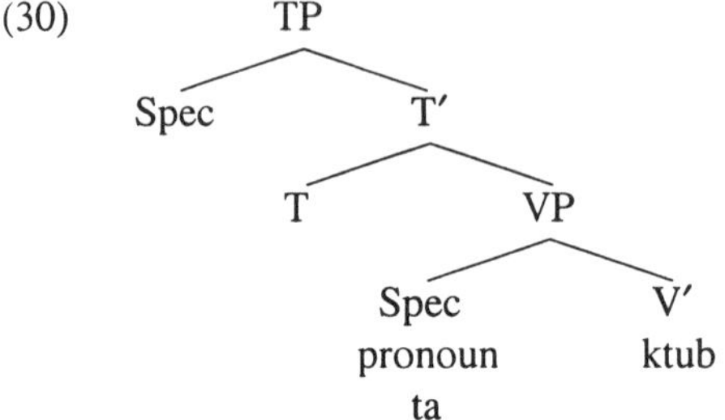

This is admittedly highly tentative and should be taken as a first approximation. More work needs to be done in this area, which I leave for future research.

4.5 Word Order Alternations

The evidence from negation suggests that in the past tense the verb must raise to T, while in the present tense it may remain in a position lower than TP. However, the evidence from idioms and the distribution of person agreement affixes argue for a stronger position, namely that in the past tense, on the one hand, the subject raises to a position higher than the subject, hence the VSO order. In the present tense, on the other hand, the subject seems to be in a higher projection than the verb, hence the SVO order.

This conclusion is confirmed by the fact that some speakers of Moroccan Arabic agree that in the past tense the VSO order is preferred, while in the present tense the SVO is strongly favored.

(31) a. nəʕs-u   lə-wlad   MA
        sleep.past-p the-children
        'The children slept.'

     b. lə-wlad   ta-y-ləʕbu
        the-children asp-3m-play
        'The children are playing.'

This difference between past tense sentences and present tense sentences is readily explained within the present analysis. In the past tense, the T head is specified for both [+V] and [+D] features. On the one hand, there is only one candidate to check the [+V] feature—namely, the verb. The [+D] feature, on the other hand, can be checked primarily by the subject. But it can also be checked by the verb, thanks to the agreement features it carries, assuming Borer's 1986 I-subject theory. According to

Borer, in null subject languages the agreement inflection acts as the subject. Updated to the minimalist terms, the inflection on the verb can check the [+D] feature of tense (see also Alexiadou and Anagnostopoulou 1999). Turning to the past tense in Arabic, since the verb must move to tense to check the [+V] feature, it can also check the [+D] feature for free, thus obviating the movement of the subject to the Spec of TP. This results in the VSO order with the verb in tense and the subject in a lower projection (either VP or AspP).

(32)

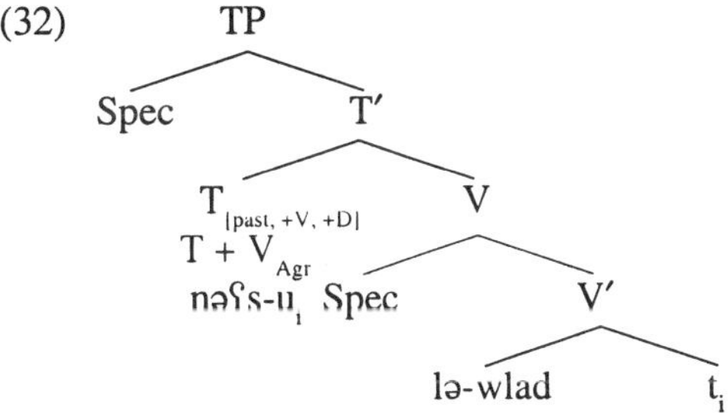

Turning now to the present tense, the T head is specified for a [+D] feature only. This feature can be checked by the subject. The verb, however, though a potential checker, is not attracted to T by the main feature it can check, namely, [+V].

(33)

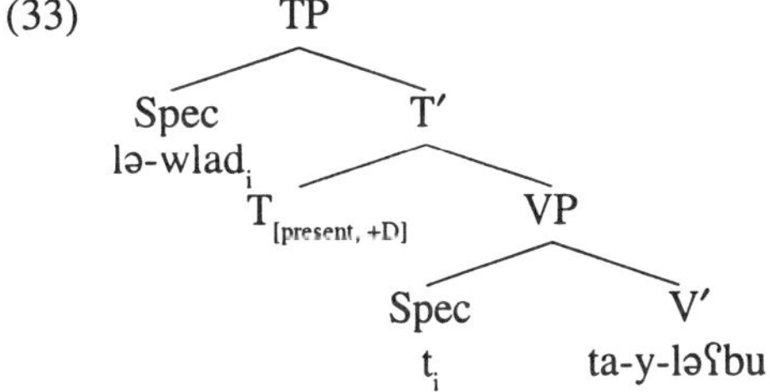

If this analysis is correct, we have a principled explanation for the contrast between the status of word order options available in the present and past tense. Assuming that the VSO order involves movement to TP, I have argued that this situation only arises in the context of the past tense because the latter contains a [+V] feature that attracts the verb. The obligatory movement of the verb to tense puts it in a position where it can check the [+D] feature as well. In the present tense, by contrast, there is only one [+D] feature in T to check that attracts the subject.

Given this analysis, we are now in a position to explain why the other orders, though available are less preferred. The SVO order in the past tense entails a redundancy. The subject moves to tense to check its [+D] feature, while the verb moves to check its [+V] feature. However, the verb, which must move to tense anyway can fulfill the same function as the subject. Therefore, the movement of the subject results in a representation where there is one categorial feature to check but two possible checkers, the subject in the Spec of TP and the verb in tense.

(34)

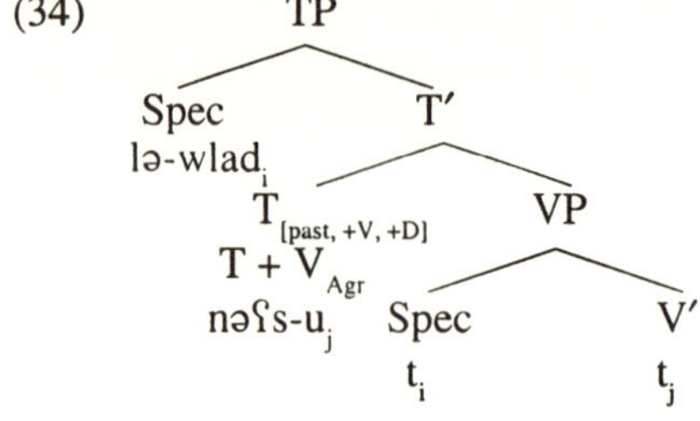

This is clearly redundant, which could explain why it is less optimal than the representation where the [+D] feature of tense is paired with one single checker. In the present tense, the VSO order is less preferred, probably because the movement of the NP only involves the necessary feature [+D] while the movement of the verb involves the movement of a superfluous feature [+V].

4.6   Position of the Subject in Verbless Negative Sentences

This analysis provides a straightforward answer to a puzzle within Arabic syntax. The puzzle concerns word order in the context of sentential negation. As introduced briefly in the previous chapter, sentential negation in Moroccan Arabic consists of two morphemes: the proclitic *ma* and the enclitic *š*. If they attach to a verb, *ma* occurs as a prefix and *š* as a suffix.

(35)   Omar ma-qra-š   lə-ktab
        Omar neg-read.past.3ms-neg the-book
        'Omar did not read the book.'

I will assume that *ma-š* is a complex head of a negative projection located between TP. The evidence for this analysis of sentential negation will be presented in detail in the next chapter. Verb movement to tense proceeds through the negative projection (to circumvent minimality).

(36)

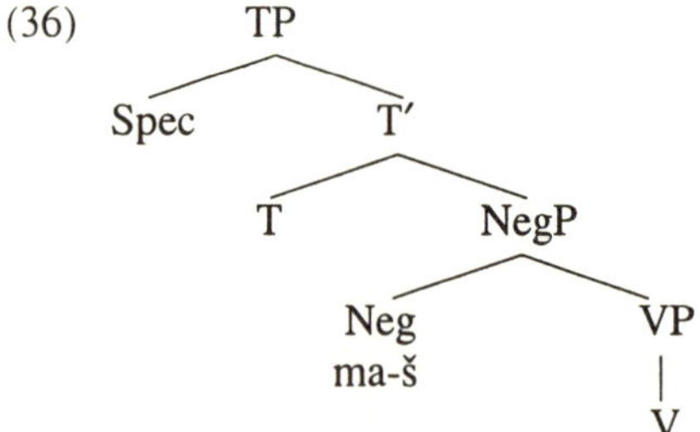

In verbless sentences, *ma* merges with *š*.

(37) a. Omar ma-ši f-d-dar
       Omar neg-neg in-the-house
       'Omar is in the house.'
   b. Omar ma-ši kəddab
      Omar neg-neg liar
      'Omar is not a liar.'
   c. Omar ma-ši mriḍ
      Omar neg-neg sick
      'Omar is not sick.'

With this brief background in mind, let us consider the distribution of the sentential subject in the context of sentential negation. In sentences with a verbal head, the subject can either follow or precede the verb, though preference is given to the VSO order in the past tense.

(38) a. Omar ma-qra-š   lə-ktab
       Omar neg-read.past.3ms-neg the-book
       'Omar did not read the book.'
   b. ma-qra-š   Omar lə-ktab
      neg-read.past.3ms-neg Omar the-book
      'Omar did not read the book.'

The alternative orders have already been accounted for. Interestingly, this alternative ordering is not possible in verbless sentences. In these contexts, the subject must precede sentential negation.

(39) a. Omar ma-ši mriḍ   MA
       Omar neg-neg sick
       'Omar is not sick.'
   b. * ma-ši Omar mriḍ
       neg-neg Omar sick

Previously, this fact has been taken as an argument that the subject must always move to the Spec of TP (Benmamoun 1996). This, in turn, has forced the stipulation that in the VSO order the verb must be in a projection higher than TP.

The present analysis provides a principled alternative explanation for why in verbless sentences the subject must precede sentential negation. The reason is that there is no other head to check the [+D] feature of tense. Alternative orders are available with verbal predicates because the latter contain agreement features that can check the [+D] feature of tense. In verbless sentences, the only contender for checking the [+D] feature of tense is the subject.

Consider the derivation of (39a). The underlying representation is as in (40).

(40)

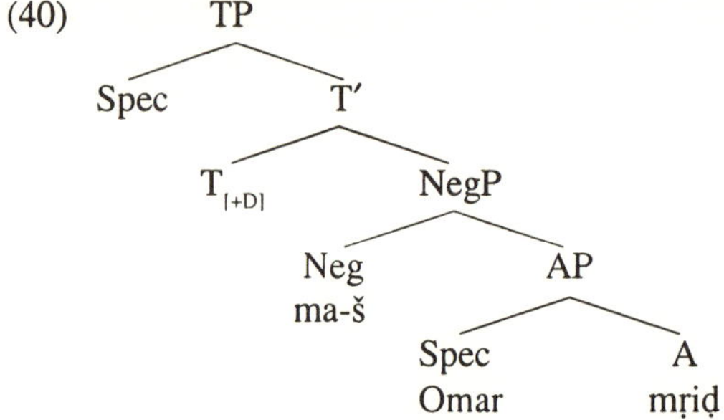

The NP *Omar* is generated in the Spec of the lexical projection, where it gets its thematic role—namely, the AP. If it stays in situ, the [+D] feature of tense will remain unchecked. This sharply contrasts with (38b), where the verb can check the [+D] feature of tense, thus obviating the need for NP movement to Spec TP.

4.7   Conclusion

In this chapter, I have proposed that the functional category TP is specified for different categorial features depending on tense type. In the present tense T is [+D], while in the past tense it is [+V] and [+D]. This has allowed me to account for various asymmetries that characterize the syntax of verbs in the present and past tense. These asymmetries are summarized in the following table.

(41)

	V to T (EA)	V+Neg (EA)	Person Agr	Independent Neg	Idiom
$T_{[present]}$	Not obligatory	Optional	Prefix	Possible	SV
$T_{[past]}$	Obligatory	Obligatory	Suffix	Not possible	VS

II

The Feature Structure of Negation

5

Sentential Negation in Modern Arabic Dialects

In this chapter, I discuss two issues that arise in the context of sentential negation. The first issue is the representation of sentential negation, particularly in dialects where it is realized by two formatives. The second issue is the feature structure of negation. I will argue that sentential negation is specified for the categorial feature [+D], which must be checked by an inherently [+D] head or phrase or by a head that carries agreement features. Arabic dialects diverge with respect to the checking configuration they adopt, resulting in variation in word order and the morphological realizations of sentential negation. In some contexts, the two-part negative is realized as a discontinuous element (one part a proclitic and the other part an enclitic). In other contexts, it is realized as a single complex element augmented with agreement. I will argue that the two realizations of sentential negation (discontinuous and nondiscontinuous morphemes) receive a unified analysis in terms of how categorial features are checked, thus obviating analyses whereby the two realizations instantiate two independent sentential negatives in the modern Arabic dialects. The analysis of how the categorial [+D] feature of negation is checked will further support the analysis provided in chapter 4 where it was argued that a head that carries agreement can check categorial [+D] features. I will demonstrate that the same situation obtains in the context of sentential negation.

5.1   Representation of Sentential Negation

Sentential negation in Moroccan Arabic, Egyptian Arabic, Palestinian Arabic (Shlonsky 1997), and Yemeni Arabic, particularly the Sanʔaani dialect (Watson 1993), is realized by two morphemes, the proclitic *ma* and the enclitic *š*, as illustrated in (1).

(1)   a.   ma-ža-t-š   Nadia   MA
            neg-come.past.3fs-neg Nadia
            'Nadia didn't come.'

      b.   Nadia ma-ža-t-š
            Nadia neg-come.past-3fs-neg
            'Nadia didn't come.'

In other dialects, such as Sudanese Arabic and Hassaniyya (the dialect of Tan Tan in Morocco, Iaaich 1996), sentential negation is expressed by one single element, *ma*.

(2)   a.   Omar ma dža   Sudanese Arabic
             Omar neg come.past.3ms
             'Omar didn't come.'

       b.   maa štɣal-t   Hassaniyya
             neg work.past-1s
             'I didn't work.'

The other possibility—namely *š* by itself—also exists, as shown in (3) from one Lebanese dialect of Baskinta (Abu-Haidar, 1979: 110) and one Jordanian dialect mentioned in Palva (1972: 42), respectively.[1]

(3)   a.   bi-t-ḥib-š   siɣl il-bayt   Lebanese
             asp-3f-likes-neg work the-house
             'She does not like housework.'

       b.   bədd-i-š   Jordanian
             want-my-neg
             'I don't want.'

In this section, I explore the syntactic representation of sentential negation in the modern Arabic dialects. Current syntactic analyses of sentential negation, particularly in Romance languages (Pollock 1989; Laka 1990; Ouhalla 1990; Zanuttini 1997; Cinque 1999), allow for two possibilities to account for languages where negation is realized by two separate markers. One possibility is that the two negative markers occupy different syntactic projections. Another possibility is that both are located within the same projection, one as Specifier and the other as head. In this section, I will argue that the markers *ma* and *š* in the modern Arabic dialects constitute a complex head; that is, both are in the head position of the negative projection.

5.1.1   Distribution of the Two Negative Morphemes *ma* and *š*

Assuming that sentential negation occupies a projection between TP and VP, the facts in dialects where negation is realized by one element, *ma* or *š* is relatively straightforward. Either *ma* or *š* could be represented as a head of the negative projection which is merged with the verb when the latter moves through the negative projection to T or a projection higher than TP.

(4)

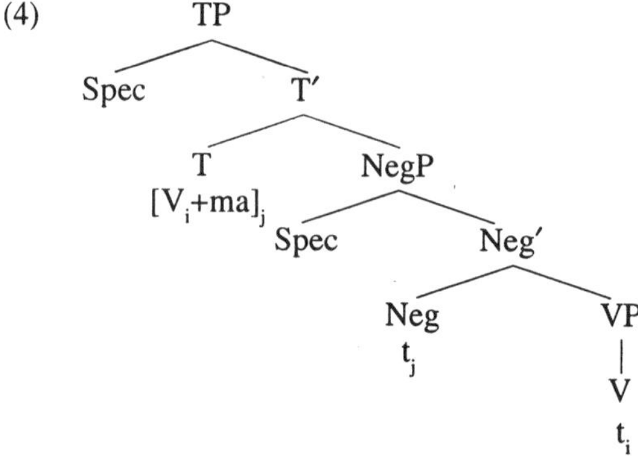

Merger between the negative head and the verb is evident from the fact that in Sudanese, on the one hand, nothing can intervene between them.

(5) * Omar ma ʔamis   dža   Sudanese Arabic
       Omar neg yesterday come.past.3ms

The facts in Egyptian Arabic, Moroccan Arabic, and Sanaanii Arabic, on the other hand, are more complex. The complexity is due to the fact that sentential negation is expressed by two elements that seem to be independent: the proclitic *ma* and the enclitic *š*. In this respect, the three dialects pattern with Standard French, where sentential negation is also expressed by two negative elements, *ne* and *pas*.

(6)   Nadia n'est pas venu
       Nadia ne-is-neg come
       'Nadia didn't come.'

The similarities with French do not stop here. As in French, in Moroccan Arabic (Benmamoun 1992, 1997) and Sanʕaanii Arabic (Watson 1993: 258), the second expression of negation does not surface in the context of negative quantifiers.[2]

(7)   a.   J'ai   vu   personne
            I have seen no one
            'I haven't seen anyone.'

       b.   ma-ža   fiətta wafiəd   MA
            neg-come.past.3ms. any   one
            'Nobody came.'

(8)   maa maʕi   zalaṭ   Sanʕaanii Arabic
       neg with.me money
       'I have no money'

5.1.2   *š* as Spec of NegP

As far as French is concerned, Pollock (1989), Ouhalla (1990), and Moritz and Valois (1994) advanced an analysis whereby *ne* occupies the head and *pas* the Spec of a negative projection located between TP and VP.

(9)   NegP

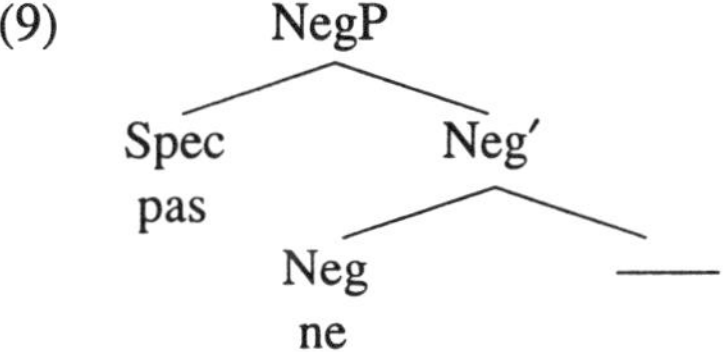

It follows from the representation in (9) that *ne* and *pas* are expressions of a single sentential negation (no double negation). The fact that *ne* overtly precedes *pas* follows as a consequence of head movement that proceeds through the negative projection and thus takes *ne* to a position higher than the negative projection that contains *pas*. Also, by putting *pas* in the Spec of NegP one can derive the complementary distribution between negative quantifiers and *pas* under the assumption that these elements must be licensed in the Spec of NegP either overtly or covertly (Moritz and Valois 1994).

(10)   Je n'ai   (*pas) vu   personne
       I   neg have   seen no one
       'I have seen no one.'

Thus, *pas* can only occur in the context of elements that are not subject to this licensing requirement. Now, given the similarities between sentential negation in Moroccan Arabic and Sanaanii Arabic, on one hand, and French sentential negation, on the other hand, we could extend the analysis of French to the Arabic dialects with two-part negation. Under this analysis, *ma* corresponds to *ne* and therefore is the head of NegP. By contrast, *š*, corresponds to *pas* and therefore is in the Spec of NegP. As in French, NegP in the above dialects is located between TP and VP (Mohamed and Ouhalla 1995; Shlonsky 1997: 92).

(11)

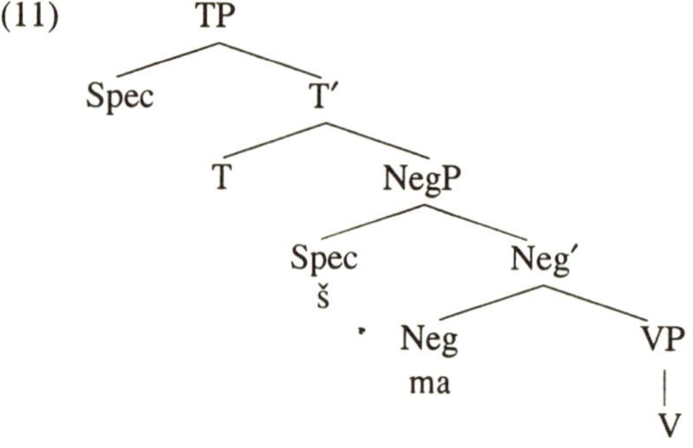

Recall from chapter 4 that verb movement in Standard Arabic and the modern Arabic dialects takes place in the overt syntax. All we need to do, then, is allow verb movement to go through the negative projection on the way to tense. Due to this movement, the verb merges with negation and the whole complex moves up to tense.

(12)

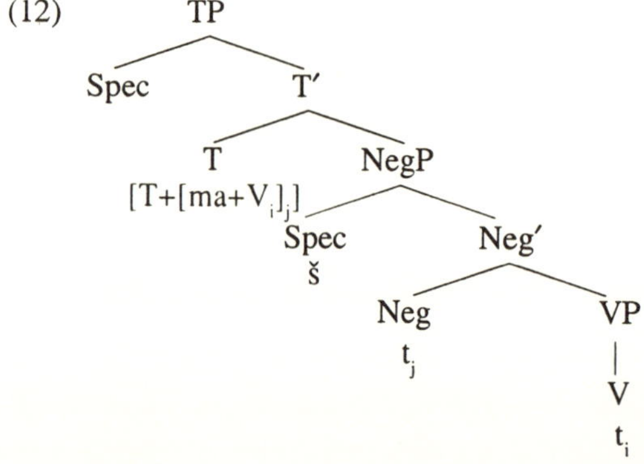

Notice that verb movement through the negative projection is necessary to circumvent a violation of minimality since the intervening negative head would block antecedent government of the verbal trace (Ouhalla 1990; Benmamoun 1992). As far as the enclicization of *š* is concerned, one hypothesis is that this obtains in PF by simple merger between the verbal complex in tense and the Spec of NegP that follows it (Mohamed and Ouhalla 1995: 73, Ouhalla forthcoming).

5.1.3 Arguments Against *š* as Spec of NegP

While this analysis derives the distributional facts already mentioned, particularly the merger of the verb and the negative elements, it makes some predictions that are not borne out.

One problem with the configuration in (11) comes from the distribution of sentential negation in the context of verbless sentences (nominal sentences). As noted in the previous chapter, in these sentences the two negative elements cliticize onto each other.

(13) Nadia ma-ši   fə-l-madrasa   MA
      Nadia neg-neg in-the-school
      'Nadia is not at school.'

Given that there is no verb movement through the negative projection, the putative specifier of NegP merges with the putative head of NegP. However, the order is reversed; the output has the head following the putative specifier, which is exactly the opposite of the Spec-Head sequencing predicted by the configuration in (11). This clearly cast doubt on the representation in (11).

This fact leads us to question the central argument for the representation in (11). The main reason that *š* is treated as Spec of NegP is because it patterns with *pas* in French as far as its interaction with negative quantifiers goes.[3] Both can be in complementary distribution with these elements. This assumption, however, is problematic because there are instances in some Arabic dialects where this complementary distribution is optional. Moreover, there are situations where the element in complementary distribution with *š* is clearly not in Spec of NegP.

The optionality of dropping *š* in the context of negative quantifiers is attested in Eastern Libyan Arabic, described in Owens (1984). Thus, while in Moroccan Arabic *s* cannot occur in the context of *ħadd*, according to Owens (1984: 161-162), in Eastern Libyan Arabic, *š* is optional, though it seems that the forms without *š* are "more emphatically negative" (Owens does not provide the example with *š*.) Similarly, in Egyptian Arabic *š* does not get dropped in the context of negative quantifiers.

(14) ma-šuf-ti-š   ħad   EA
      neg-see.past-1s-neg anyone
      'I didn't see anyone.'

The facts in these dialects cast doubt on the analysis that takes the complementary distribution between *š* and negative quantifiers in Moroccan Arabic and Sanʕaanii

Arabic as an argument for the former being in the Spec of NegP, where licensing can take place (due to the Neg Criterion).

Further arguments that the absence of *š* is not related to the requirement that negative polarity items or quantifiers move to the Spec of NegP (either overtly or covertly) come from the distribution of negative predicates in Moroccan Arabic (the same facts obtain in other dialects). The element that corresponds to the English negative adverbial *never* is a verbal element in Moroccan Arabic, *ʕəmmər*, as shown by the fact that it can take nonnominative clitics (Benmamoun 1992: 147–148).

(15) ʕəmmr-u ma-ža   MA
      never-him neg-come.past.3ms
      'He never came.'

The distribution of this element in Moroccan Arabic is quite complex, but suffice it to say that the predicate in the negative clause that follows *ʕəmmər* cannot contain *š*. Significantly, *ʕəmmər* is clearly higher than NegP in the embedded clause, which indicates that if there is any licensing relationship between this negative predicate and sentential negation it cannot involve the embedded NegP (except if we stipulate an adhoc process of LF lowering). Consequently, the absence of *š* is not related to the requirement that NPIs or negative quantifiers move to the Spec of NegP.[4]

With these facts in mind, one could argue that *š* occupies the Spec of or is adjoined to a lower projection.[5] This essentially means that *š* and *ma* are different expressions of negation located in different syntactic positions.

(16)

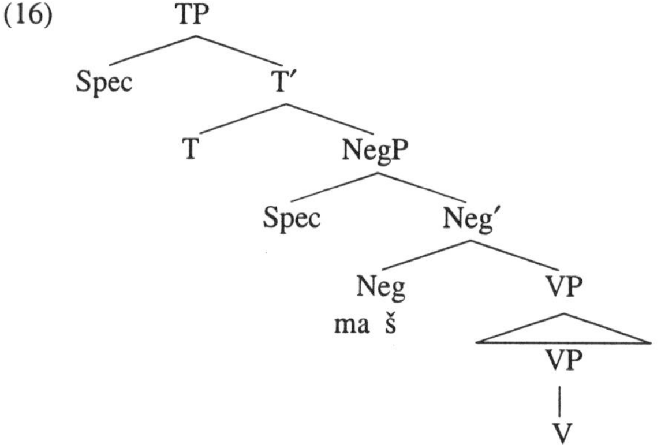

A serious piece of evidence that militates against this analysis comes from Sanaanii Arabic. This dialect differs from Moroccan Arabic in that the negative complex *maa-ši* can be used on its own as a response to a question, for example. This is illustrated by the following exchange (Watson 1993: 266).

(17) a. zawžiš   yi-safir   al-yaman   SanʕaaniiArabic
          husband.your 3m-travel the-Yemen
          'Will your husband go to Yemen?'

b. maaši (maa y-saafur-š   al-yaman)
    no   neg 3m-travel-neg the-Yemen
    'No, he will not go to Yemen.'

This form is also used in elliptical contexts (Watson 1993: 121).

(18) bih   naas   yi-šill-u   l-zild   u-naas maaši
      there people 3m-take-p off the-skin and people no
      'There are people who take off the skin and some people who don't.'

Here we see *maa* and *š* making up a single negative element, which goes to show that the two parts of negation do not belong to different syntactic positions that are subsequently brought together by a syntactic process. This is undoubtedly the case in instances where *maašii* is followed by a negative sentence, as in (17b), ruling out any alternative where *maašii* is within an elliptical sentence with enough space for movement and merger.

The same conclusion can be reached when we consider the fact that in some dialects, such as Egyptian Arabic, the two negative elements can merge with a quantifier to derive a negative quantifier (Jelinek 1983, 103).

(19) ma-ḥaddi-š   yi-staʕmil maktabi wi ana ɣaayib   EA
      neg-someone-neg 3m-use   my office and I absent
      'Nobody is to (let nobody) to give orders.'

It could be argued that the negative quantifier has merged with the negative head *ma* and moved higher to the Spec of TP, as illustrated in (20).

(20)

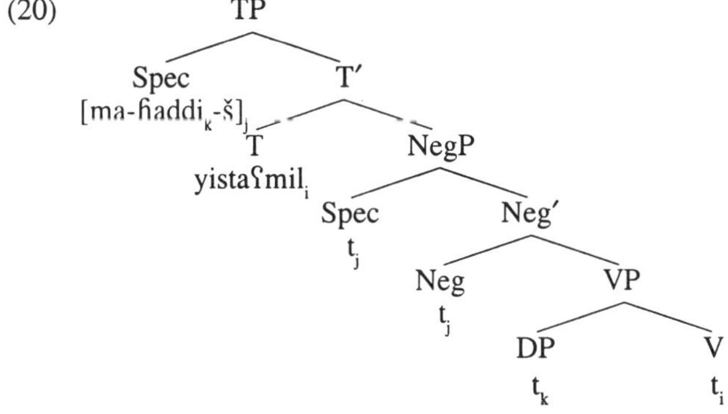

For this analysis to be maintained a host of auxiliary assumptions must be made, however. First, suppose that the verb in (20) is in T.[6] This means that in (20) the verb has moved across the negative head, in violation of minimality. Second, under this analysis it is surprising that the Spec of NegP cannot be left behind to subsequently merge with the verb that derives an output as in (21).

(21)* ma-ħaddi   yistaʕmil-š maktabi   wi ana ɣaayib
      neg-someone use-neg   my office and I absent

At any rate, it is not even clear that the negative quantifier in (19) should be derived in the syntax because it can co-occur with sentential negation, as illustrated in (22) from Woidich (1968: 73).

(22) ma-ħaddi-š   min il-bašar   ma-lu-š   mafiaasin   EA
      neg-someone-neg of   the-humanity neg-has-neg attributes
      'No human being lacks good qualities.'

The same problem arises in the context of constituent negation in Moroccan Arabic. As shown in (23) *š* again surfaces as a suffix on *ma*.

(23) ma-ši kull   wəld ža   MA
      not   every child come.past.3ms
      'Not every child came.'

Assuming that constituent negation is not derived in the syntax, the fact that both *ma* and *š* are needed to express it suggests that these two elements do not belong to different syntactic positions (say Spec and head) within a single projection or belong to different projections. Rather, it suggests that they form a single discontinuous element, as I propose in the next section.

5.1.4   *ma—š* as a Complex Head of NegP

Given that there is no strong evidence for a complex structure in (17b), (18), and (19) that would allow for generating the two negative elements separately in different syntactic positions and bringing them together with the quantifier by movement, the most plausible analysis is that these elements form a single complex unit, a kind of a discontinuous morpheme.

(24)

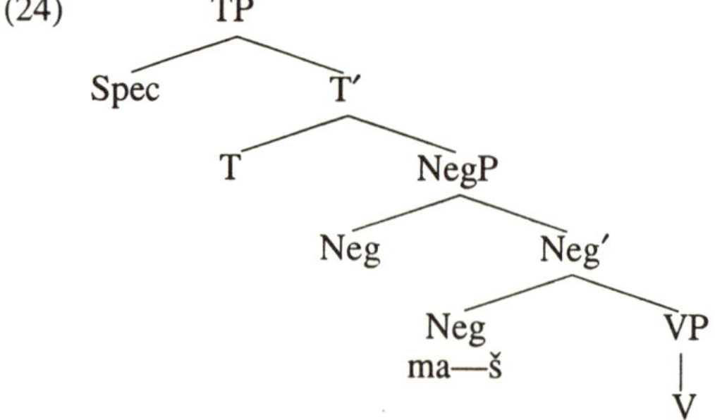

Treating *ma* and *š* as part of a negative head solves all the problems mentioned here and can adequately deal with the interaction between negation and head movement. With a single unit, made up of a proclitic and enclitic, we account for the fact that both markers always occur on the same lexical host. In addition, we account for the fact that they can occur independently of any lexical host or of any evidence of a negative projection in the syntax (i.e., as constituent negation or part of a negative quantifer/NPI).

Further evidence that this analysis may be on the right track comes from Moroccan Arabic quantifiers. As is well-known, the negative element *š* evolved from the word *šay?* (thing).[7] Interestingly, as observed in Ouhalla (forthcoming), there are other constituents in Moroccan Arabic that contain *š*. These are existential positive quantifiers (25) and Wh-words (26).

(25) ši   ktab   MA
      some book

(26) škun šnu   ʕlaš kifa-š
      who   what why   how

According to Chomsky (1964), Katz and Postal (1964), and Klima (1964), Wh-words in English such as *who* and negative polarity items such as *anything* are made up of an existential quantifier and a functional feature such as [+Wh] and [+Neg]. Thus, *who* can be decomposed into [Wh+someone] and *anything* into [Neg+someone]. In some languages, these two features are realized by different elements in the syntax. For example, Aoun and Li (1993) provide an analysis whereby the element that occupies the argument position in Chinese questions is the existential quantifier, while the element that is in CP is the Wh-operator.[8] In other languages, such as English, these features are combined within a single lexical item; hence movement must carry all these features even though the target of movement may be only the [+Wh] part. Assuming with Ouhalla (forthcoming) that we are dealing with the same element in (25) and (26), I would like to argue that the same decomposition can be applied to Moroccan Arabic where negation is made up of an interpretable feature realized by *ma* and an existential quantificational feature realized by *š*, which has evolved to express the existential operator part of negation, positive quantifiers, and questions.[9] The same decomposition also extends to Wh-words in (26). In both negation and Wh-words, the functional interpretable feature is generated together with the existential quantificational feature as a single lexical item though the two features are realized by separate morphemes.[10] In this respect, the representation of sentential negation in the modern Arabic dialects in (24) is more consistent with the representation of Wh-words and positive existential quantifiers.

To sum up, in this section we explored the representation of sentential negation in the modern Arabic dialects. In dialects where sentential negation is expressed by both the proclitic *ma* and the enclitic *š*, these two elements seem to occupy the head position of NegP. The surface distribution of sentential negation in these dialects depends on whether some lexical head has moved to or through the negative projection. If, on the one hand, a head moves to the negative projection, it provides a host for the complex negative head. If, on the other hand, no lexical head moves to or through the negative projection, the complex negative head surfaces on its own with *ma* and *š* supporting each other. This analysis presupposes that we are dealing with the same negative element.

A plausible alternative hypothesis is that the two realizations of sentential negation in the modern dialects are due to the fact that there are two independent formatives that express sentential negation. One realization consists of the discontinuous elements *ma* and *š*, and another realization consists of one single element: *maši*. This is the way descriptive studies of negation in the modern Arabic dialects have approached the problem. In the next section, I will argue that the two realizations of sentential negation are identical in that both consist of *ma+š* and some other element. This element can be a verb, an adjective, an inflected preposition, a noun, a pronoun, or an agreement morpheme. In short, it is an element that reflects the [+D] categorial feature of Negation. The two realizations are then reduced to how sentential negation checks its categorial [+D] feature.

5.2   The Feature Structure of Negation

Within minimalist syntax the standard assumption is that tense and probably the complementizer are specified for categorial features that attract heads such as verbs and maximal projections such as NPs. What is not clear is whether sentential negative heads also have categorial features as part of their feature matrices. In this section, I will argue that negation carries a categorial [+D] feature. This, in turn, will help provide a unified analysis for the two realizations of sentential negation in the dialects.

5.2.1   The Categorial Feature of Sentential Negation

As before, I will take agreement with the subject to imply that the agreeing head carries a [+D] EPP feature that is checked by the subject. In this respect, sentential negation in Arabic seems to be specified for the categorial feature [+D]. This explains why the Standard Arabic negative *laysa* discussed in chapter 4 agrees with the subject.

(27) a.   laysa   ṭ-ṭaalib-u   mariiḍan   SA
           neg.3ms the-student-nom sick
           'The (male) student is not sick'

      b.   lays-at ṭ-ṭaalibat-u   mariiḍatan
           neg-3fs the-student-nom sick
           'The (female) student is not sick.'

We will discuss this negative in more detail in chapter 6, but the main point that is relevant to the present discussion is that the negative carries agreement with the subject, which indicates that negation is [+D].

Another set of facts that suggest that negation is [+D] comes from the fact that negation can merge with pronominals in Moroccan Arabic and Egyptian Arabic, as the following paradigms from Caubet (1996: 83) and Eid (1991: 50) illustrate.[11]

(28) Moroccan Arabic   Egyptian Arabic
         ma-ni-š   ma-nii-š   I + neg
         ma-nta-š   ma-ntaa-š   you.ms + neg
         ma-nti-š   ma-ntii-š   you.fs + neg

ma-huwa-š	ma-huwwaa-š	he + neg
ma-hiya-š	ma-hiyyaa-š	she + neg
ma-fina-š	ma-finaa-š	we + neg
ma-ntuma-š	ma-ntuu-š	you.p + neg
ma-huma-š	ma-hummaa-š	they + neg

These facts follow automatically if we assume that negation is specified for a [+D] feature. Then merger with the pronominal subject is one way to check this feature.

The morphological form of the negative in dialects such as Maltese and the dialects spoken in the Gulf region also supports the idea that the negative is [+D].

In Maltese Arabic, the negative when merged with a predicate is *ma—x* but is realized as *mhux* when independent (Borg and Azzopardi-Alexander 1997).

(29) a. il-fenek   ma qatltu-x   b'sikkina   Maltese Arabic
        thc-rabbit ncg-killcd.3fs-ncg with-knifc
        'She didn't kill the rabbit with a knife.'

   b. Hutek   mhux sejrin ghalissa
        siblings.2s neg   going for-now
        'Your brother and sisters are not leaving.'

mhux is composed of the discontinuous negative *ma-x* and the pronominal *hu,* which carries the third masculine singular features. The latter features are exactly the features that realize expletive pronouns in Arabic and are plausibly a realization of the [+D] feature of negation.

The dialects spoken in the Gulf region display relatively similar patterns. As discussed in Matar (1976: 89–95), the negative is realized as *ma* when affixed to verbs or pronominals.[12]

(30) a. ma-dri
        neg-know.1s
        'I don't know.'

   b. ?anaa ma-ni braayi
        I   neg-I leaving
        'I am not leaving.'

However, when the negative is not merged (i.e., is independent) it surfaces as *mhub,* which Matar decomposes into the negative *mu,* the pronoun *hu,* and the emphatic particle *b.*[13]

(31) ?anaa mub yaay
        I   neg coming
        'I am not coming.'

In fact, according to Holes (1990: 73), in some dialects in the Gulf region, the negative may vary according to gender. Thus, with masculine subjects *mu* is used, while with feminine subjects negation is realized as *mi.*

(32) haadhi mi zoojti
     this   not wife-my
     'This is not my wife.'

Holes then states that the negative *mu* is made up of *ma* and the third masculine singular pronoun *hu* and *mi* is made up of *ma* and the third feminine singular pronoun *hi*. Within the present analysis, the difference between dialects where *mu* is used regardless of the gender of the subject and dialects where negation varies according to gender has to do with the feature structure of negation. In the former dialects negation is not specified for gender while in the latter it is specified for gender. This is exactly what we expect if negation carries categorial nominal features.

Finally, it is worth mentioning that in some dialects, such as Hassaniyya (Iaaich 1996: 168), the negative merges with a genitive pronominal clitic rather than the independent nominative pronouns, as is the case in both Moroccan Arabic and Egyptian Arabic

(33)	maani	my+neg	Hassaniyya
	maanaak	your.S+neg	
	maahu	his+neg	
	maahi	her+neg	
	maanna	our+neg	
	mankum	your.P+neg	
	maahum	their+neg	

This again could be taken to show that the negative is [+D] in this dialect and therefore takes genitive clitics on a par with nominals in Arabic.

In brief, there is strong evidence that sentential negation in Arabic is specified for a [+D] feature, which must be checked in the syntax. Two types of evidence were given to support this proposal. The first type of evidence comes from agreement: negation carries agreement on a par with functional categories that carry the [+D] categorial feature such as tense. The second type of evidence comes from the merger between negation and pronominals. If merger is driven by feature checking, then the fact that negation attracts NPs suggests that the latter are able to check some feature in negation. NPs usually check Case and/or categorial [+D] features. Given that pronominals do not carry [+Neg] (they are not NPIs or negative quantifiers), the only remaining candidate is the [+D] feature. This, I contend, is at the heart of the existence of two alternative realizations of sentential negation in the modern dialects. There are two realizations because the [+D] feature of negation can be checked in different ways, as I argue in the next section.

5.2.2 Checking the Categorial Feature of Negation

In this section, I discuss how the [+D] feature is checked. I will suggest that in addition to Spec-head agreement with the subject, movement of a head that carries subject agreement features is another way to check the [+D] features of negation in Moroccan Arabic.

5.2.2.1 Checking the Categorial Feature of Negation in the Context of Past Tense

As discussed in chapter 4, in both Moroccan Arabic and Egyptian Arabic merger between the verb inflected for past tense and negation is obligatory. The merger between the verb and negation is indicated by the fact that *ma* occurs as a proclitic on the verb, while *š* occurs as an enclitic.

(34) a. Omar ma-ktəb-š   lə-bra   MA
          Omar neg-write.past.3ms-neg the-letter
          'Omar didn't write the letter.'

      b. Omar ma-katab-š   ig-gawaab   EA
          Omar neg-write.past.3ms-neg the-letter
          'Omar didn't write the letter.'

(35)

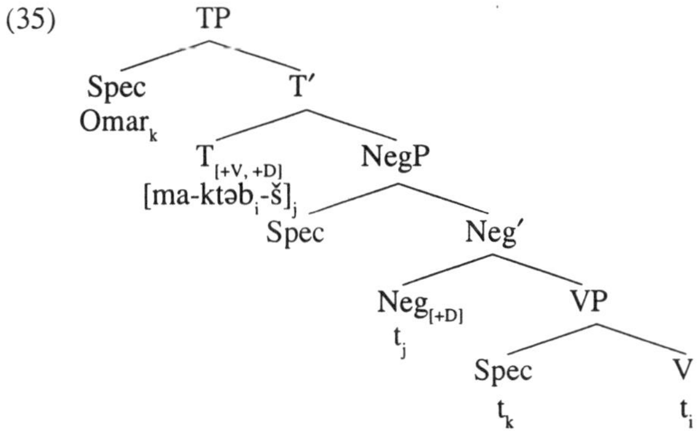

(36) a. * Omar ma-ši   ktəb   lə-bra   MA
             Omar neg-neg write.past.3ms the-letter

      b. * Omar mi-š   katab   ig-gawaab   EA
             Omar neg-neg write.past.3ms the-letter

      The ungrammaticality of (36) follows immediately from the analysis we provided earlier—namely, that the node containing the past tense has a [+V] feature that must be checked overtly by the verb. In (36) the V feature of tense has not been checked, as is evident from the fact that the verb has not merged with the head of the negative projection that intervenes between TP and VP. By contrast, in (34) the verb has moved through the negative projection where it merged with the negative head and then to tense, where it checked the V feature of tense. The third possibility—namely, the verb moves to tense to check the V features but skips the intervening negative head results in ungrammaticality.

(37) a. * Omar ktəb   ma-ši lə-bra   MA
             Omar write.past.3ms neg-neg the-letter

      b. * Omar katab   mi-š   ig-gawaab   EA
             Omar write.past.3ms neg-neg the-letter

These sentences are ill-formed because of minimality. In the theory of Chomsky (1995), minimality effects in the context of head movement are limited to instances where the intervening head shares a checking feature with the moved head. In that situation, the attractor with a feature that needs to be checked targets the closest head that carries the relevant feature. Within the present context, this implies that negation carries some feature that attracts the verb. In other words, the verb carries a feature that can check the categorial feature of negation; otherwise there is no reason that negation should block verb movement to tense. If this is correct, then the question that arises is: what feature on the verb is attracted by negation? If the only categorial feature on negation that needs to be checked is the [+D] feature, one feature on the verb that is capable of checking it is agreement, particularly the person feature, which, adapting the insight of Ritter (1995), I will take to be [+D]. The standard assumption is that agreement is a nominal element, particularly in null subject languages such as Arabic. Therefore, I will assume, in the spirit of Borer's (1986) I-subject theory, that agreement on the verb enables the latter to check the [+D] features of functional heads. Thus, the sentences in (37) are ill-formed because the verb did not merge with negation, though the verb carries a feature that can potentially check the [+D] feature of negation.

(38)

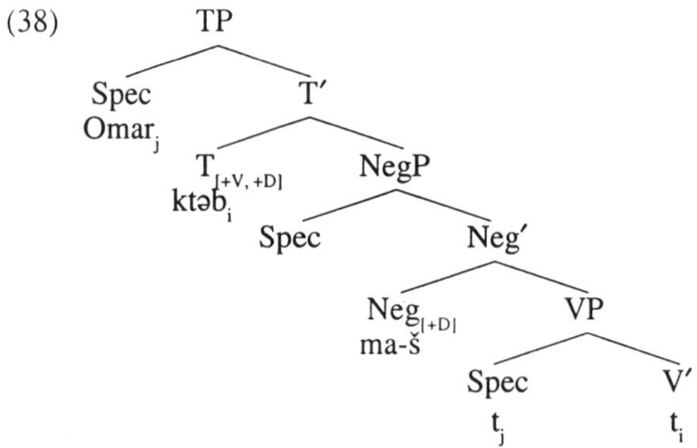

Notice that when the past tense verb merges with negation the latter is realized as a discontinuous element. In particular, in no dialect that I know of is the alternative nondiscontinuous realization of the negative possible. This generalization can now be readily explained if we allow the agreement features on the verb to check the [+D] feature of negation. In other words, agreement on the verb fulfills the same function that subject and pronominals in Moroccan Arabic, Egyptian Arabic, Hassaniyya, Maltese, and the Gulf dialects fulfill—namely, checking the [+D] feature of negation.

5.2.2.2 *Checking the Categorial Feature of Negation in the Context of Present Tense*

While the dialects mentioned in the preceding section pattern together as far as the morphosyntactic distribution of negation in past tense sentences is concerned, they display variation in negative present tense sentences. In Moroccan Arabic, the verb must merge with negation in the present tense, as shown in (39).

(39) a.   Omar ma-ta-y-šrəb-š   MA
            Omar ma-asp-3m-drink-neg
            'Omar does not drink.'

      b. * Omar ma-ši   ta-y-šreb
            Omar neg-neg asp-3m-drink

In Egyptian Arabic, by contrast, particularly the Cairene dialect, both options
are available (Wise 1975: 6). The negative may merge with the verb, as illustrated in
(40a), or the negative may be independent from the verb, as illustrated in (40b).

(40) a.   ma-bi-yi-ktib-š   EA
            neg-asp-3m-write-neg
            'He isn't writing.'

      b.   miš   bi-yi-ktib
            neg-neg asp-3m-write
            'He isn't writing.'

(41) Merger of Negation and Verb Present Tense
      Moroccan Arabic   Obligatory
      Egyptian Arabic   Optional

I argued in chapter 3 that the present tense node in all dialects is specified for a
[+D] feature only. This allowed us to account for the fact that the copula is not inserted in the so-called verbless sentences. The copula is only inserted in contexts where
a [+V] feature needs to be checked. Thus, in both dialects there is no V feature in T in
the present tense that would force verb movement. As shown in chapter 4, the facts
in Egyptian confirm this analysis; merger with negation is obligatory when T is [+V]—
namely, in the context of the past tense. In present tense sentences, this merger is not
obligatory. What is surprising from the present perspective is the obligatory merger
of negation and the verb in the present tense in Moroccan Arabic and its optionality
in Egyptian Arabic.
      However, before dealing with verbs let us look at another contrast between
Moroccan Arabic and Egyptian Arabic. When the predicate is a bare nominal or adjective, merger with negation is optional in Moroccan Arabic but ruled out in Egyptian Arabic (Eisele 1988: 188).

(42) a.   Omar ma-ši   kbir   MA
            Omar neg-neg big
            'Omar is not big.'

      b.   Omar ma-kbir-š
            Omar neg-big-neg
            'Omar is not big.'

   c. Omar ma-ši   mudir
      Omar neg-neg director
      'Omar is not a director'

   d. Omar ma-mudir-š
      Omar neg-director-neg
      'Omar is not a director.'

(43) a. mifiammad mi-š   kibir   EA
        Muhammad neg-neg big
        'Muhammad is not big.'

     b. * mifiammad ma-kbir-š
        Muhammad neg-big-neg

     c. mifiammad mi-š   mudir
        Muhammad neg-neg director
        'Muhammad is not a director.'

     d. * mifiammad ma-mudir-š
        Muhammad neg-director-neg

Predicative prepositions inflected for agreement can merge with negation in both Moroccan Arabic and Egyptian Arabic (44a from Wise 1975: 10 and 44b from Gary and Gamal-Eldin 1982: 39).[14]

(44) a. ma-tafit-uu-š   EA
        neg-under-it-neg
        'not under it'

     b. ma-ʕand-ii-š   ʔik-kitaab
        neg-at-me-neg the-book
        'I don't have the book'

(45) a. Omar ma-ši   fi-ha   MA
        Omar neg-neg in-it
        'Omar is not in it.'

     b. Omar ma-fi-ha-š
        Omar neg-in-it-neg
        'Omar is not in it.'

Thus, we have the following facts that we need to account for. Merger between negation and verbs is obligatory in Moroccan Arabic but optional in Egyptian Arabic. Merger between negation and nonverbal predicates is optional in Moroccan Arabic but generally ruled out in Egyptian Arabic except in the context of inflected prepositions (44–45). All the generalizations that govern the merger between predicates and negation are summarized in the table in (46).

(46)

	[Past-V+Neg]	[Present-V+Neg]	[Inflect P+Neg]	[Adj/N+Neg]
MA	Obligatory	Obligatory	Optional	Optional
EA	Obligatory	Optional	Optional	Not Possible

The obligatory merger between negation and the verb in the past has already been dealt with. In both dialects, the verb must move to tense to check its [+V] feature, merging with negation and checking its [+D] feature in the process. Turning to the verbs in present tense sentences, I would like to suggest that the difference between Moroccan Arabic and Egyptian Arabic has to do with how the [+D] feature of negation is checked.

(47) Moroccan Arabic

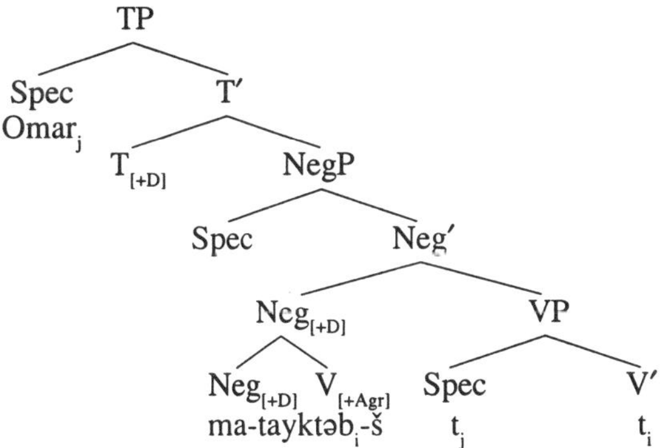

(48) Egyptian Arabic

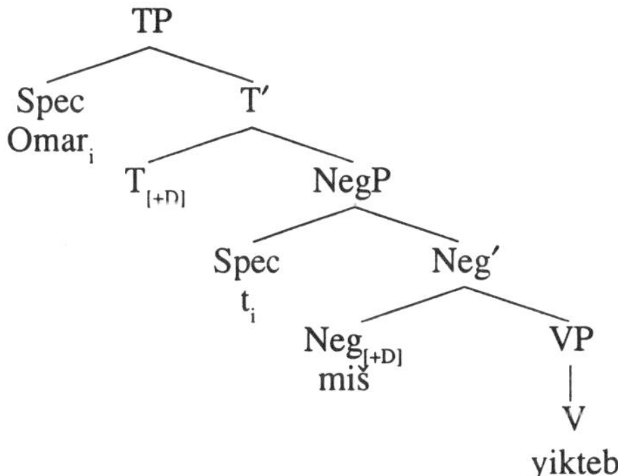

Notice that either the subject or the verb can check the [+D] feature of negation. The subject is a potential checker by virtue of the fact that it is inherently [+D]. The verb qualifies as a checker because it carries subject agreement features, particularly the person feature which is a nominal [+D] element. Thus, negation can in principle have its [+D] feature checked either by merger with the subject, which moves to the Spec of NegP or by merger with the verb, which moves to the head of NegP. Moroccan Arabic seems to require merger with the verb as a first option, while Egyptian Arabic seems to equally allow for either option. As far as nonverbal predicates are concerned, the main question is why in Egyptian Arabic the nonverbal predicates, except inflected prepositions, cannot optionally merge with negation. Jelinek (1981) suggests that the crucial feature is person. The idea is that there is a morphological stipulation of Egyptian Arabic that requires that a lexical head that moves to the negative head be specified for person features.

(49)* [W$_{[-person]}$ +Neg]

What this constraint says is that a head that merges with negation must be specified for person agreement. This is exactly what we should expect. The person feature corresponds to the [+D] feature, which can check the [+D] feature on negation. As to why predicate adjectives and nouns cannot merge with negation in Egyptian, this could be due to a morphological constraint on the type of lexical elements that can host negation. In Egyptian Arabic only verbs and inflected prepositions can support negation, while in Moroccan Arabic all predicates can do so.[15] This is a morphological difference between the two dialects that does not seem to be reducible to syntactic factors. However, even in Moroccan Arabic the merger between nonverbal predicates and negation is not obligatory. The question then arises as to how negation checks its [+D] feature. Two options seem to be available. The first option obtains when the subject moves to the Spec of NegP and checks the [+D] feature of Neg. In PF, the negative, with its checked [+D] feature, is spelled-out as *ma-ši*, while in other dialects the negative may carry default third masculine singular agreement or gender agreement as already shown. The second option, I contend, obtains when the nominal predicates (nouns and adjectives) merge with negation and check its [+D] feature. This latter option is only available in languages where the morphology allows it, which is the case in Moroccan Arabic as opposed to Egyptian Arabic.[16] Therefore, the discontinuous and nondiscontinuous negatives display different checking options for the same sentential negative. In the case of the past tense, only one option is available given that verb movement to tense is obligatory. In the present tense, by contrast, particularly verbless sentences, merger with the nominal predicate, or Spec-head relation with the subject fulfills the checking requirement.

5.3.2.3 *Checking the Categorial Feature of Negation in the Context of the Prospective Present/Future*

In this section, I explore the relation between negation and the predicate in the context of the so-called prospective present. Here again, Moroccan Arabic and Egyptian Arabic differ. In Egyptian Arabic, in the prospective present the verb and the reduced form of the participle do not merge with negation (Wise 1975: 6).

(50) mi-š   ha-n-saafir   bukra   EA
      neg-neg going-1P-travel-travel tomorrow
      'We shan't leave tomorrow.'

As in Moroccan Arabic, the Egyptian motion predicate is derived from the active participle *raayih*. Thus, the motion predicate patterns with active participles in that it cannot merge with negation (Eisele 1988: 188), unlike their counterparts in Moroccan Arabic.

(51) a.   miħammad mi-š   šaayif   EA
           Mohammad neg-neg seeing
           'Mohammad does not see.'

b. * miħammad ma-šaayif-š
Mohammad neg-seeing-neg

The facts in Moroccan Arabic are more complicated and require some digression. As pointed out in chapter 2, the prospective present in Moroccan Arabic is realized by the motion predicate ɣadi (going) which is followed by the imperfective form of the verb. This participle form, which is derived from the bilateral root ɣd, can inflect only for gender and number agreement.

(52) a.   ɣadi n-safər
           going 1-travel
           'I am going to travel.'

      b.   ɣad-a   t-safər
           going.fs 3f-travel
           'She is going to travel.'

      c.   ɣad-yn n-safr-u
           going-p 1-travel-p
           'We are going to travel.'

In addition to this full form, there is a second form of this participle (Benmamoun 1992: 71-72) which does not inflect for number or gender.

(53) a.   ɣadi n-safər
           going 1-travel
           'I am going to travel.'

      b.   ɣadi t-safər
           going 3f-travel
           'She is going to travel.'

      c.   ɣadi n-safr-u
           going 1-travel-p
          'We are going to travel.'

The third form is a reduced version of the participle that consists of the first syllable only.

(54) a.   ɣa   n-safər
           going 1-travel
           'I am going to travel.'

      b.   ɣa   t-safər
           going 3f-travel
           'She is going to travel.'

      c.   ɣa   n-safr-u
           going 1-travel-p
          'We are going to travel.'

Interestingly, in the context of sentential negation different patterns emerge. If the first form is used, ɣ*adi* with agreement inflections, negation must merge with it. The facts are clearer when the participle is evidently inflected for gender and number, which is the case if the subject is feminine or plural.

(55) a.   ma-ɣad-a-š   t-safər
           neg-going-fs-neg 2f-travel
           'She is not going to travel.'

     b.   ma-ɣadə-yn-š   n-safr-u
           neg-going-p-neg 1-travel-p
           'We are not going to travel.'

Failure to merge with negation results in ungrammaticality.

(56) a. * ma-ši   ɣad-a   t-safər
           neg-neg going-fs 3f-travel

     b. * ma-ši   ɣadə-yn n-safr-u
           neg-neg going-p 1-travel-p

In the context of the second form, two options present themselves. Either the negative merges with the participle only or it merges with both the participle and the verb.

(57) a.   ma-ɣadi-š   n-safər   *or*   a′.   ma-ɣadi n-safər-š
           neg-going-neg 1-travel   neg-going 1-travel-neg
           'I am not going to travel.'   'I am not going to travel.'

     b.   ma-ɣadi-š   t-safər   b′.   ma-ɣadi t-safər-š
           neg-going-neg 2-travel   neg-going 2-travel-neg
           'She is going to travel.'   'She is going to travel.'

     c.   ma-ɣadi-š   n-safr-u-š   c′.   ma-ɣadi n-safr-u-š
           neg-going-neg 1-travel-p   neg-going 1-travel-p-neg
           'We are not going to travel.'   'We are not going to travel.'

The option of merging the negative with both the participle and the verb is not possible in the context of the first form, especially if the participle is inflected for number.

(58) a.?/*ma-ɣad-a   t-safər-š
           neg-going-fs 3f-travel-neg

     b. * ma-ɣadə-yn n-safr-u-š
           neg-going.p 1-travel-p-neg

In the context of the third form, the phonologically reduced form, the negative

must merge with both the participle and the verb. Merger with the participle only is
not possible.

(59) a.   ma-ɣa   n-safər-š   a′. * ma-ɣa-š   n-safər
           neg-going-neg 1-travel-neg   neg-going-neg 1-travel
           'I am not going to travel.'

      b.   ma-ɣa   t-safər-š   b′. * ma-ɣa-š   t-safər
           neg-going 3f-travel-neg   neg-going-neg travel
           'She is not going to travel.'

      c.   ma-ɣa   n-safr-u-š   c′. * ma-ɣa-š   n-safr-u
           neg-going 1-travel-p-neg   neg-going-neg 1-travel-p
           'We are not going to travel.'

These generalizations are summarized in the table in (60).

(60) Participle   [Neg+part] V   [Neg+part+V]   [Neg] part V
      Form I: ɣadi+Number   Yes   No   No
      Form II: ɣadi   Yes   Yes   No
      Form III: ɣa   No   Yes   No

One striking fact about the prospective present in Moroccan Arabic is that the
motion predicate must merge with negation. However, ɣadi is radically different from
other motion predicates such as *maši* (going) and *maži* (coming) in that it can be reduced and incorporated into a verb. I will take this to mean that the motion predicate
ɣadi is in the process of evolving into a pure future marker, with one form of ɣadi
and its reduced counterpart ɣa being the overt form of the future morpheme and another form of ɣadi being a motion predicate generated within the VP while T hosts an
abstract future tense morpheme. Thus, suppose that at the present stage of Moroccan
Arabic future tense is realized either as ɣa(di) or as an abstract future tense morpheme,
which is reinforced by a motion predicate.

(61)

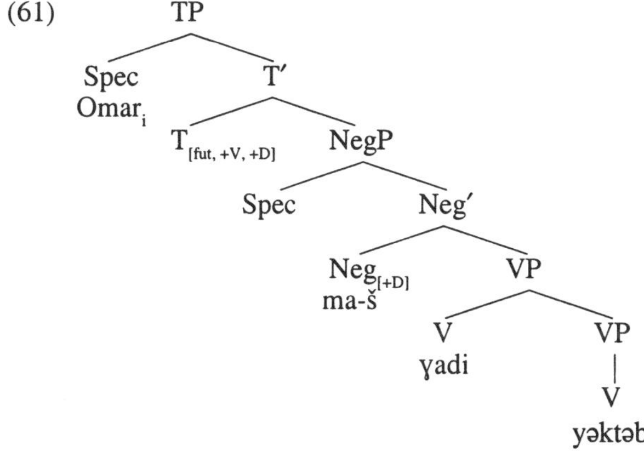

(62)

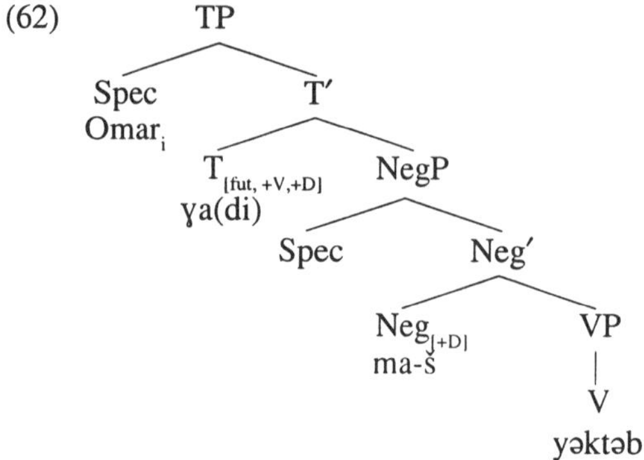

In (61), the motion predicate γadi heads a VP. It then raises to T to check features of the abstract future tense. In (62), however, γa(di) is generated directly in T. Since future tense is [+V] the lexical verb then raises to check its [+V] feature. Thus, we account for merger between γadi alone and negation on the one hand and γa(di), negation, and the lexical verb on the other hand.

This analysis leads us to say that in Egyptian Arabic though the prospective present marker is a reduced form, there is no future tense feature in T. T is still realized as present tense, which does not force raising of a verbal head as argued in chapter 4.

To summarize this section, I have discussed the relation between negation and predicates in Egyptian and Moroccan Arabic. While in the former dialect negation merges only with verbs and some inflected prepositions, in Moroccan Arabic all predicates can merge with negation. I have attempted to provide an explanation for this contrast by proposing that negation carries a categorial [+D] feature that must be checked. Checking can be either by an NP or by a head that carries agreement. Checking interacts crucially with verb movement to tense. In the context of the past tense, movement to tense is obligatory and therefore merger with negation is obligatory due to minimality. In the context of the present tense, if the predicate is a verb, merger is optional in Egyptian because checking of the [+D] feature of negation can be either by an NP or by the verb that carries agreement. In Moroccan Arabic, merger with the verb is obligatory. This analysis has allowed us to achieve two goals: (1) to reduce the inventory of sentential negation in the modern dialects to one single negative with alternative checking options, and (2) to explain the morphology of negation in the modern dialects, particularly why it attracts heads that carries agreement and nominal elements and also why it enters into agreement relation with the subject. All these properties follow from the categorial [+D] feature of negation.

5.3 Merger between Negation and Nonverbal Predicates: Syntax or PF?

So far, we have argued that the merger with negation takes place in the syntax. This is clearly the case in the context of past tense verbs in all the dialects already discussed given that verb movement to tense is driven by the requirement to check the [+V] feature of the past tense. With respect to verbal and nonverbal predicates in the present tense we suggested that merger with negation takes place to check the [+D] feature of negation. In this section, I will attempt to show that the merger between negation and nonverbal predicates is syntactic, which is what we should expect if it is driven by feature checking, a syntactic operation. However, if it turns out that the merger between negation and nonverbal predicates takes place postsyntactically, then it cannot be driven by feature checking.

Now suppose we say that instances of merger between negation and nonverbal predicates in Moroccan Arabic obtain in PF. Then we need to show that this merger is sensitive to the vocabulary of PF only (such as adjacency, Marantz 1988). Since the issue of PF merger will be dealt with in greater detail in chapters 8 and 9, here I am going to touch only on aspects that are immediately relevant to negation.

The kind of evidence we are looking for is the following. We want an element that usually cannot move in the syntax but can merge with negation. The Semitic genitive construction, the so-called Construct State (CS), is exactly the construction we need. As shown by Borer (1988), the members of the CS in Semitic behave prosodically as simple words, yet in the syntax the two members are clearly independent because each can be accessed separately (they do not constitute an anaphoric island). Moreover, the merger of the two members of the CS violates various conditions on movement such as structure preservation (see chapter 9).

One aspect of this merger in Moroccan Arabic that makes it appealing to the PF merger hypothesis is the fact that negation and the projection containing the lexical head that merges with it are adjacent. Starting with the CS if the two members of the CS make up a single word in PF, we expect them to be able to merge with negation. Yet this merger is not possible, as shown in (63).

(63)   a.   Omar ma-ši   ʕəmm Nadia
            Omar neg-neg uncle Nadia
            'Omar is not Nadia's uncle.'

       b. * Omar ma-ʕəmm-Nadia-š
            Omar neg-uncle-Nadia-neg

Under the PF merger hypothesis it is difficult to rule (63b) out. In PF, the two members of the CS display properties of heads. Notice also that merger with the first member is also ruled out, though the first member of the CS and negation are adjacent and therefore can undergo merger by rebracketing under adjacency.

(64)* Omar ma-ʕəmm-š   Nadia
      Omar neg-uncle-neg Nadia

However, the syntactic merger hypothesis can easily explain away both ill-formed sentences. The merger in (63b) can only obtain by moving the whole CS, clearly a maximal projection, into the head of NegP. That movement is not structure-preserving (Chomsky 1995) because it involves the adjunction of an XP to a head. Thus, it cannot take place in the syntax. (64) also cannot be derived in the syntax, because that would entail movement out of NPs. As is well known, this type of movement is independently ruled out in Arabic (and Semitic in general). For example, pied-piping is obligatory in Wh-questions and relatives.[17]

(65) a. * škun qri-ti   ktab
         who read.past-2s book

      b.   ktab mən qri-ti
           book who read.past-2s
           'Whose book did you read?'

      c.   škun qri-ti   ktab-u
           who read.past-2s book-his
           'Whose book did you read?'

Thus, (64) is ruled out on a par with (65a); both violate the ban on extraction out of NPs in Arabic.

The same explanation extends to (66), where the preposition is followed by a lexical complement.

(66) a.   Omar ma-ši   f-d-dar
           Omar neg-neg in-the-house
           'Omar is not at home.'

      b. * Omar ma-fi-d-dar-š
           Omar neg-in-the-house-neg

(66b) is ruled out by structure preservation like (63b).

Conjoined nominal predicates also resist merger with negation.

(67) a.   Omar ma-ši   mudir ʔaw muʕəllim
           Omar neg-neg director or   teacher
           'Omar is not a director or teacher.'

      b. * Omar ma-mudir-š   ʔaw muʕəllim
           Omar neg-director-neg or   teacher

Again under the PF merger hypothesis, (67b) in particular should be well-formed. The nominal predicate, which is usually an eligible host for negation, is clearly adjacent to it. However, if this merger is syntactic, (67b) is ill-formed because of the Coordinate Structure Constraint.

Finally, a nonverbal head that merges with negation can be fronted in questions.

(68) ma-mʕa-k-š   Omar
      neg-with-you-neg Omar
      'Isn't Omar with you?'

Assuming that this fronting involves syntactic movement to C, the fronted negative+preposition must have merged in the syntax prior to movement to C.

In brief, merger between negation and nonverbal predicates obeys syntactic locality conditions and feed syntactic movement. This strongly suggests that it takes place in the syntax. In turn, this conclusion is consistent with the theory advanced in this chapter—namely, that the merger between negation and the predicates, verbal and nonverbal, is driven by the requirement to check the [+D] feature of negation.

5.6   Conclusion

In this chapter, I investigated two main properties of sentential negation in the modern
Arabic dialects: (1) its syntactic status, and (2) its categorial feature structure. With respect to the syntactic status of negation, I have argued that the two morphemes that make
up the sentential negative constitute a complex head, with one morpheme being a proclitic
and the other an enlitic. With respect to the categorial features of negation, I have proposed that it is specified for the categorial feature [+D], which must be paired with (or
checked by) the subject, a nominal head (adjectival or nominal predicate), or a head that
carries subject agreement features. On the one hand, if it is paired with the subject, we
get the standard Spec-head configuration, in which case negation is spelled-out as a
nondiscontinuous element. On the other hand, if it is paired with a head, we get the head
adjunction configuration, in which case negation surfaces as a discontinuous element.
Dialects differ as to which options to use, with Moroccan Arabic requiring head adjunction
if the predicate is a verb that carries subject agreement feature and either spec-head agree
ment or adjunction in the context of nonverbal predicates. Egyptian Arabic (particularly
the Cairo dialect), however, opts for either the Spec-head schema or the head adjunction
schema when the predicate is a verb. With the nonverbal predicate it almost exclusively
opts for the Spec-head option. Crucially, the non-discontinuous option exists only in the
context of the present tense. I have shown that this follows automatically from the analysis in chapters 3 and 4 where I argued that the present tense is not [+V], and therefore
does not force the movement of the verb through the negative projection. The past tense,
by contrast, is [+V] and therefore the verb must move through the negative projection,
merging with the negative head in the process. Thus, we correctly account for the fact
only the discontinuous form of sentential negation is possible in the context of the past
tense. One advantage of this analysis is that we no longer need to postulate two independent negatives in the modern Arabic dialects. There is one complex head, which is spelled-
out differently depending on the temporal features of the head of T and the checking options that the relevant dialect opts for.

6

Negation in Standard Arabic

In this chapter, I focus on sentential negation in Standard Arabic. The same analysis that I applied to sentential negation in the modern Arabic dialects will be extended to sentential negation in Standard Arabic. Morphologically, there are five main sentential negatives.[1] These are *laa, lam, lan, laysa,* and *maa.* These negatives can be divided into two groups: *laa* and its variants, *lam, lan,* and *laysa,* on one hand, and *maa,* on the other. The variants of *laa* can in turn be divided according to their inflections, *lam* and *lan* inflect for tense but not agreement while *laysa* inflects for agreement but not tense. *laa* inflects for neither tense nor agreement. The fact that there are multiple realizations of sentential negation in Standard Arabic makes this dialect appear radically different from the modern colloquial dialects analyzed in chapter 5. I shall argue that this difference is superficial. On close inspection, it will emerge that there are only two negatives in Standard Arabic—namely, *laa* and *maa.* The other three negatives, *lam, lan,* and *laysa,* are all inflected variants of *laa.*

Adopting the analysis that the sentential negatives in Standard Arabic are located between TP and VP, I shall argue that the distribution of each negative can be derived given the assumptions that have been made so far, particularly that tense and negation carry categorial features that need to be checked. Whether a verb can carry tense in the context of sentential negation depends on the features of negation and its syntactic status (as head or Spec). If the negative can carry tense, the verb is precluded from doing so since the complex head that moves to tense is headed by negation. With respect to the two sentential negatives that do not inflect for tense, *laa* and *laysa,* I shall argue that these elements occur in contexts where no verb movement to tense takes place (present tense sentences). Finally, with respect to *maa,* I shall argue that it is generated in the Spec of NegP. This explains why it does not inflect for tense or agreement, on one hand, and why it can merge with lexical subjects, on the other. The descriptive part of this chapter relies substantially on the detailed analysis of sentential negation in Standard Arabic in Moutaouakil (1993: 79–119).

6.1   *laa, lam,* and *lan*

The negative *laa* has two tensed counterparts, *lam* and *lan. laa* occurs in sentences with present tense interpretation. *lam* has a past tense interpretation, and *lan* has a future tense interpretation (Benmamoun 1992; Ouhalla 1993; Shlonsky 1997).

(1)   a.   ṭ-ṭullaab-u   ya-drus-uu-n
            the-students   3m-study.mp-ind
            'The students study.'

    b. ṭ-ṭullab-u   **laa** ya-drus--uu-n
       the-students neg 3m-study-mp-ind
       'The students do not study.'

(2) a. ṭ-ṭullaab-u   ðahab-uu
       the-students-nom go.past-3mp
       'The students left.'

    b. ṭ-ṭullaab-u   **lam**   ya-ðhab-uu
       the-students-nom neg.past 3m-go-mp
       'The students did not go'

(3) a. ṭ-ṭullabu   sa-ya-ðhab-uun
       the-students fut-3m-go-mp
       'The students will go.'

    b. ṭ-ṭullabu   **lan**   ya-ðhab-uu
       the-students neg.fut 3m-go-mp
       'The students will not go.'

Notice that the verb in (1–3) occurs in the imperfective form with each negative occurring with a particular variant of the imperfective: *laa* occurs with the indicative, *lam* with jussive, and *lan* with subjunctive. For the rest of the chapter, I will focus on the negatives, putting aside the issue of the difference between the three imperfective paradigms (see chapter 2 for discussion).

6.1.1   Representation of *laa* and Its Variants

I will adopt the same representation I posited for negation in the modern dialects whereby the negative projection that hosts the tensed negative occurs between TP and VP.[2]

(4)

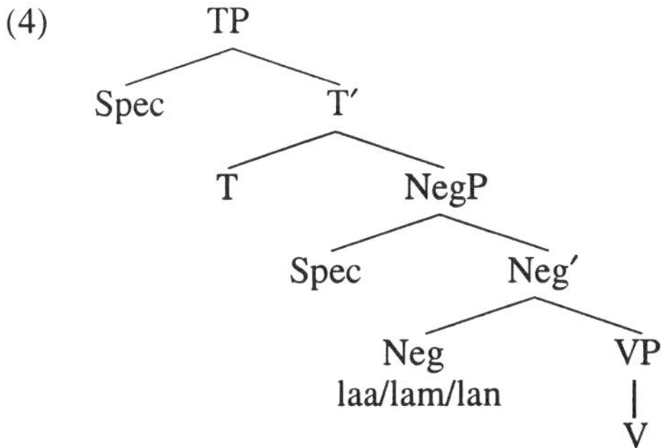

I will also assume that the negative *laa*, which is used in present tense contexts, is the default form of negation (see also Ouhalla 1993). That it does not inflect for present tense is evident from the fact that it can be used as the negator in answers to questions.

(5) a. hal ħaḍara   ṭ-ṭullab-u
          q   come.past.3ms the-students
          'Did the students come?'

     b. laa, lam   ya-ħiḍur-uu
          No, neg.past 3m-come-mp
          'No, they didn't come.'

Moreover, unlike *lam* and *lan*, *laa* can occur in constituent negation (6a is from Moutaouakil 1993: 87).

(6) a. laa ražula fii d-daari
          no man   in the-house
          'There is no man in the house.'

     b. * lam   ražula fii d-daari
            neg.past man   in the-house

     c. * lan   ražula fii d-daari
            neg.fut man   in the-house

These facts can be easily explained since a tensed negative automatically entails that it must be in the head position of TP (either to support or to check tense). However, in (6b,c) negation is within a noun phrase and therefore is not accessible to check the tense features in T. Movement of the whole phrase to T would violate structure preservation because it would involve the movement of an XP to a head position. By contrast, this problem does not arise in the context of *laa* because the latter is not specified for any tense feature that needs to be supported and checked.

6.1.2   Complementary Distribution between Tensed Negatives and Tensed Verbs

Tensed verbs are in complementary distribution with tensed negatives. When the negative inflects for tense the verb cannot do so.

(7) * ṭ-ṭullaab-u   **lam**   ðahab-uu
        the-students-nom neg.past go-past-3mp

(8) * ṭ-ṭullabu   **lan**   sa-ya-ðhab-uu-n
        the-students neg.fut fut.3m-go-mp-ind

In (7) and (8), both the negatives and the verbs are inflected for the same tense, past and future, respectively. Since negation in Arabic can carry tense this obviates the need to duplicate the same information on the verb.

However, suppose we use the default form of the negative, namely, *laa,* and allow the verb to inflect for tense. Given that the [+V] feature of future and past tense must be checked overtly, verb movement is obligatory. This movement must take place across the negative, which in turn violates minimality.

(9) * ṭ-ṭullaab-u   ðahab-uu   **laa**
    the-students-nom go.past-3mp neg

(10)* ṭ-ṭullabu   sa-ya-ðhab-uu-n   **laa**
    the-students fut-3m-go-mp-ind neg

(11)

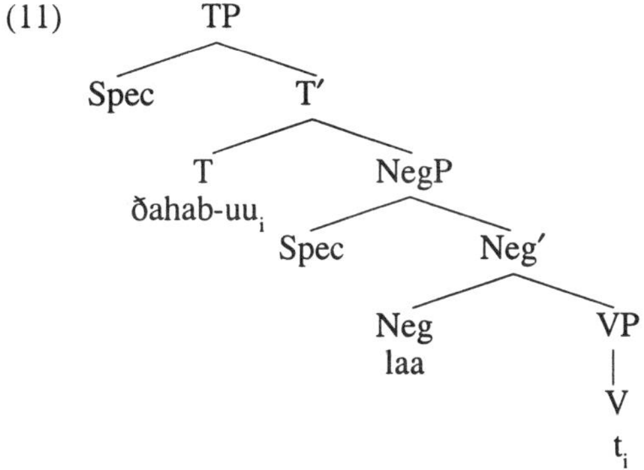

In this respect, it appears that *laa* is different from *ma--š* in Moroccan Arabic and the other dialects. *Ma--š* allows the verb to move through the negative projection. However, we will show that *laa* behaves exactly like *ma--š* in the modern dialects. The two negatives differ in how their agreement features are spelled-out.

6.1.3   Problems with the Minimality-Based Analysis

The preceding analysis of the difference between Standard Arabic and the modern dialects such as Moroccan Arabic is basically a reformulation in minimalist terms of the account given in Benmamoun (1992). However, there are problems left unresolved in that analysis. The first problem concerns the fact that the negative and the verb must be adjacent (Hassan 1973, vol. 4: 409; Fassi Fehri 1993: 164; Moutaouakil 1993: 83). This indicates some kind of merger or incorporation between negation and the verb (Moutaouakil 1993, 83, and Shlonsky 1997, 103). Thus, neither a subject (12a) nor an adverb (12b) can intervene between the verb and the negative (12b from Moutaouakil 1993).

(12)   a. * **lam**   ṭ-ṭullaab-u   ya-ðhab-uu
              neg.past the-students-nom 3m-go-mp

       b. * lam   l-baariḥat   yu-saafir   xaalid
              neg.past the-yesterday 3m-travel Khalid

This merger between negation and the verb is not predictable in the minimality-based account as formulated in Benmamoun (1992). Under that analysis, there is no motivation for the merger of the verb and the negative *laa* and its variants. The second problem is that as pointed out in Fassi Fehri (1993: 164) and Moutaouakil (1993: 82-88), *laa* and its variants *lam* and *lan* cannot occur in verbless sentences as shown in (13) from Moutaouakil (1993: 82–84).

(13) a. * lam   hindun kaatibatun
         neg.past Hind   writer   (intended meaning: Hind was not a writer.)

     b. * lan   ʕamr ʔustaað
          neg.fut Amr   professor

The only way to negate past and future copular sentences is by inserting the copular
verb *kaana* (be).

(14) a.   lam   ya-kun ṭaaliban
          neg.past 3m-be student
          'He wasn't a student.'

     b.   lan   ya-kuun-a sahlan
          neg.fut 3m-be-subj easy
          'It won't be easy.'

If head movement to tense is only to merge a bare head with a tense morpheme,
the preceding facts remain a mystery. There is no reason that there should be a verb
in (14) nor that this verb should be adjacent to negation. I take up these problems in
the next two sections.

6.1.4   *laa* and Its Variants Do Not Select a VP

One possible way to account for the presence of the verb in the context of the past
and future tense is to resort to selection. Fassi Fehri (1993) proposes that *lam*, which
is a modal that carries tense as well, for example, "selects a present form of the verb."
We could capitalize on these insights and assume that the negative *laa* and its variants, *lam* and *lan*, have some property that forces the presence of the VP. However,
there is strong evidence that it is tense rather than negation that determines whether a
VP must be present; the selectional properties appear to come from the negative simply because the latter carries tense.

   First, notice that the copula is necessary in affirmative future and past tenses.

(15) a.   kaana   ṭaaliban
          be.past.3ms student
          'He was a student.'

     b.   sa-ya-kuunu fi-l-bayti
          fut-3m-be   in-the-house
          'He will be in the house.'

Second, in Moroccan Arabic (see chapter 5 for more details) where the same
negative is used in both verbal and verbless sentences (16), essentially without a VP,
the copula is also obligatory in both affirmative and negative past and future (prospective present) clauses.

(16) a. Omar ma-ši   hna   MA
         Omar neg-neg here
         'Omar is not here.'

     b. Omar ma-hna-š
         Omar neg-here-neg
         'Omar is not here.'

(17) a. ma-kan-š   hna
         neg-be.past.3ms-neg here
         'He wasn't here.'

     b. ma-γadi-š   y-kun hna
         neg-going-neg 3m-be here
         'He won't be here.'

Third, a negative such as *laysa* may or may not take a VP (both sentences are from Moutaouakil (1993: 85).

(18) a. lays-at zaynab fii l-bayt
         neg-3fs Zeinab in the-house
         'Zeinab is not in the house.'

     b. laysa   xaalid ya-ktubu š-šiʕr
         neg.3ms Khaild 3m-write the-poetry
         'Khalid does not write poetry.'

If the presence of a VP in the contexts of negation is due to some property of the negative then one would have to say that *laysa* optionally selects VP, which would lead to an analysis that treats both as a modal and nonmodal.

At any rate, the fact that a VP is obligatory in copular constructions in the past and future tense in Moroccan Arabic negative sentences shows clearly that its presence in negative sentences headed by *lam* and *lan* may not be due to the negative itself but to the tenses involved. The proposal I will present in the next section will adequately deal with this construction in terms of categorial feature checking without appealing to modal properties of negation.

6.2   Complementary Distribution, Feature Checking, and Morphological Blocking

6.2.1   Merger and Feature Checking

Recall that for the checking theory, future and past tenses are specified for two types of features: a V feature and a D Feature. The V feature must be checked by verbal heads, while the D feature can be checked by nominal heads or by verbs that carries agreement. Recall also that in chapter 3 we motivated the insertion of the copula in past and future tense constructions by the requirement to check the V feature of these tenses.

Since past and future nodes are each specified for a V feature, then in the context of tensed negatives the negative by itself cannot check that feature. This is due to the fact that the tensed negatives are not [+V] in Arabic. Thus, for the V feature of tense to be checked, the verb must move through the negative projection and merge with negation and then the whole complex can move to tense. The output at the point of spell-out is as in (19), where the T head contains the negative, tense, and the verb.

(19)

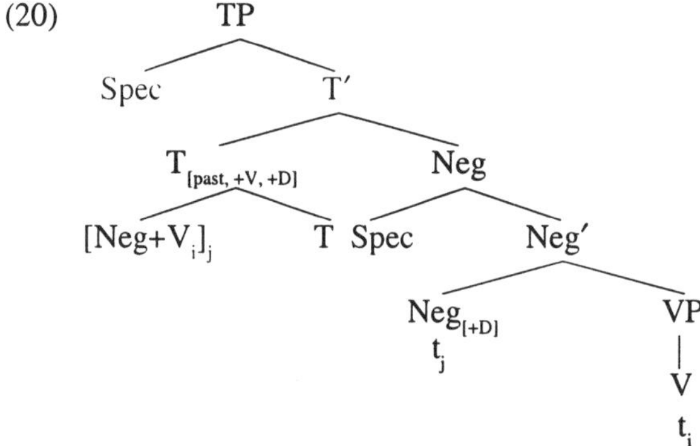

This analysis automatically accounts for both the obligatory presence of the verb in the context of tensed negatives and its merger with negation. The tensed negative carries the temporal features of tense while the verb checks its [+V] features. This, in turn, explains why the two lexical heads are adjacent. They are both in tense supporting the tense feature and checking the categorial [+V] feature.

(20)

To sum up, we have discussed the behavior of the tensed negatives *lam* and *lan* in Standard Arabic. These two negatives are peculiar in two ways: (1) they always require the presence of a verbal head, and (2) they merge with that verbal head. I proposed that the presence of the verbal head has to do with tense rather than negation. As far as the merger between negation and verb is concerned, I attributed it to the requirement that the verb must move to tense to check its [+V] features while the tensed negative moves to tense to check its temporal features.

However, the merger between negation and the verb seems to serve another purpose—namely, checking the [+D] feature of negation. This certainly seems to be the case with *laa*, which occurs in the present tense. Since in the present tense there is no [+V] feature to check, merger between *laa* and verb must be due to some property of *laa* itself. The property in question is the categorial [+D] feature of *laa*. The merger between *laa* and the verb, carrying subject agreement, allows the latter to check the categorial [+D] feature on the negative on a par with the verb in the present tense in Moroccan Arabic.

(21)

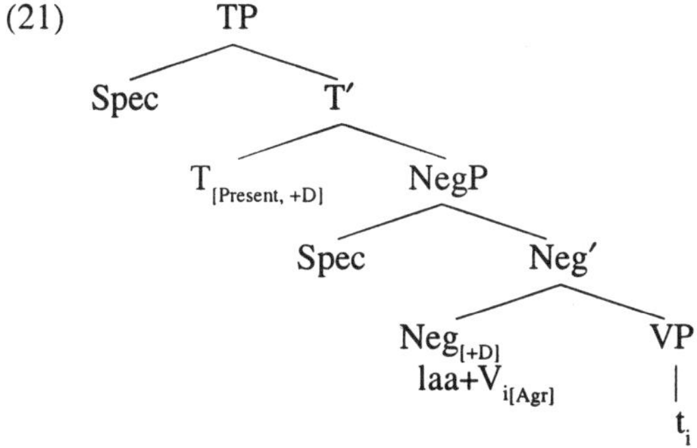

To summarize this section, I have provided a principled analysis for the adjacency requirement on the verb and the negative *laa* and its tensed variants, *lam* and *lan*. The adjacency in question follows because the verb carries agreement features that can check the [+D] categorial feature on negation. With respect to tensed negatives, *lam* and *lan*, the adjacency also follows from the requirement to check the [+V] feature of tense.

6.2.2   The Derivation of Tensed Negatives

Having derived the adjacency relation between *laa* and its variants and the verb, we turn to the interaction between *laa* and tensed verbs. In particular, we want to account for the fact that this negative cannot co-occur with tensed verbs.

(22)   a. * ṭ-ṭullaab-u   **laa** ðahab-uu
              the-students-nom neg go.past-3mp

        b. * ṭ-ṭullabu   laa   sa-ya-ðhab-uu-n
              the-student neg   fut-3-go-mp-ind

As already pointed out, one possible way to account for (22) is in terms of minimality. For the verb to check the [+V] feature of tense, it must move across the intervening negative head, which induces a violation of minimality. That analysis needs to be refined given that minimality can be circumvented by merging the verb and the negative and taking the whole complex to tense.

Suppose that in Standard Arabic the tense morpheme is generated independently of the verb. That is, suppose that the verb does not enter the derivation specified for tense. This idea is due to an original proposal of Aoun (1981), who argues that in Standard Arabic tense is expressed independently of the verb while in the modern dialects it may be realized directly on the verb.[3] The tenses that are relevant here are the past and the future. The future tense is realized by the particle *sa*, and the past tense is realized by an abstract tense morpheme specified for agreement. Assuming Aoun's proposal about the morphology of tense in Standard Arabic, we can account for why negation carries tense in this language. After merger of the negation and the verb, it is the negative that moves to tense; hence tense is spelled-out on the head of the complex Neg+V—namely, the negative.

(23)

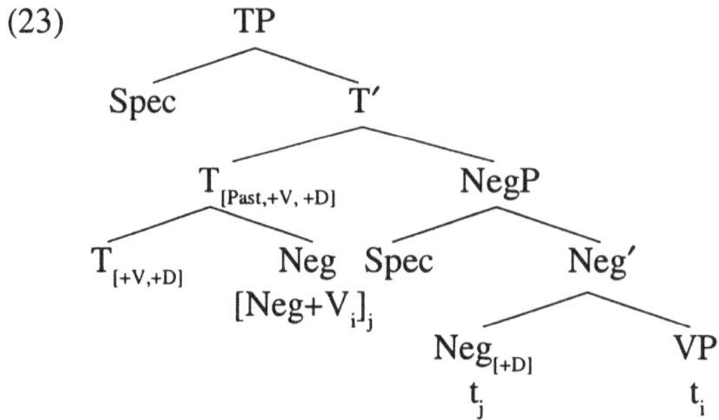

Thus, (22 a) and (22b) are ill-formed because the tense feature is morphologically realized on the verb rather that the negative, which is the head of the complex X^0 that moves into tense.[4]

6.3 The Negative *laysa*

This negative occurs in two main contexts: (1) in verbless sentences as illustrated in (24a) and (2) in sentences with present tense interpretation as in (24b). Both sentences are from Moutaouakil (1993: 85).

(24) a. lays-at zaynab fii l-bayt
          neg-3fs Zeinab in the-house
          'Zeinab is not in the house.'

      b. laysa   xaalid ya-ktubu š-šiʕr
          neg.3fs Khaild 3m-write the-poetry
          'Khalid does not write poetry.'

This negative differs from *laa* and its tensed variants in two crucial properties: First, *laysa* carries agreement, as illustrated by the paradigm in (25).

(25)

Person	Number	Gender	Affix	
1	Singular	F/M	-tu	las-tu
2	"	M	-ta	las-ta
2	"	F	-ti	lasti-ti
3	"	M	-a	lays-a
3	"	F	-at	lays-at
2	Dual	M/F	-tumaa	las-tumaa
3	"	M	-aa	lays-aa
3	"	F	-ataa	lays-ataa
1	Plural	M/F	-naa	las-naa
2	"	M	-tum	las-tum
2	"	F	-tunna	las-tunna
3	"	M	-uu	lays-uu
3	"	F	-na	las-na

Second, *laysa* is mobile in the sense that it can be separated from the verb by the subject. Moreover, it displays the same word order alternations as verbs—namely, Neg Subject order and Subject Neg order (24). Thus, unlike *laa* and its tensed variants, *laysa* is a free morpheme and can carry agreement. I will argue in the next section that these properties are related.

6.3.1   *laysa* as Head of NegP

I will follow Ouhalla (1993) and argue that *laysa* is a variant of *laa* and therefore occupies the head position of the negative projection between the predicate and tense.

(26)

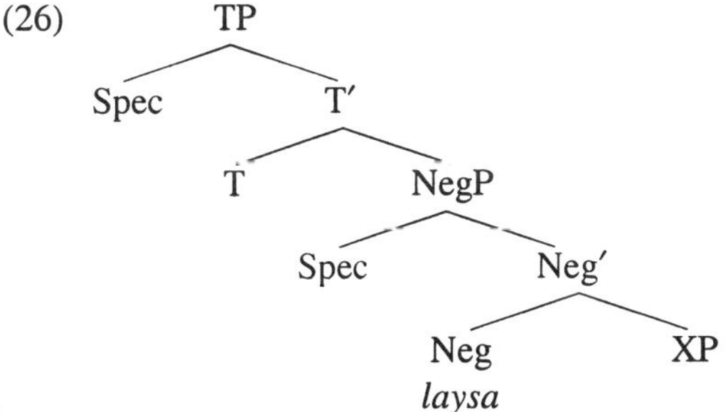

As just noted, one property that singles out *laysa* from the other negatives is its mobility. In particular, it does not have to be adjacent to the predicate. As shown in (24), it can be separated from the predicate by the subject. According to the analysis we provided in chapter 4, this means that the subject is in a projection lower than NegP.

6.3.2   Agreement on *laysa*

On the one hand, the availability of *laysa* in copular constructions with nonverbal predicates precludes the presence of *laa* (27). On the other hand, in verbal sentences with present tense either *laa* or *laysa* could be used (28).

(27)   a. * laa zaynab fii l-bayt
       neg Zeinab in the-house

     b. * zaynab laa fii l-bayt
       Zeinab neg in the-house

(28)   a.   laysa   xaalid ya-ktubu š-šiʕr
       neg.3ms Khalid 3m-write the-poetry
       'Khalid does not write poetry.'

     b.   laa ya-ktubu xaalid š-šiʕr
       neg 3m-write Khalid the-poetry
       'Khalid does not write poetry.'

Notice that while either *laa* or *laysa* is possible (28), in (27) only the option with *laysa* is available (Fassi Fehri, 1993: 170–171). This contrast between *laa* and *laysa* has been dealt with by stipulating that *laa* selects a VP, a solution that is not available to us. As argued earlier, it is tense, rather than negation, that determines whether a VP must be present.

Fortunately, there is another way to account for *laa* and *laysa*. Recall the analysis we provided for negative sentences in the modern dialects. I argued that in sentences such as (29) from Egyptian Arabic and (30) from Moroccan Arabic we are dealing with the same negative whose [+D] features are checked differently.

(29) a. ma-bi-yi-ktib-š   EA
          neg-asp-3m-write-neg
          'He isn't writing.'

      b. mi-š   bi-yi-ktib
          neg-neg asp-3m-write
          'He isn't writing.'

(30) a. Omar ma-ši   mudir   MA
          Omar neg-neg director
          'Muhammad is not a director.'

      b. Omar ma-mudir-š
          Omar neg-director-neg
          'Omar is not a director.'

To account for the optionality of merger with negation and the predicate, I proposed that in both options we have the same negative whose [+D] feature is checked differently depending on what element it is merging with. The [+D] feature can be checked by an agreement morpheme on the verb (29a), by the subject (29b, 30a), or by a nominal predicate (30b). The same analysis carries over to *laa* and *laysa*. Suppose, following the insight of Ouhalla (1993), that we are dealing with the same element *laa* specified for a [+D] feature. On the one hand, if the [+D] feature is checked by the subject and the negative does not merge with any element, it is spelled-out as *laysa*, essentially *laa* plus agreement. On the other hand, if the [+D] feature is checked by merger with the verb inflected for agreement, it is spelled-out as *laa*. The agreement on the verb effectively spells-out the agreement features of negation (see chapter 8 for arguments that agreement features can be spelled-out by merger with a lexical element). In other words, we are dealing with one single negative element that has alternative realizations depending on how the [+D] feature is checked.

If this analysis is correct, then the fact that *laa* cannot occur in verbless sentences follows automatically. In those contexts, the agreement features of *laa* have not been spelled-out.[5] However, in present tense sentences that contain verbal predicates Standard Arabic patterns with Egyptian Arabic. Checking of the [+D] feature is carried out either by the subject, in which case the negative is spelled-out as *laysa*, or by the verb, in which case the negative is spelled-out as *laa*. The first option corresponds to the Egyptian one where the verb does not raise to negation (29b). The second option parallels the Egyptian sentence in (29a) and the Moroccan sentence in (30a), where the verb and the nominal predicate, respectively, do not raise and merge with negation.

6.3.3 *laysa* and Its Absence in the Context of Tensed Verbs

As pointed out by Fassi Fehri (1993: 208 n25), *laysa* is not compatible with future tense interpretation, nor can it co-occur with a verb inflected for past tense. It is only compatible with present tense interpretation.

(31) a. laysa   r-ražulu ya-ʔkulu
         neg.3ms the-man 3m-eat
         'The man does not eat (now).'

    b. * laysa   r-ražulu ʔakala
         neg.3ms the-man eat.past.3ms

    c. * laysa   r-ražulu sa-ya-ʔkulu ɣadan
         neg.3ms he-man fut-3m-eat tomorrow

Starting with (31b), suppose that *laysa (laa+Agr)* has raised to TP while V remains in situ. Since past tense is [+V] its feature cannot be checked by *laysa*. Moreover, if we assume that tense is generated independently of the verb, (31b) could only arise from lowering the tense inflection to the verb, an option that is not available to us since it leaves unbounded traces.

(32)

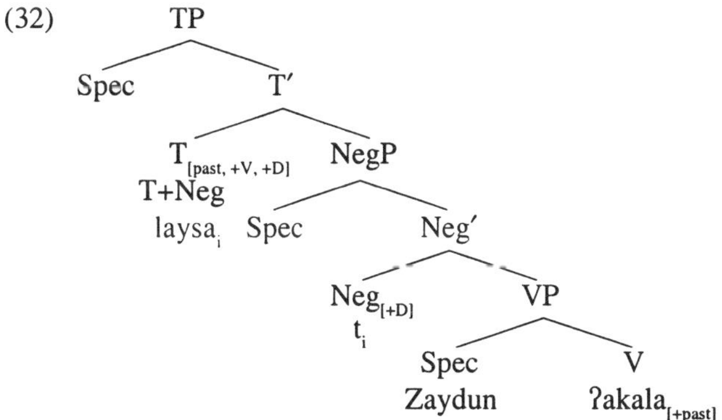

Suppose that the negative stays in situ within its own NegP and the verb moves to tense.

(33)* ʔakala   r-ražulu laysa
      eat.past.3ms the-man neg.3ms

The [+V] feature of tense is successfully checked and the tense inflection supported. However, the derivation violates minimality since the lexical verb moves across the negative head as illustrated in (34).

(34)

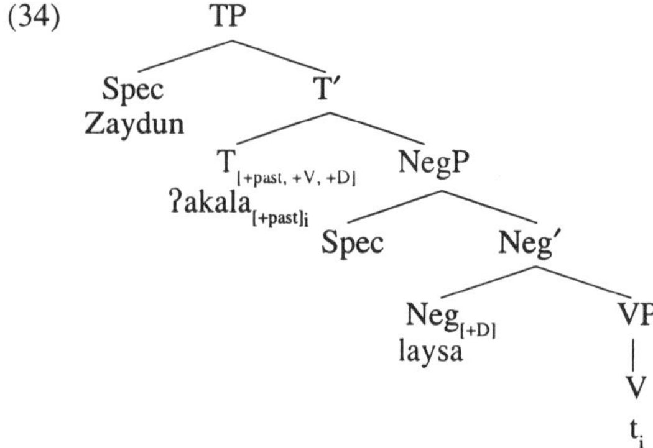

With respect to (31c), the ill-formedness of this sentence is captured in the same way as (31b).

In brief, the fact that *laysa* is a free morpheme explains why it carries agreement. Negation in Standard Arabic is specified for a [+D] feature, which is checked by the subject NP and spelled-out as a free morpheme with its own agreement features, *laysa*. Alternatively, the [+D] feature is checked by the verb, which carries agreement features. In this context, the negative is spelled-out as *laa*. Negation can also support tense—namely, past and future—which carry a [+V] feature. This ensures that the verb must still merge with negation to check the [+V] feature of tense. In this context, negation is spelled-out as *lam* and *lan*. This analysis allowed us to postulate one single basic negative—namely, *laa*, which can have alternative morphological realizations depending on the formal features it carries and how its categorial feature is checked.

6.3.4   Projections, Competition, and Last Resort

One option to repair (27) that we still need to exclude would consist of an analysis that would insert a dummy verb—say the copula—with agreement features. The agreement features on the copula could then check the [+D] feature of negation, which would be spelled out as laa+Copula in PF. However, the result is still not well formed under a nongeneric (deictic) interpretation.

(35) a. * laa takuunu zaynab fii l-bayt
         neg is   Zeinab in the-house

      b. * zaynab laa ta-kuunu fii l-bayt
         Zeinab neg 3f-be   in the-house

This seems to be a standard case of last resort processes such as Do-support. If we assume Chomsky (1995: chapter 4), where the initial numeration determines the competition or reference set, it is not clear why (36) is ungrammatical (with no emphatic reading).[6]

(36)* John did leave.

However, according to Chomsky (1991) sentences such as (36) are ruled out

because there is a competing derivation that does not involve the insertion of a dummy
verb (does not involve a repair strategy).

(37)   John left.

In Standard Arabic, the situation is somewhat identical. In both cases, we have
the insertion of a dummy verb to check the [+D] features of negation. If we assume
that these verbs project their own VPs whose head merges with tense in English and
negation in Arabic, we can rule this derivation out provided we have a competing
successful derivation/representation that can do without an extra VP. Basically, this
means that a sentence without a dummy VP is preferred over a sentence with one except
if there is an overriding reason for having the VP. Compare the competing derivations/
representations. In one derivation, *laysa* occupies its own NegP. So we have the following projections.

(38)   TP Neg$_{[+neg]}$ PP

In the derivation with *laa* and the copula, we have the following projections.

(39)   TP NegP VP PP

NegP introduces the negative feature while the VP projection is introduced for
the sole purpose of checking the D feature of negation. Thus, two projections are
needed. Clearly, (38) is more economical than (39) since the [+D] feature of negation
can be checked by the subject without the need to insert a dummy element to achieve
the same task. This seems to me to be the main reason that the sentences in (34) are
ill-formed; they lose to a more economical representation. A projection should be only
introduced if necessary. This situation arises in the context of the negatives *lam* and
lan in Standard Arabic, which inflects for past and future tense, respectively. Here
both a negative projection and a VP projection are needed. The VP projection introduces the head that checks the [+V] feature of tense.[7]
       This analysis may be able to explain why either *laa* or *laysa* is available in (30).
This may be because each derivation contains the same number of projections. Each
sentence has a TP, NegP, and VP.

(40)   a.   TP NegP$_{laa}$ V
       b.   TP NegP$_{laysa}$ V

The fact that they have the same number of projections and none is superfluous accounts for the free variation. The variation has more to do with how the features are
spelled-out, as argued earlier.

6.4   *maa*

The last negative we will consider is *maa*. This negative occurs mostly in the context
of past tense (Moutaouakil, 1993: 81) but it can also occur in the present tense. This

is illustrated in (41) (a from Moutaoukil 1993: 81, and b from Fassi Fehri, 1993: 173).

(41) a.   ma ɣaadara   Zaydun ʔal-madiinata
          neg leave.past.3ms Zayd   the-city
          'Zayd did not leave the city.'

     b.   maa ʔu-ṣallii
          neg 1s-pray
          'I do not pray.'

I will assume that *maa* is in the Spec of NegP. In the past tense, the verb must move to tense to support tense and check its V features. Since the verb carries agreement features that can check the [+D] feature of negation, it moves through the negative projection and merges with its Spec.

One potential argument that *maa* is in the Spec of NegP comes from the fact that it can merge with the subject as shown in (49) from Moutaouakil (1993: 81).[8]

(42) maa muḥammadun kaatibun
      neg Mohammad   writer
      'Mohammad is not a writer.'

Assuming that this is not an instance of constituent negation, the derivation of (42) is as follows. In verbless sentences, the only way to check the [+D] feature of tense is by moving the subject to the Spec of TP. Since the Spec of NegP is also specified for [+D] feature, the subject moves first to the Spec of NegP, where it merges with *maa*. The two stages of the derivation are given in (43) and (44).

(43)

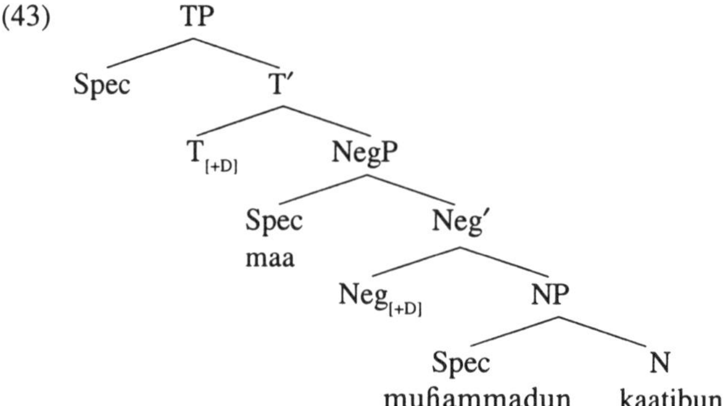

The situation with *maa* is the mirror image of the situation with *lam*. On the one hand, *maa* does not carry past tense, but the verb does. On the other hand, *lam* carries past tense, but the verb does not. However, notice that in both options, we have a complex head that contains a negative+T+V. The difference between the two situations is that with *lam* the negative inflects for tense, which precludes the verb from doing so, while *maa* cannot carry tense, which allows it to be spelled-out on the verb.

However, the same situation does not obtain in the context of future tense, where *maa* is ruled out.

(44)

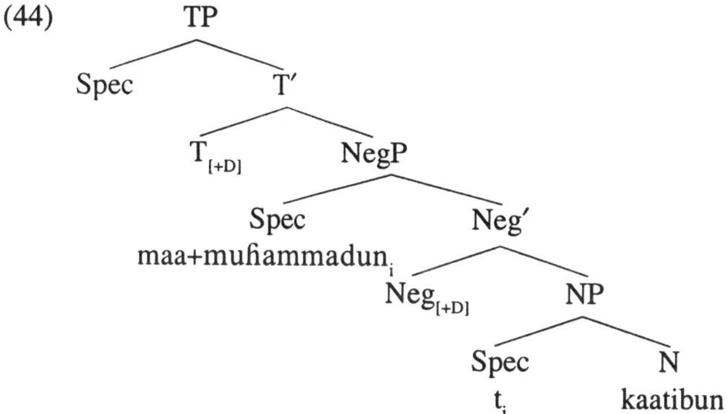

(45)* maa sa-ya-ðhabu
  neg fut-3m-go

To deal with this problem, I will rely on the important insight of Ouhalla (1993) that *maa,* as opposed to *laa,* carries both negative and focus features. This is supported by the fact that *maa* is considered a stronger denial (associated with contrastive focus) than *laa.*[9] In this respect, a sentence with *maa* is probably equivalent to a sentence with the emphatic particle *qad.*[10]

(46) qad   ðahaba
   indeed go.past.3ms
   'He did good indeed.'

Interestingly, *qad* as an emphatic particle cannot be used in future tense.[11]

(47)* qad   sa-ya-ðhabu
   indeed fut-3m-go

I will assume that whatever rules out (47) rules out (45).

6.5   Conclusion

In this chapter, I have discussed the distribution of the main sentential negatives in Standard Arabic. I have argued that the inventory of sentential negatives can be reduced to two: *laa* and *maa. lam, lan,* and *laysa* are variants of *laa* that carry either tense (*lam* and *lan*) or agreement (*laysa*). The difference between *laa* and *maa* has to do with their syntactic status, *maa* is generated in the Spec of NegP, while *laa* is generated in the head of NegP. Apart from *maa* and the ability of *laa* to inflect for tense, sentential negation in Standard Arabic patterns with its counterpart in the modern dialects. In both, there are alternative realizations of negation depending on how the [+D] feature is checked. As in the dialects, the alternative realizations seem to be in free variation in the present tense because the latter is specified for [+D] features only, which opens up the option of checking the [+D] feature of negation by the subject or by the predicate that carries subject agreement. However, in both Standard Arabic and the modern dialects only one realization is possible in the past tense, because the [+V] feature of the latter forces verb movement, which must proceed through the negative projection and check its [+D] in the process.

7

Negation and Imperatives

7.1   The Syntactic Distribution of the Imperative

Verbs in imperative sentences syntactically pattern with their tensed counterparts.
Thus, in English the presence of the sentential negative *not* in imperative sentences
forces Do-support.

(1)   a.   Go.

       b.   Don't go.

       c.   * not go

The presence of Do in negative imperatives can be explained on a par with its
presence in past and present tense sentences. Following and updating the analysis of
Lasnik (1981: 167), we can posit a functional projection in imperative sentences headed
by an Imp feature (Lasnik 1981, 167).

(2)

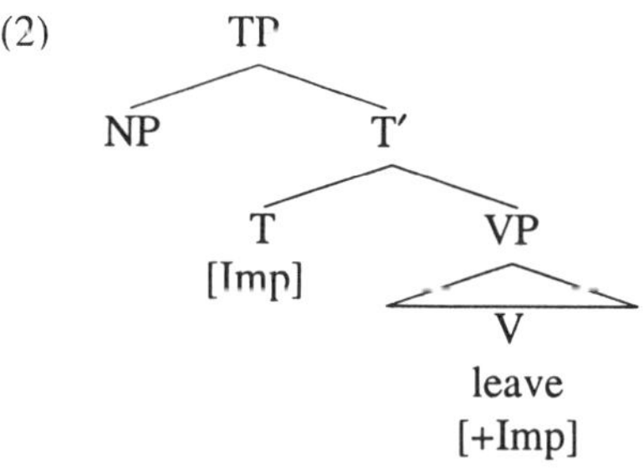

By projecting a functional head Imp in the same space as tense, we expect imperatives to pattern with tensed clauses as far as the interaction between the element
Imp in tense and the verb is concerned. Thus, the sentential negative *not,* which is
located between this functional projection and the VP, blocks the merger of the verb
and Imp.

I will adopt this analysis, particularly the idea that there is an Imp feature located in TP.[1] Naturally, once we take this step, the question that arises is: what is the
categorial feature composition of Imp?

(3)

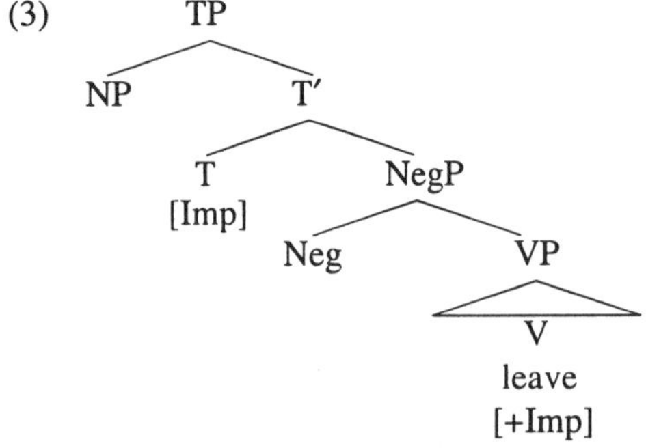

The fact that Do-support is forced in imperative sentences suggests that Imp carries a [+V] categorial feature, which must be checked by/be paired with a verbal head. The dummy verb *do* is inserted to check its [+V] feature, hence the ungrammaticality of (1c). The question is whether the imperative is also [+D]. I explore this question in the next section.

7.2   Positive Imperatives vs. Negative Imperatives

In many languages, different paradigms are used in positive imperatives and negative imperatives. As Palmer (1986: 29) points out, the positive imperative "is also often unmarked or minimally marked even in inflected languages, where the declarative (the indicative) has a full set of inflections". Within Government and Binding/Minimalist syntax, this specific issue has been addressed with focus on various Romance and Balkan languages (see Kayne 1992; Rivero 1994; Rivero and Terzi 1995; Harris 1997; Zanuttini 1997). In most of these languages, the difference between positive imperatives and negative imperatives has to do with mood. A language may have one form that is exclusively used in positive imperatives and another form that is used in both negative imperatives and nonimperative sentences (indicative, subjunctive, or infinitive).[2]

In Arabic, this characterization obtains in one respect. There is a form that is exclusive to the positive imperative, while the negative imperative has exactly the same form as the verb in the context of sentences negated by the past tense negative *lam* in Standard Arabic and simply as the bare imperfective verb in Moroccan Arabic and Egyptian Arabic.

Standard Arabic[3]

(4)	ktub	ktub-ii	ktub-aa	ktub-uu	ktub-na
	write.ms	write-fs	write.d	write-mp	write-fp
	'Write.'	'Write.'	'Write.'	'Write.'	'Write.'

(5)	* ta-ktub	* ta-ktub-ii	* ta-ktub-aa	* ta-ktub-uu	* takutb-na
	2-write.ms	2-write-fs	2-write-d	2-write-mp	2write-fp

(6) laa ta-ktub   laa ta-ktub-ii   laa ta-ktub-aa
     neg 2-write.ms   neg 2-write-fs   neg 2-write-d
     'Do not write.'   'Do not write.'   'Do not write.'

     laa ta-ktub-uu   laa takutb-na
     neg 2-write-mp   neg 2-write-fp
     'Do not write.'   'Do not write.'

(7) * laa ktub   * laa ktub-ii   * laa ktub-aa
       neg write.ms   neg write-fs   neg write-d

     * laa ktub-uu   laa ktub-na
       neg write-mp   neg write-fp

Moroccan Arabic

(8) ktəb   kətb-i   kətb-u
     write.ms   write-fs   write-p
     'Write.'   'Write.'   'Write.'

(9) * tə-ktəb   * t-kətb-i   * t-kətb-u
       2-write.ms   2-write-fs   2-write-p

(10) ma-tə-ktəb-š   ma-t-kətb-i-š   ma-t-kətb-u-š
     neg-2-write.ms-neg   neg-2-write-fs-neg   neg-2-write-p-neg
     'Do not write.'   'Do not write.'   'Do not write.'

(11) * ma-ktəb-š   * ma-kətb-i-š   * ma-kətb-u-š
        neg-write.ms-neg   neg-write-fs-neg   neg-write-p-neg

As noted in chapter 2, one important difference between positive imperatives
and negative imperatives is that the former lack the person prefix; they are identical
in all other respects. The same facts obtain in other Semitic languages such as Amharic
and Hebrew. For this reason, the difference between the two forms in Arabic cannot
be characterized in terms of mood but rather in terms of person agreement. In fact, in
Standard Arabic, where verb endings seem to partition the verbs into different moods,
the verb has the same form in the positive and negative imperative—namely, with no
vowel or *na/ni* endings (5–6). According to the traditional characterization, they are
both in the jussive.[4] Thus, mood does not seem to be the relevant feature that distinguishes positive imperatives from negative imperatives.

Taking into account the facts from the Romance, Balkan, and Semitic languages,
the generalization in (12) seems to characterize imperatives.

(12) In languages where imperatives carry person agreement, a temporal inflection or
     mood inflection it is more likely that to be true of negative imperatives than of
     positive imperatives.

In most, if not all, languages, if the verbal paradigm that is used in negative imperatives is different from the paradigm used in positive imperatives the former usually
carries person agreement or some inflection that is used in other tenses and moods.

7.3   Previous Accounts of the Difference between Negative Imperatives and Positive Imperatives

The inflectional difference between positive imperatives and negative imperatives has
been dealt with mainly from the perspective of the relation among negation and mood
and modality (Laka 1990; Kayne 1992; Rivero 1994; Zanuttini 1997). Thus, Zanuttini
(1997) observes that in some Romance languages, such as Italian, Catalan, and Spanish, negative imperatives that use preverbal negatives, as opposed to positive imperatives, require the presence of subjunctive or indicative moods. In other dialects, an
auxiliary may be present along with a true imperative, an infinitive, or a gerund.

Italian (Zanuttini 1997: 106–108)

(13) a.   telefona[5]   (true imperative)
           call.2s
      b. * non   telefona   (true imperative)
           don't call.2s
      c.   non   telefonare   (same as indicative)
           don't call.2s

Zanuttini's insightful analysis consists of the following crucial assumptions: (1)
imperatives, whether positive or negative, involve a projection (probably a CP) that
contains an Imp feature and this projection dominates the negative projection headed
by the preverbal negative; (2) the preverbal negative head dominates a mood phrase,
which must be activated (essentially filled) by either a verb that carries mood (such
as the subjunctive) or an auxiliary verb (overt or covert); (3) both the features of Comp
and of the head of MoodP (when active) must be checked. Let us see how these assumptions derive the facts summarized previously. Consider the representation that
Zanuttini proposes for imperative sentences (ignoring specifiers and irrelevant parts
of the structure).

(14)

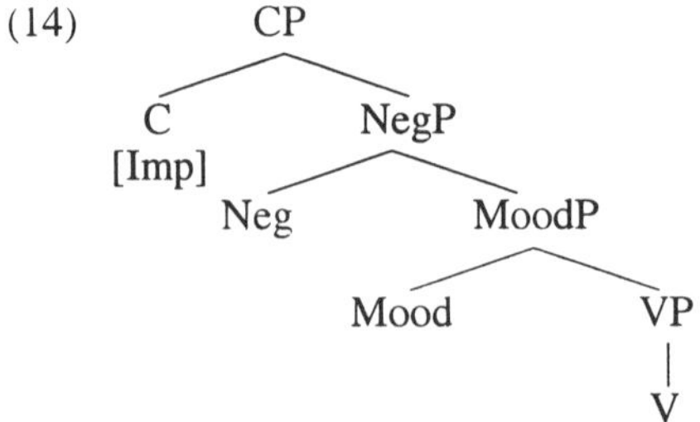

In positive imperatives, the negative projection is obviously absent and MoodP
is probably inert. Crucially, this means that it does not have a feature that needs to be

checked by the imperative verb. The verb may move to CP to check some feature of the C head. In some other languages, a complementizer may occupy the C position and thus fulfill the checking requirement (Zanuttini 1997: 144).

(15) Que me den el libro.   (Spanish)
      that me give the book
      'Give me that book.'

In negative imperatives, the situation is more complicated. Here there are three heads with three requirements. The C head that contains the Imp feature has some feature to check. The negative requires an active MoodP and the latter, when active, has some feature that needs to be checked. The feature on C can be checked by negation, though it is not clear what property negation has that enables it to check the relevant feature. The main problem is the feature in MoodP. It cannot be checked by the true imperative verb because it does not carry mood. This leaves languages with two options: (1) generate a lexical verb with the proper mood such as subjunctive; or (2) insert an auxiliary verb in MoodP. Presumably, the auxiliary has the right feature specifications to check the feature in MoodP. In either case, the feature in MoodP is properly checked.

This analysis enables Zanuttini to derive an impressive array of facts in various Romance languages. However, this analysis cannot be extended to the distribution of person agreement in negative imperatives in Arabic for two reasons.

First, not all negatives require an active MoodP. Nonimperative sentences use the same negative heads and yet do not require the specific moods or auxiliary that occur in negative imperatives. Zanuttini deals with this problem in Romance languages by postulating two negative heads, one in the imperative and one in nonimperative sentences. While this is true for some Arabic dialects spoken in the Gulf region it is not true for the three dialects studied here. The same negative that is used in imperatives is used in other sentences in all the three dialects.

(16) a. laa ta-ktubu   b. laa ta-ktub   SA
          neg 2-write   neg 2-write
          'You are not writing.'   'Don't write.'

(17) a. ma-ta-t-ktəb-š   b. ma-t-ktəb-š   MA
          neg-asp-2-write-neg   neg-2-write-neg
          'You are not writing.'   'Don't write.'

(18) a. ma-bi-ti-ktib-š   b. ma-ti-ktib-š   EA
          neg-asp-2-write   neg-2-write-neg
          'You are not writing.'   'Don't write.'

Second, it is clear that in Arabic the difference between positive and negative imperatives does not have to do with mood. In Standard Arabic, the mood ending on the positive imperative verb is the same as the ending on the negative imperative verb. The only difference between positive and negative imperatives has to do with person agreement. Positive imperatives do not carry person agreement, but negative imperatives do. Therefore, the choice of a different verb form could not be due to a checking requirement by a functional projection headed by mood.

The solution that I will suggest relies on the insight of Kayne (1992) and Zanuttini (1997)—namely, that the verb form used in negative imperatives satisfies some property of negation that cannot be satisfied by the form used in positive imperatives.[6] However, I would like to explore an alternative account that implements this insight in terms of the formal features of Imp and sentential negation in Arabic.

7.4 Analysis of the Difference between Positive and Negative Imperatives

Let us consider the difference between the two forms in Arabic again. One form has person agreement, and the other form does not. Person agreement is a relational feature that usually reflects a property of the subject of the verb. The same goes for number and gender agreement. However, the two sets of features are different semantically— the person feature maybe used deictically, while the other features may not.[7] In addition, Ritter (1995) suggests that the person feature implies definiteness. Shlonsky (1997: 122) also suggests that the person feature carries definiteness. Within the feature system adopted for functional categories, this means that person expresses the [+D] feature.

Returning to imperatives, the absence of person agreement in positive imperatives in languages where verbs are usually marked for this feature naturally follows if we assume that Imp is [+V] only and that the subject in imperative sentences is not syntactically projected.[8]

Being a [+V] functional head, Imp only requires a verb to check its [+V] feature; it does not require the presence of a lexical element with a [+D] feature. The representation of positive imperatives is given in (19), where the T head is specified for the [+V] categorial feature.

(19)

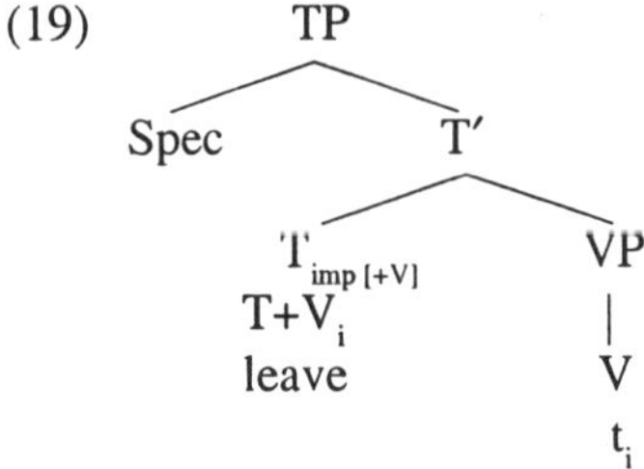

This analysis correlates with another fact in English. In negative imperatives, the subject, when overt, can occur after Do (see Schmerling 1982: 202; and Beukema and Coopmans 1989: 423–424).

(20) a. Don't the rest of you say anything.
   b. Don't you open the window.

There are two possible derivations for these facts. They could be instances of

Subject Aux Inversion, whereby Do is in C and the subject is in the Spec of TP. However, this solution predicts that we should have the same situation with positive imperatives. But this is clearly not the case, as indicated by the fact that Do-support is not forced in positive imperatives. Alternatively, Do is in T to check the [+V] feature of Imp and the subject is in a lower projection, probably the Spec of NegP. Thus, the subject can remain in a lower projection because Imp does not have a [+D] feature that needs to be checked.

Turning to negative imperatives, since the verb carries person agreement, the analysis suggested so far leads us to say that there is a head with a [+D] feature. It cannot be the Imp head of TP because this feature is absent in positive imperatives. Moreover, we want the Imp head to have the same formal feature value in affirmative and negative sentences, on a par with the other heads of TP such as present, past, and future. The only other candidate is negation. We have already seen in chapters 5 and 6 that negation carries a categorial [+D] feature. Part of the evidence comes from the Standard Arabic negative *laysa*, which carries subject agreement (21a), and Egyptian Arabic and Moroccan Arabic negation (21b, c) which merges with pronominal subjects.

(21) a.   lays-at ṭ-ṭaalibatu fii l-bayti   SA
         neg-3fs the-student in the-house
         'The student is not in the house.'

    b.   ma-nta-ši   ḥiməq   MA
         neg-you-neg crazy
         'You are not crazy.'

    c.   ma-nii-š saakna hina   EA
         neg-I-neg living here
         'I am not living here.'

Assuming that negation is [+D], we can now explain why person agreement is present in negative imperatives. Person agreement on the verb allows for the [+D] feature of negation to be checked. The verb moves and checks the [+D] feature of neg and then moves to tense to check its [+V] feature. In positive imperatives, there is no head with the categorial [+D] feature and therefore the person feature does not have to present.

This analysis, if correct, provides further support for the theory that both relational and intrinsic features are able to check categorial features. A head that carries a [+D] feature, such as person, checks the categorial [+D] feature on another head, such as negation.[9]

7.5   Conclusion

In this chapter, I have investigated the syntax of imperatives with particular focus on the morphological asymmetry that arises in the context of positive and negative imperatives. In Arabic, this asymmetry relates to the distribution of the person feature. Only negative imperatives carry the person feature. I have argued that this morphological difference between the two imperative paradigms reflects a requirement of negation. The requirement in question involves the [+D] feature of sentential negation. The person feature, being nominal in nature, is inserted to check the [+D] feature of the negative head. This is due, in turn, to the absence of (null) subjects in imperatives. As far as the imperative feature is concerned, I have argued that it is [+V] only. In this respect, it contrasts with the present tense in Arabic, which is [+D], and the past tense, which is both [+D] and [+V]. This property of the imperative head explains why the person feature is absent and why a subject, when overtly realized, does not have to enter into Spec-head agreement relation with the imperative head because the imperative does not have an EPP [+D] feature to check.

III

AGREEMENT ASYMMETRIES

8

Subject Verb Agreement Asymmetries

8.1 Agreement Paradigms

Agreement between the verb and the subject in Standard Arabic varies according to word order. When the subject follows the verb, the latter carries person and gender agreement. I will refer to this as partial agreement.

(1) a. ʔakal-**at**   ṭ-ṭaalibaat-u   SA
       eat.past-3fs the-students.fp-nom
       'The students ate.'

   b. * ʔakal-**na**   ṭ-ṭaalibaat-u
       eat.past-3fp the-student.fp-nom

   VSO = Partial Agreement: Person and Gender

When the subject precedes the verb, the latter carries all features: number, person, and gender. I will refer to this as full agreement.

(2) a. ṭ-ṭaalibaat-u   ʔakal-**na**
       the-student.fp-nom eat.past-3fp
       'The student ate.'

   b. * ṭ-ṭaalibaat-u   ʔakal-**at**
       the-student.fp-nom eat.past-3fs

   SVO = Full Agreement: Person, Gender, and Number

In the modern dialects, such as Moroccan Arabic, this agreement asymmetry does not arise. The verb carries full agreement in both orders as shown in (3).

(3) a. kla-w   lə-wlad   MA
       eat.past-3p the-children
       'The children ate.'

   b. lə-wlad   kla-w
       the-children eat.past-3p
       'The children ate.'

Absence of number agreement with the postverbal subject is ruled out.

(4)   * kla   lə-wlad
           eat.past.3s the-children

There is no question that the postverbal subject is syntactically plural in (1) and (2). This is evident from the fact that the plural feature on the subject is syntactically visible. The subject can bind a plural anaphor (5a), occur with the quantifier *kull* (all), which always requires a plural NP (5b), can be the subject of a collective predicate (5c), and can be modified by a plural adjective (5d).

(5)   a.   ʔiʕtamada   ṭ-ṭullaabu   ʕalaa ʔanfusihim   SA
            rely.past.3ms the-children on   themselves
            'The students relied on themselves.'

      b.   žaaʔa   kull-u   ṭ-ṭullaab-i
            come.past.3ms all-nom the-students-gen
            'All the students came.'

      c.   ʔižtamaʕa   ṭ-ṭullaab-u
            gather.past.3ms the-students-nom
            'The students met.'

      d.   žaaʕa   ṭ-ṭullab-u   l-mužtahid-uun
            come.past.3ms all-nom the-students the-diligent-mp
            'The hard working students came.'

Predictably, when the lexical subject occurs between an auxiliary verb and the main verb, it partially agrees with the auxiliary but fully agrees with the main verb, as illustrated in (6) and (7) and schematized in (8).

(6)   a.   kaanat   ṭ-ṭaalibaat-u   ya-ʔkul-**na**
            be.past.3fs the-students.fp-nom 3-eat-fp
            'The students were eating.'

      b.   ṭ-ṭaalibaat-u   kun-**na**   ya-ʔkul-**na**
            the-students.fp-nom be.past.3fp 3-eat-fp
            'The students were eating.'

(7)   a. * kun-**na**   ṭ-ṭaalibaat-u   ya-drus-**na**
            be.past.3fp the-students.fp-nom 3-study.fp

      b. * ṭ-ṭaalibaat-u   kaan-**at**   ya-drus-**na**
            the-students.fp-nom be.past-3fs 3-study-fp

(8) $AUX_{Num/Gen}$ NP_{subj} $V_{Per/Num/Gen}$

8.2.   Previous Accounts

8.2.1   Two Agreement Paradigms

If we confine our attention to (1) and (2), we may be tempted to posit two agreement affixes in Standard Arabic, one affix specified for person and gender and another affix specified for person, number, and gender. The choice of a particular affix would then depend on word order.

(9)   Agreement Affix 1   Agreement Affix 2
         Person and Gender   Person, Gender and Number

Thus, in the VSO order the verb carries agreement affix 1 and in the SVO order it carries agreement affix 2. In minimalist terms, one could capitalize on the weak versus strong diacritic feature specifications to account for the correlation between a particular agreement pattern and word order. For example, the agreement affix 1 could be characterized as a weak feature, while agreement affix 2 could be characterized as a strong feature.[1]

(10) a. V_S+Agr$_{[Weak]}$ Subject$_P$
      b.   Subject$_P$ V_P+Agr$_{[Strong]}$

Consequently, the fact that full agreement obtains in the SVO order could be attributed to the requirement that strong features must be checked overtly, a situation that presumably obtains in the SVO order but not in the VSO order.

However, the idea that there are two agreement paradigms in Standard Arabic (regardless of how they are characterized) is not empirically valid, because a verb with the putative weak agreement in the context of a postverbal plural subject, as in (11a) and (12a), has the same form as a verb in the singular with the putative strong agreement, as in (11b) and (12b). This situation obtains in both the imperfective (11) and the perfective paradigms (12).

(11) Imperfective
      a.   **ta-ʔkulu** ṭ-ṭaalibaat-u   SA
            3fs-eat   the-students.f-nom
            'The students are eating.'

      b.   ṭ-ṭaalibat-u   **ta-ʔkulu**
            the-student.f.nom **3fs**-eat
            'The student is eating.'

(12) Perfective
      a.   ʔakal-**at**   ṭ-ṭaalibaat-u
            eat.past-**3fs** the-students-nom
            'The students ate.'

      b.   ṭ-ṭaalibat-u   ʔakal-**at**
            the-student.f.nom eat.past-**3fs**
            'The student ate.'

The fact that in both paradigms the same agreement inflection is used with both a singular preverbal subject and a plural postverbal subject suggests that the two agreement patterns in both the VSO order and the SVO order draw on the same paradigms. This implies that the weak-strong dichotomy has no lexical or morphological content as far as Standard Arabic agreement is concerned.[2] In the context of postverbal lexical subject, only the singular cells of the paradigms are spelled-out.

In addition to this problem, it is crucial for this type of account that the verb cannot check strong features (full agreement) before it raises past the subject. Since we have argued in chapter 4 that in the VSO order the verb is in TP, according to this account one must assume that both Spec VP and intermediate lower projections that might host the subject are not positions where strong agreement can be checked.

(13)

$$
\begin{array}{c}
\text{TP} \\
\diagup \diagdown \\
\text{T} \qquad \text{VP} \\
| \qquad \diagup \diagdown \\
\text{T+V}_{s_i} \quad \text{Spec} \qquad \text{V}' \\
\qquad | \qquad | \\
\qquad \text{Subj}_p \quad \text{V}_s \\
\qquad\qquad | \\
\qquad\qquad t_i
\end{array}
$$

In other words, according to the preceding account (14) is ill-formed because the verb carries strong agreement features that have not been checked by spell-out.

(14)

$$
\begin{array}{c}
\text{TP} \\
\diagup \diagdown \\
\text{T} \qquad \text{VP} \\
| \qquad \diagup \diagdown \\
\text{T+V}_{p_i} \quad \text{Spec} \qquad \text{V}' \\
\qquad | \qquad | \\
\qquad \text{Subj}_p \quad \text{V}_p \\
\qquad\qquad | \\
\qquad\qquad t_i
\end{array}
$$

In minimalist terms, this is as ill-formed as a sentence in English with the subject remaining in the Spec of VP (15a) or a sentence in French with the tensed verb remaining within the VP (15b).

(15) a. * has John left

b. * Jean ne pas aime Marie
Jean neg   love Marie

In both instances, the sentences are ungrammatical because there is a strong feature (the [+D] feature on tense in English and the [+V] feature on tense in French) that has not been checked by spell-out (Chomsky 1995).

This assumption is not correct given that when the subject occurs between an auxiliary and a main verb the latter carries full (strong) agreement as schematized in (9). This implies that the putative strong agreement features on the lexical verb have been successfully checked within the VP or whatever projection contains the subject and the main verb. Therefore, the fact that the verb in the VSO order does not carry the number affix is still a mystery under any account that posits two separate agreement paradigms. Consequently, the ill-formedness of (1b) is still left unexplained. This very same point is made by Aoun, Benmamoun, and Sportiche (1994), who argue that in the VSO order the verb has been at some point in the derivation prior to spell-out in a Spec-head relation with the subject. Then they went on to suggest that the number feature that is present on the verb, at least at the point in the derivation when it is in Spec-head relation with the subject, is not retained when the verb raises to a projection higher than the projection that contains the subject. The account I will suggest adopts the spirit of this analysis but gives a different explanation for the absence of the number affix.

8.2.2   Partial Agreement as Agreement with Expletive

One nonmovement approach that does not rely on the weak-strong dichotomy would consist of positing an expletive argument chain when the subject is postverbal. The expletive would be specified only for gender and person, which it acquires through a chain relation with the lexical subject. In the SVO order, we have an argument trace chain, in which case the verb must carry all the agreement features, particularly number.

(16) Expletive Argument (Contentive) Chains in SA
      $Expletive_{FS}$ V_{FS} $Argument_{FP}$

(17) Argument Trace Chains in SA
      $Argument_{FP}$ V_{FP} $Trace\ (copy)_{FP}$

In Moroccan Arabic, where full agreement is required regardless of word order, the putative expletive would be specified for all features.

(18) Expletive Argument Chain in MA
      $Expletive_{FP}$ V_{FP} $Argument_{FP}$

This analysis is problematic as well because if there is an expletive it seems to be the same in Moroccan Arabic and Standard Arabic—namely, a third person singular masculine (null) pronominal.

(19) a.   ya-žibu   ʔan ya-fiḍuru-uu   SA
           3m-must that 3-come-mp
           'They must come.'

      b.   ta-y-ḍhər   bəlli kan-u   hna
           asp-3m-seems that be.past.3p here
           'It seems that they were here.'

Of course one could posit a different type of expletive in the VSO order in Moroccan Arabic and Standard Arabic, but so far there doesn't seem to be any independent motivation for such an expletive.[3]

8.2.3   Full Agreement as Incorporated Pronominal

Another analysis that seems problematic is one that treats full agreement as the incorporation of a pronominal. The fact that we are dealing with the same agreement paradigms and the fact that the asymmetry affects number agreement only show that we cannot resort to pronominal incorporation to account for the complementary distribution of number agreement and a postverbal lexical subject.[4] This is because one would have to explain why person agreement occurs in the context of the postverbal lexical subject. Since there is a lexical subject, pronominal incorporation could not be the origin of the person inflection on the verb. Therefore, it must be due to a genuine agreement relation. But if that is the case, then pronominal incorporation is not a viable alternative to explain the complementary distribution between number agreement and the postverbal lexical subject. Moreover, as I illustrate in (20), full agreement can occur on the both the auxiliary and the main verb when the subject is a null pronominal.

(20) a.   kun-**na**   ya-ʔkul-**na**   SA
            be.past.3fp 3-seat-fp
            'They were eating.'

      b. * kaan-**at**   ya-ʔkul-**na**
            be.past.3fs 3-eat.fp

To account for (20a) the incorporation analysis would have to posit two pronominal subjects.[5]

To sum up this section, both partial agreement and full agreement reflect a genuine agreement relation between the verb and the subject. Moreover, both agreement patterns are drawn from the same paradigm. Therefore, the main issue is the absence of the plural cells of the agreement paradigm in the VSO order.

8.3   Distribution of Number Agreement

Though the two agreement patterns, partial agreement and full agreement, draw on the same paradigms, number and person are dissociated morphologically. In the imperfective, each affix carries a different type of information, either person or number. Moreover, each affix seems to have a different distribution from the other. For example, in the VSO order it is the suffix that does not show up. In positive imperatives, discussed in chapter 7, it is the person prefix that does not show up.

(21) ktub   ktub-ii   ktub-uu   ktub-na   SA
      write.ms   write.fs   write-mp   write-fp
      'Write.'   'Write.'   'Write.'   'Write.'

When we take all these facts together, subject verb agreement in Arabic seems to display different patterns, number agreement, and person agreement. While person agreement obtains regardless of word order, the distribution of number agreement is more restricted. Thus, any analysis of agreement in Arabic will have to explain why only number agreement has such restricted distribution—that is, why only number agreement is in complementary distribution with postverbal lexical subjects. To do that we need to discuss all other environments where number agreement is obligatory.

In addition to SVO sentences with overt subjects, number agreement is also obligatory when the subject is a Wh-trace, as illustrated in (22), or a null pronominal, as illustrated in (20) repeated as (23).[6]

(22) a. žaaʔa   l-ʔawlaadu lladiina nažaɦ-**uu**   SA
         come.past.3ms the-children that   pass.past-3mp
         'The children who passed came.'

    b. * žaaʔa   l-ʔawlaadu llaðiina nažaɦ a
         come.past.3ms the-children that   pass.past.3ms

(23) a. kun-**na**   ya-ʔkul-**na**
         be.past.3fp 3-eat-fp
         'They were eating.'

    b. * kaan-**at**   ya-ʔkul-**na**
         be.past.3fs 3-eat.fp

(24) $AUX_{Per/Num/Gen}$ $V_{Per/Num/Gen}$

Notice that in (23a), in particular, full agreement on the auxiliary cannot be due to a requirement that the features of a null pronominal subject must be recoverable from agreement on the verb because the lexical verb carries all the features that are required to identify the null pronominal.

Full agreement is also obligatory when the postverbal subject is an overt pronominal, as illustrated in (25) from Fassi Fehri (1988: 109).

(25) žaaʔ-uu   hum laa ʔixwatu-hum   SA
      come.past-3mp they not brothers-their
      'They came, not their brothers.'

However, the overt pronominal does not seem to be the real subject. The subject is probably a null pronominal focused by the overt pronominal. That this may be the case is supported by the fact that accusative clitics can also be focused by the same nominative form of the pronoun in (25) (Fassi Fehri 1988: 112).

(26) ʔiltaqay-tu bi-hi   huwa
      meet.past-1s with-him.gen he.nom
      'I met him.'

Taking all the facts in (1), (2), (22), and (23) into account, we can draw the following empirical generalizations.[7]

(27) *Number Suffix Distribution (Version 1)*
The number suffix is obligatory when:
(i)   The lexical subject precedes the verb.
(ii) The subject is null (null pronominal or trace).

The two contexts in (27) can be collapsed into a single generalization.

(28) *Number Suffix Distribution (Version 2)*
The number suffix is obligatory whenever the postverbal subject position is
phonologically null.

Thus, it is the phonological matrix of the postverbal subject position that determines whether a singular cell or plural cell of the agreement paradigm is chosen. In the next section, I will provide an analysis for the generalization in (28).

8.4   Analysis of the Distribution of Number Agreement

Instead of treating the agreement asymmetry in Standard Arabic as a syntactic problem I would like to explore an alternative morphological analysis that is consistent with the lexicalist spirit of the Minimalist Program (Chomsky 1995) and other constraint based analyses of agreement.[8] In particular, suppose that the verb is fully specified for all agreement features throughout the syntactic derivation. In minimalist terms, that amounts to saying that the verb enters the syntactic derivation specified for agreement features. Thus, regardless of word order, in the context of a plural subject the verb carries plural agreement, while in the context of a singular subject it carries singular agreement features.

(29) a.   Subject$_p$ V$_p$
      b.   Subject$_s$ V$_s$

In simple sentences, the agreement features on the verb can be checked in either the Spec of VP or the Spec of TP, depending on whether we allow for features to be checked within the thematic shell (Chomsky 1995). Recall that we argued earlier that the subject in the SVO order may be in the Spec of TP. By contrast, in the VSO order the subject is in the Spec of VP or a projection intermediate between VP and TP.[9]

(30)

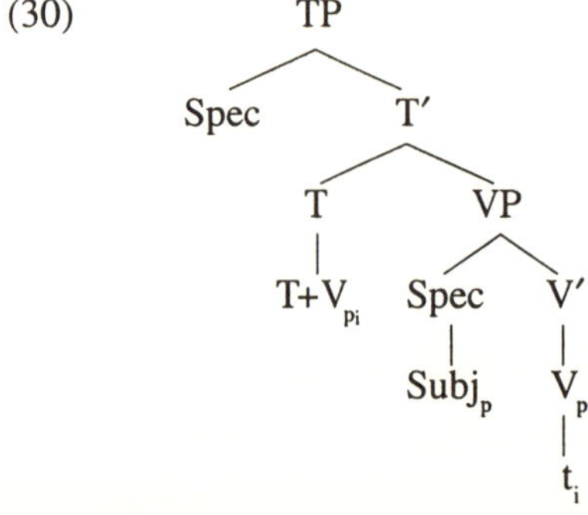

(31)

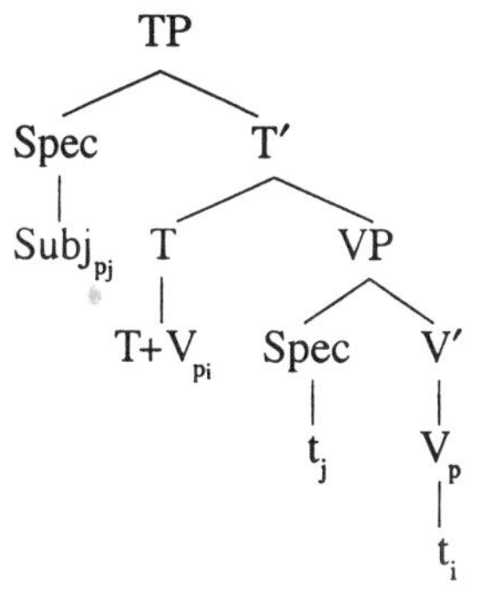

[tree diagram:
TP
  Spec   T′
  Subj$_{pj}$ T   VP
          T+V$_{pi}$ Spec   V′
                       t$_j$ V$_p$
                               t$_i$]

I will assume that agreement features can be checked whenever the verb and the subject are in a Spec-head relation.[10] Thus, in sentences with auxiliary verbs, if the verb remains in the VP its agreement features can be checked within the thematic shell. The problem then becomes why number agreement does not surface in the VSO order with an overt subject. Since I am assuming that the verb carries number agreement throughout the syntactic derivation, we can sharpen the question as follows.

(32)   Why doesn't the number feature for which the verb is already specified and which has been checked by the subject get spelled-out by a number affix when the subject is postverbal?

This seems to me to be the question one needs to ask about subject verb agreement in Arabic. Most of the answers discussed earlier in this section and others that have previously been advanced adopt the position that the number suffix is absent because at the point of Spell-out the verb does not carry the (plural) number feature for various syntactic reasons. I would like to contend that the answer to this question must be in terms of how morphosyntactic features are spelled-out in the morphology. The answer I will suggest assumes that the verb always carries plural agreement features when the subject is plural. This is the null hypothesis. Given that the language has rich agreement paradigms with singular, dual, and plural cells, the simplest assumption is that, as in the majority of languages, when the verb has a plural external argument it is specified for plural features. Obviously, any analysis will have to tie the absence of the number affix to the subject being in the postverbal position.

8.4.1   Absence of the Number Suffix due to Merger between the Verb and Subject

Most analyses of agreement assume that agreement features are spelled-out/realized by agreement affixes. However, this assumption does not extend to other morphosyntactic features. Thus, tense features can be realized either by affixes or periphrastically by independent words (auxiliaries and modals). For example, in French the compound past (*passé composé*) realized by an auxiliary verb and a main verb stands in a paradigmatic relation with tenses realized by a single word that carries a tense affix.

(33)   Compound Past   Present
       J'ai vu   Je vois

Similar examples can be duplicated in other languages. In such instances, it seems that
we have a paradigm "with both single words and groups of words among its members," to quote Mathews (1974: 171).[11]

My proposal is that this is exactly the situation that arises in the VSO order in
Standard Arabic; the number feature on the verb is not spelled-out by an affix but by
the lexical subject, which merges with the verb. Since the subject is inherently specified for number features, its merger with the verb amounts to spelling-out those features on the latter, thus making the number suffix redundant. In other words, the fact
that the subject carries number as an intrinsic (as opposed to relational) feature effectively turns it into a potential exponent of the relational number feature on the verb. If
this is correct, it essentially means that there are two alternative ways to spell-out
number agreement in Standard Arabic, either as a single word (verb plus affix) or
periphrastically (verb plus postverbal subject). The latter option is only available in
the VSO order. In the SVO order, only the affixation option is possible.

If this analysis is on the right track, we can immediately explain the generalization in (28). Recall that number is realized by an affix whenever the postverbal subject position is not filled by a lexical NP. This now follows automatically because a
phonologically null element (a Wh-trace, as in (22), or a null pronominal, as in (23))
cannot spell-out the number feature, given that they do not have a phonological matrix. The only elements that can compete for spelling- out number agreement are the
number suffix and the lexical subject. In Standard Arabic, the latter wins because the
language allows for merger of the verb and the subject. Since the merged subject is
already available as an argument of the verb, the option of using the number suffix
just to spell-out number is redundant.

(34)   *Standard Arabic Number Agreement Spell-out in the Morphology*

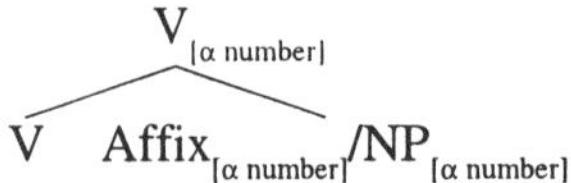

However, once we adopt this analysis the following questions arise: 1) Why is
person realized by an affix even when the verb and the subject merge? 2) Where does
this merger take place: syntax or PF? 3) Why don't intervening elements block the
verb subject merger? I take up each question in turn.

8.4.2   Distribution of Person Agreement

While number agreement can be spelled-out by the lexical subject, person agreement
must be spelled-out by an affix. One possible explanation is that this could follow from
the fact that lexical NPs do not carry person as an inherent feature realized morphologically by an affix.[12] Verbs, by contrast, do carry person affixes, which in Arabic
vary according to first, second, and third.

One fact that may be significant in this connection is that person agreement is
the only feature that sometimes distinguishes verbs from nouns. This situation arises

particularly in nominal forms derived from imperfective verbs. The only difference between the nominal and the verbal form is the substitution of a nominal prefix for the person prefix.

(35) a. yu-ʕallim-uun   yu-saaʕid   SA
         3-teach-mp   3-help
         'They teach/are teaching.'   'He helps.'

    b.   mu-ʕallim-uun   mu-saaʕid
         n-teach-mp   n-help
         'teachers'   'helper'

These facts suggest that the person prefix carries the categorial feature of the verb. It is the feature that signals that the lexical head is a [+V] element as opposed to a [+N] element.[13] This seems to be a fundamental difference between person agreement and number agreement; the former is a categorial and relational feature, while the latter is a purely relational feature. If this characterization of the person prefix is correct, then it is not surprising that merger with the lexical subject does not preclude the presence of the person affix. The lexical subject is a [+N] head, which cannot spell-out the categorial feature of a [+V] head. Therefore, the person feature on the verb must be spelled-out by an affix.

8.4.3 Verb/Subject Merger: Syntactic or PF

Turning to the issue of where this merger takes place, it is unlikely that the merger between the verb and the subject takes place in the syntax, because the distribution of number in the context of the postverbal lexical subject is oblivious to the syntactic complexity of the latter. Thus, the postverbal subject can head a maximal projection as complex as a genitive construction (36a) or relative clause (36b).

(36) a. žaaʔa   muʕallimuu t-tullab-i   SA
         come.past.3ms teachers.mp the-students
         'The students' teachers came.'

    b.   t-tullabu   llaðiina nažaħ-uu   fi lʔ-imtiħaani
         the-students who   pass.past-3mp in the-exam
         'the students who passed the exam'

The putative syntactic merger of the verb and the subject in (36) would violate structure preservation, merger of a head and a maximal projection.

However, allowing this merger to apply in the morphology (or the component that interfaces with the syntactic component and spells-out the terminal elements of the phrase marker) allows for a more plausible account for the generalization in (28). It is in a component that distinguishes between elements that have a phonological matrix and those that do not have one that we can adequately account for the generalization in (28), which frames the correlation between the presence of the number affix and the subject in terms of whether the latter has phonological features.[14]

8.4.4   Merger and Adjacency

One fact that challenges the merger solution to the agreement asymmetries is the ability
of other elements, such as complements, to intervene between the subject and the verb.

(37) a. ʔakala   t-tuffaaḥata l-ʔawlaadu   SA
         eat.past.3ms the-apple   the-children
         'The children ate the apple.'

   b. ʔiltaqaa   bi-l-muʕallim-i   ṭ-ṭullab-u
       meet.past.3ms with-the-teacher-gen the-students-nom
       'The students met the teacher.'

One option is that in the spirit of Aoun and Benmamoun (1999) merger can be
between copies of the verb and the subject. That is, suppose that when an element (XP)
intervenes between the verb and the subject the verbal chain consists of at least three
members, one in VP, one in TP, and one in a projection higher than the position that
hosts XP.

(38) V_1 XP V_2 Subject V_3

In this sequence, the highest copy (V1) of the verb is pronounced. However, the
morpho-syntactic feature number is spelled-out on V_2 by merger with the subject,
which is adjacent to it. This ensures that the plural feature of the copy that ultimately
gets pronounced is spelled-out by the subject. In other words, all this amounts to is
that merger with one copy entails merger with all other copies.

   Now, we may wonder why the same situation cannot obtain in the context of
the preverbal subject. More precisely, consider a SVO sequence that contains at the
least the following copies with pronunciation of the highest copy of each of the verb
and subject chains.

(39) $Subject_1$ V_1 $Subject_2$ V_2

We need to explain why when $Subject_1$ gets pronounced the verb must have its number feature spelled-out by an affix. What we need to rule out, then, is the scenario
whereby, say, V_1 merges with $Subject_2$, thus incorrectly precluding the need for the
number affix.

   Notice that while all copies of the verbal chain carry the morphosyntactic feature number throughout the syntactic derivation, only one copy of the subject—namely,
the merged copy—spells-out the number feature. In other words, spelling-out the
number feature of the verb is not a property of the subject chain. Therefore, only the
merged copy can spell-out this feature. Crucially, the other copies cannot do so.[15]

8.5   Agreement in Moroccan Arabic

As noted above, in Moroccan Arabic full agreement is obligatory regardless of word
order.

(40) a. kla-w   lə-wlad   MA
         eat.past-3p the-children
         'The children ate.'

     b. lə-wlad   kla-w
         the-children eat.past-3p
         'The children ate.'

     c. * kla   lə-wlad
         eat.past.3s the-children

According to the analysis of partial and full agreement in Standard Arabic, the facts
in Moroccan Arabic suggest that the only option to spell-out number agreement is
affixation. The difference between the two dialects with respect to the presence versus absence of the number affix is due to how morphosyntactic features are spelled-
out in the morphology rather than to some syntactic condition, primitive, or operation
that distinguishes the two dialects. In this regard, the present analysis is consistent with
the theoretical claim that language variation must be due to lexical and morphological differences. In the present context, Moroccan Arabic has one single option to spell-
out number agreement on the verb, while Standard Arabic has two options, affixation
and merger between the verb and the subject.

8.6   Agreement and Interpretation

One important consequence of the present analysis is that it can readily explain an
agreement asymmetry that arises in the context of coordination. As first discussed in
Mohammad (1989) in the context of coordinated postverbal subjects, on the one hand,
the verb may carry either partial agreement or full agreement. On the other hand, when
the coordinated subject is in the preverbal position, agreement is with the whole conjunct. This topic has received a great deal of attention recently (see Benmamoun 1992;
Bahloul and Harbert 1993; Aoun, Benmamoun and Sportiche 1994, forthcoming; Aoun
and Benmamoun 1999; Camacho 1997; Mohammad 1998; and Munn forthcoming).[16]
The crucial facts are illustrated here with examples from Moroccan Arabic (Aoun and
Benmamoun 1999).

(41) a. ža   Omar w   Karim
         come.past.3ms Omar and Karim
         'Omar and Karim came.'

     b. Omar w   Karim ža-w
         Omar and Karim come.past-3p
         'Omar and Karim came.'

     c. * Omar w   Karim ža
         Omar and Karim come.past.3ms

     d. ža-w   Omar w   Karim
         come.past.3p Omar and Karim
         'Omar and Karim came.'

The different patterns of agreement can be schematized as in (42).

(42) a. V_s NP_s+NP_s c. * NP_s+NP_s V_s
      b. NP_s+NP_s V_p d. V_p NP_s+NP_s

At first glance, the agreement pattern schematized in (42a) suggests that this is one instance where Moroccan Arabic patterns with Standard Arabic—that is, where an agreement asymmetry is sensitive to word order. Thus, one is tempted to extend to Moroccan Arabic the same analysis provided for partial agreement in Standard Arabic. Accordingly, the agreement pattern in (42a) could be one case of merger where number agreement on the verb is spelled-out by merger with the coordinated subject. As far as the possibility of full agreement with postverbal conjoined subjects schematized in (42d) goes, one could argue that merger is optional.

This account rests on a fundamental assumption—namely, that in both (42a) and (42d), we have instances of phrasal coordination, i.e., the coordination involves the two NP subjects (NP and NP). This analysis makes the prediction that elements that require plural subjects should be equally licensed in (42a) and (42d) since in both cases that requirement obtains.

This prediction is not borne out, as shown in Aoun, Benmamoun and Sportiche (1994, forthcoming) and Aoun and Benmamoun (1999). For example, collective predicates, anaphors, and PRO are all ruled out in the context of partial agreement.

Collective Predicates
(43) a. * tlaqa   Omar w   Karim   MA
             meet.past.3ms Omar and Karim

      b.   tlaqa-w   Omar w   Karim
           meet.past-3p Omar and Karim
           'Omar and Karim met.'

      c.   Omar w   Karim tlaqa-w
           Omar and Karim meet.past-3p
           'Omar and Karim met.'

(44) a. * tqasəm   Omar w   Karim l-ɣalla
             divided.3ms Omar and Karim the-harvest

      b.   tqasm-u   Omar w   Karim l-ɣalla
           divide.past-3p Omar and Karim the-harvest
           'Omar and Karim devided the harvest.'

      c.   Omar w   Karim tqasm-u   l-ɣalla
           Omar and Karim divide.past-3p the-harvest
           'Omar and Karim divided the harvest.'

Anaphors
(45) a. * gləs   Omar w   Karim ħda bəʕdhum
             sit.past.3ms Omar and Karim near each other

b. gləs-u   Omar w Karim fida bəʕḍhum
    sit.past-3p Omar and Karim near each other
    'Omar and Karim sat near each other.'

c. Omar w Karim gləs-u   fida bəʕḍhum
    Omar and Karim sit.past-3P near each other
    'Omar and Karim sat near each other.'

Control

(46) a. *rfəḍ   Omar w Karim y-mši-w
          refuse.past.3ms Omar and Karim 3-go-p

      b. rəfḍ-u   Omar w Karim y-mši-w
          refuse.past-3p Omar and Karim 3-go-p
          'Omar and Karim refused to go.'

Aoun, Benmamoun and Sportiche (1994) and Aoun and Benmamoun (1999) then argue
that the facts in (43–46) can be explained if each NP in the context of first conjunct
agreement is the subject of its own clause. In other words, (42a), (43a), (44a), (45a),
and (46a) display cases of clausal coordination that invole either VPs or functional
projections lower than TP. Thus, a more accurate representation of first conjunct agreement (the pattern in 42a) is as in (47) where each NP is the subject of an independent
predicate.[17]

(47) [$_{IP}$ tlaqa$_i$ [$_{VP}$ Omar t$_i$ [$_{VP}$ Karim GAP]]]

Thus, on the one hand, the requirement that the subject of the collective predicate in (43–44), the antecedent of the anaphor in (45) and the controller of PRO in
(46) is plural is not met. On the other hand, in (42d) no problems arise because we
have phrasal coordination.

One important consequence of this analysis is that we can now have a uniform
analysis of agreement in Moroccan Arabic. The verb always fully agrees with the
subject regardless of word order and whether the subject is a simple NP or a coordinated NP.

Interestingly, in Standard Arabic, elements that require a plural subject are allowed in the context of partial agreement.

(48) a. ʔiʕatamada   Karim wa Marwan ʕalaa nafsayhimaa   SA
          rely.past.3ms Karim and Marwan on   themselves
          'Karim and Marwan relied on themselves.'

      b. Karim wa Marwan ʔiʕatamad-aa ʕalaa nafsayhimaa
          Karim and Marwan rely.past.3md on   themselves
          'Karim and Marwan relied on themselves.'

(49) a. ʔaraada   Marwan w Karim ʔan ya-nžaḥ-aa
          want.past.3ms Marwan and Karim to 3-pass-md
          'Karim and Marwan wanted to pass the exam.'

   b.   Marwan w   Karim ʔaraadaa   ʔan ya-nžaħ-aa
      Marwan and Karim wanted-3md to   3-pass-md
      'Karim and Marwan wanted to pass the exam.'

(50) a.   ʔižtamaʕa   Marwan w   Karim
       meet.past.3ms Marwan and Karim
       'Marwan and Karim met.'

   b.   Marwan w   Karim ʔižtamaʕ-aa
      Marwan and Karim meet.past-3md
      'Marwan and Karim met.'

These facts now follow. The fact that partial agreement on the verb in the context of postverbal coordinated subjects does not affect interpretation is due to how agreement is spelled-out postsyntactically. The verbs in (48a), (49a), and (50a) carry plural agreement features throughout the syntactic derivation. Therefore, they display the pattern in (42d). The only idiosyncratic property of Standard Arabic is that the number feature on the verb is spelled-out by merger with the postverbal conjoined subject. In Moroccan Arabic, spell-out of verb subject agreement by merger is not an option; the only option is affixation of the number morpheme. However, in the next section I will discuss one case where agreement seems to be spelled-out by merger in Moroccan Arabic. This case will highlight an important feature of postsyntactic merger.

8.7   Agreement between Demonstratives and Nouns

Interestingly, there are instances where we find the opposite situation, where Moroccan Arabic seems to spell-out a feature by merger while Standard Arabic does it by affixation only. The facts in question come from the agreement between demonstratives and nouns. In Standard Arabic, demonstratives must agree with the noun in number and gender.

(51) a.   haaða l-walad   SA
       this   the-boy
       'this boy'

   b.   haðihi l-bint
      this.f the-girl
      'this girl'

   c.   haʔulaaʔ l-ʔawlaad
      these   the-children
      'these children'

(52) a.   ðaalika l-walad
       that.ms the-boy
       'that boy'

   b.   tilka   l-bint
      that.fs the-girl
      'that girl'

c.   ʔulaaʔika l-ʔawlaad
     those   the-children
     'those children'

In Moroccan Arabic, the proximate demonstrative agrees with the noun only if it precedes it.[18] If the proximate demonstrative follows the noun, agreement is not allowed.

(53) a.   had l-wəld   l-wəld hada   MA
           this the-boy   the-boy this
           'this boy'   'this boy'

      b.   had l-bənt   l-bənt had**i**
           this the-girl   the-girl this.f
           'this girl'   'this girl'

      c.   had lə-wlad   lə-wlad   had**u**
           this the-children the-children these
           'these children' 'these children'

This agreement asymmetry in terms of word order parallels the asymmetry we find in the context of verb subject agreement in Standard Arabic. The significance of these facts was first pointed out by Aoun and Choueiri (1997). They argue that when the demonstrative does not carry agreement features those features are retrieved from the NP. This retrieval follows the familiar pattern we have seen with verb subject agreement in Standard Arabic. Number agreement (and with demonstratives gender) is realized by an affix only when the noun does not follow the demonstrative—that is, when the post-demonstrative position is null. This recalls the generalization in (28).

Given the parallelism between demonstrative noun agreement in Moroccan Arabic and verb subject agreement in Standard Arabic, I would like to extend the analysis of the latter to the former. That is, I would like to propose that in all the cases in (53) the demonstrative enters the syntactic derivation fully specified for number and gender features. In the morphology, these features can be spelled-out either by an affix when the noun precedes the demonstrative or by the noun when it follows it. In other words, the noun and the number and gender affix stand in a paradigmatic relation exactly on a par with the postverbal subject and the verb in Standard Arabic. I will assume that demonstratives occupy the head of DP.

(54)

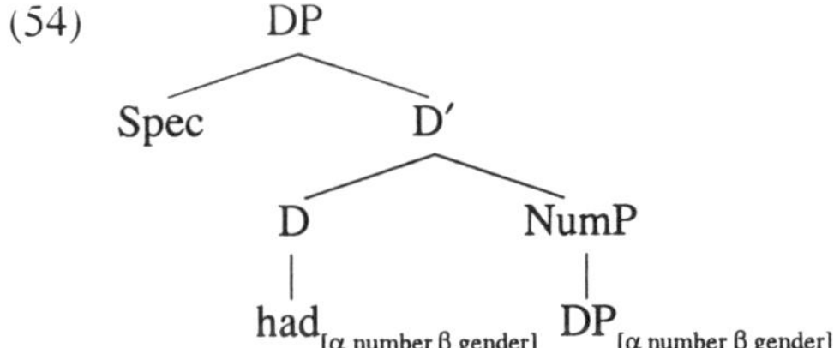

What prevents spelling-out the number and gender features on the demonstrative by merger with the head noun that follows it in Standard Arabic? I have already hinted at the possibility that this is arbitrary. In other words, being in a sequence Dem

>N is a necessary condition for merger but does not automatically mean that the language will avail itself of this option. This seems to me certainly the case of verb subject agreement in Moroccan Arabic. However, with respect to demonstrative noun agreement in Standard Arabic there is a possible explanation that the environment for spelling-out by merger may not be met after all.

The starting point for the explanation is Moroccan Arabic. As I indicated earlier, the proximate demonstrative spells-out its agreement features by merger with the head. However, this situation does not obtain in the context of the nonproximate demonstrative. In this context, the agreement features must be spelled-out on the demonstrative by an affix. Consider the following paradigm.

(55) a.   dak l-wəld   MA
           that the-boy
           'that boy'

      b.   dik/*dak l-bənt
           that.f   the-girl

      c.   duk/*dak lə-wlad
           those   the-children
           'those children'

What is most surprising about the nonproximate demonstrative is that gender and number features are realized by the same affix on the proximate demonstrative. The feminine singular affix is *i*, and the plural affix is *u*. Therefore, it is unlikely that spelling-out by merger with the noun or by an affix is a property of the morphosyntactic feature itself. That is, it is unlikely that the language has statements to the effect that the morpho-syntactic feature /plural/ is spelled out by merger with proximate demonstratives and by an affix with nonproximate demonstratives. Usually, it is the stem that determines how a morpho-syntactic feature is to be spelled-out.

This seems to be the case with the nonproximate demonstrative. One main contrast between this demonstrative and the proximate demonstrative is that the morphosyntactic features number and gender are buried within the word in the sense that they precede the nonproximate affix. Once we assume that the nonproximate affix is derivational, it is plausible that the number and gender affixes on the demonstrative are not realized by the regular rules/constraints of inflection. In other words, at the morphosyntactic component nonproximate demonstratives are inserted into the terminal phrase marker as fully inflected words while proximate demonstratives are inserted as bare stems subject to the spell-out rules of the postsyntactic component. This amounts to saying that the number and gender features in the two forms are different as far as their lexical status is concerned.[19] Most probably, the nonproximate demonstratives are stored as morphological non-compositional forms related to each other by being members of the same paradigm or network. The proximate demonstratives, however, are probably stored as bare stems whose gender and number realizations are the output of rules.[20]

If this analysis is correct, we can now explain why all Standard Arabic demonstratives do not tolerate spell-out by merger. In all Standard Arabic demonstratives, the gender and number features are followed by other morphemes.

So it is not surprising that all demonstratives have their gender and number features spelled-out by affixes on a par with Moroccan Arabic nonproximate demonstratives.

This section has shown that spell-out by merger is not limited to verb subject agreement. Demonstratives in Moroccan Arabic seem to display the same asymmetry that obtains in the context of verb subject agreement. However, spell-out by merger is sometimes precluded from applying even when the syntactic conditions are met. For morphosyntactic features to be spelled-out by merger they have to be peripheral. Morphosyntactic features that must be spelled-out word internally can only be realized by affixes. This could suggest that the two different realizations, peripheral and word internally, correspond to different mechanisms of storage and retrieval.

One significant aspect of the agreement asymmetry in the context of demonstratives in Moroccan Arabic is that it lends itself easily to an analysis of how features are spelled-out in the morphology. It is difficult to see how a syntactic analysis, whether in terms of diacritic features or in terms of different types of chains, can provide an adequate account of the difference between proximate and nonproximate demonstratives. As in the case of Wh-traces and null pronominals in the context of verb subject agreement, the difference between proximate and nonproximate demonstratives seems to be phonological at its core. A postsyntactic morphological account such as the postsyntactic merger analysis provided earlier, can easily take into account this fundamental factor. After all, spell-out is the process of pronouncing the terminal elements of the phrase marker. Thus, the phonological properties of the elements in question are expected to play a significant role.

8.8   Conclusion

In this chapter, I have discussed the well-known agreement asymmetry in Standard Arabic. I have provided an alternative analysis that attributes the absence of the number suffix when the subject is postverbal to the ability of the verb and the subject to merge and spell–out number agreement. By treating the asymmetry in morphological terms we have been able to account for the main generalization about number agreement—namely, that it is not realized by an affix when the postverbal subject position is null. The null versus overt dichotomy can be naturally stated in the postsyntactic component where morphosyntactic features are spelled-out. However, merger as a spell-out mechanism is an option that may or may not exist in a particular language. Thus, in Moroccan Arabic number agreement between the verb and the subject is always realized by an affix, regardless of word order. Moreover, merger is sensitive to how the relevant feature is spelled-out on the stem. If it is peripheral, merger is a contender. On the other hand, if it is not peripheral, merger is not an option. Spell-out by affixation of a morpheme is the only option.

To the extent that this analysis is successful it provides strong evidence for morphological processes that interpret the output of syntax and highlights key aspects of the workings of the postsyntactic morphological interface. In the next chapter, I turn to another construction that displays a similar agreement asymmetry that arises in the context of DPs and propose that the same analysis outlined in this chapter can be extended to it.

9

Agreement Asymmetries in DPs

Let us turn to another construction that seems to display properties that are strikingly similar to the VSO pattern in Standard Arabic. This construction is the so-called Construct State (CS). Among the phrasal categories in Semitic (Arabic and Hebrew), genitive NPs in the CS (1a), as opposed to non-CS NPs (1b), display the phonological and syntactic properties in (3).

(1)   a.   ktab   l-wəld   MA
                      book the-student
                      'the boy's book'

         b.   kitaab-u   ṭ-ṭaalib-i   SA
                      book-nom the-student-gen
                      'the student's book'

(2)   lə-ktab   dyal l-wəld   MA
                the-book   of   the-boy
                'the boy's book'

(3)   a.   The members of the Construct State (CS) tend be adjacent.
         b.   The CS complex constitutes a single prosodic unit.
         c.   Only the last member of the CS can carry the marker of (in)definiteness.

Example (3a) follows from (3b) as convincingly shown in Borer (1988). The CS in (1), as opposed to the non-CS sequence in (2), behaves like a word as far as phonological processes/constraints are concerned. However, it is not entirely clear where the members of the CS merge to form a prosodic unit or why only one member of the CS can carry the marker of (in)-definiteness even though both members are either definite or indefinite. In this chapter, I shall argue: (1) that on par with the merger between the verb and the subject in Standard Arabic, this merger takes place postsyntactically, specifically in the component where morphosyntactic features are spelled-out, and (2) that (3c) is a direct consequence of this postsyntactic merger. In other words, I shall argue that the merger of the members of the CS allows the last member to spell-out the (in)definiteness feature of the other members, making spell-out by a morpheme redundant.

140

9.1   The Construct State

The CS construction has been the focus of much attention within Semitic syntax (See in this connection, Aoun 1978; Borer 1984, 1988, 1996; Ritter 1987; Mohammad 1988; Ouhalla 1991; Fassi Fehri 1993; and Siloni 1997). Since there are numerous studies that deal with the CS in sufficient detail, I will focus here on the three main properties in (3) that bear on the main topic of this chapter—namely, the spelling-out of morphosyntactic features. For a particularly detailed discussion of this construction, see Borer (1996).

9.1.1   Properties of the Construct State

9.1.1.1   Definiteness

As noted earlier, only the rightmost member of the CS can carry the marker of definiteness.

(4)   a.   kitaab-u   t-taalib-i   SA
           book-nom the-student-gen
           'the student's book'

      b. * l-kitaab-u   t-taalib-i
           the-book-nom the-student-gen

The ill-formedness of (4b) is, then, due to the fact that the first member of the CS cannot carry the marker of definiteness. However, this does not mean that it is not definite. Evidence that it is definite comes from adjectives, which must agree with the noun in Arabic in all features, including definiteness.[1]

(5)   kitaab-u   t-taalib-i   l-žadiid-u   SA
      book-nom the-student-gen the-new-nom
      'the student's new book'

The same restrictions govern the distribution of the indefinite marker *–n* in Standard Arabic. Only the last member of the CS can be morphologically marked as indefinite.[2]

(6)   a.   kitaab-u   muʕallim-i-n   SA
           book-nom teacher-gen-indef
           'a teacher's book'

      b.   kitaab-u-n   muʕallim-i-n
           book-nom-indef teacher-gen-indef

9.1.1.2   Adjacency

Another restriction on the CS is that its members tend to be adjacent.

(7) * kitaab-u   l-žadiid-u   t-taalib-i   SA
       book-nom the-new-nom the-student-gen

The ill-formedness of (7) is due to the fact that the first member of the CS is not adjacent to the second member; all adjectives and modifiers must follow the CS.

(8)   kitaab-u   ṭ-ṭaalib-i   l-žadiid-u
       book-nom the-student-gen the-new-nom
       'the new book of the student'

9.1.1.3   Construct State as a Prosodic Unit

The two members of the CS phonologically pattern with words rather than phrases. As shown in Borer (1988, 1996), on the basis of similar data from Hebrew, the main stress fall on the rightmost member in CS, while the vowel of the first member is reduced.

(9)   a.   beit   mora   Hebrew
           house teacher
           'a teacher's house'

      b.   bayit   šel mora
           house of teacher
           'a teacher's house'

Borer discusses further word-level phonological processes that also take place in the context of the CS. One of these processes is also instantiated in Moroccan Arabic and concerns the feminine marker /at/. In Moroccan Arabic, the /t/ part of the feminine suffix /-at/ surfaces only when the noun has a possessive clitic or is in the CS.[3]

(10) a.   mədras-*(t)+i
           school+1s
           'my school'

      b.   mədras-ə*(t)+nadia
           school   Nadia
           'Nadia's school'

In all other contexts, only the vowel surfaces.

(11) a.   (l)-mədras-a(*t)
           (the)-school
           'the/a school'

      b.   (l)-mədras-a(*t) (ž)-ždiid-a(*t)
           (the)-school   (the)-new
           'the/a new school'

      c.   l-qiṣṣ-(*t) dyal nadia
           the-story of   Nadia
           'Nadia's story'

Descriptively the /t/ suffix "deletes" when in word-final position.

(12) $/t/ \rightarrow \emptyset / \_\#$

The fact that the CS patterns with the genitive suffix, which clearly is part of the word it attaches to, seems to indicate that the members of the CS form a single word.

Given these properties, I will assume Borer's (1988, 1996) fundamental insight that the two members of the CS merge, which explains their word-like properties.

9.1.2   Structure of the Construct State

I will adopt the structure assumed by most students of the CS with two functional projections above the lexical NP projection. There is no consensus as to the exact label of the projection between the highest functional DP projection and the lexical projection. However, I will follow Ritter (1991) and assume that it is a Number projection (NumP).

(13)

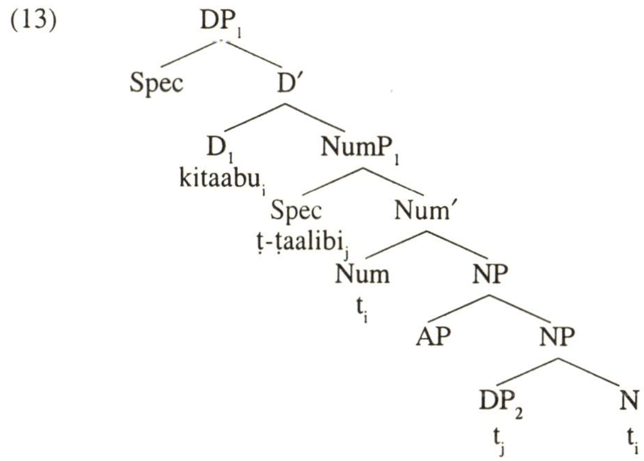

In this representation, the head noun N, which has moved successive cyclically to D_1, ends up being adjacent to DP_2, which has moved to the Spec of NumP.[4]

9.1.3   Previous Analyses

All the previous analyses that I am aware of and which have addressed the distribution of the marker of (in)definiteness have tried to account for it in syntactic terms (Ritter 1991; Fassi Fehri 1993; Siloni 1997) or in a combination of syntactic and morphological terms (Borer 1996). The accounts vary as to how syntax can explain the absence of the marker of (in)definiteness on all but the last member of the CS. I will briefly summarize the main relevant points in the analyses of Ritter (1991), Fassi Fehri (1993), Siloni (1997), and Borer (1996).

Ritter (1991) argues that the head of the CS competes for syntactic position with the marker of (in)definiteness. According to this analysis, the marker of (in)finiteness is in the head of a functional projection DP, which is also the target of N movement. This implies that both the head of the CS and the marker of (in)definiteness compete for the D position.

Fassi Fehri (1993: 229), on the one hand, seems to attribute this to the inability of the genitive NP to raise overtly to the Spec of DP (the definite article is presumably in D) or to some property of the definite article that prevents it from entering into Spec-head relation with the genitive NP either covertly or overtly.

Siloni (1997), on the other hand, posits two functional projections within the DP, the DP projection and the $Agr_{gen}P$ projection. A noun may be definite in two ways: (1) N+article, and $N+Agr_{gen}$. Both the article and Agr_{gen} realize (in)definiteness. Therefore, a noun cannot carry both. Now since in the CS the head noun must raise to Agr_{gen}, this indicates that it is specified for (in)definiteness (given checking theory).

All three accounts assume that agreement in (in)definiteness among the members of the CS is due to Spec-head agreement, which can be either overt (Siloni 1997) or covert (Fassi Fehri 1993). For example, Siloni accounts for the observed agreement in terms of a Spec-head relation that obtains between the two in the Agrgen projection. Fassi Fehri (1993: 225-232) deals with it by suggesting that agreement in the (in)definiteness obtains at LF when the genitive NP, which is specified for the relevant features, enters into Spec-head agreement with the head of the CS in D. Likewise, Ritter (1991, 41) allows the Spec-head relation to obtain within the lexical projection (NP). Movement of N to D provides the latter with the definiteness feature it has acquired through the Spec-head relation within the NP projection. In short, all three analyses assume that the configuration in (14) is what enables the head of the CS to be interpreted as (in)definite.

(14)

The analyses vary as to the details with respect to whether the head of CS is specified for (in)definiteness which must be checked by the genitive NP or whether the head noun enters the derivation unspecified for the (in)definiteness that it acquires in the Spec-head relation. The two alternatives are just notational variants of the same idea—namely, that the (in)definiteness features can only be licensed in a Spec-head relation with the genitive NP.

When we put the details of each analysis aside, the main common characteristic is that the explanation for the observed agreement in (in)definiteness among the members of the CS is due exclusively to syntactic mechanisms that exploit properties of the DP configuration and the relations that obtain within it.

Crucially, according to these analyses there is no correlation between the prosodic property of the CS and the distribution of the marker of (in)definiteness. For Borer (1988, 1996), however, the merger of the members of the CS is at the core of the agreement in (in)definiteness. According to Borer (1996), the DP projection is not specified for (in)definiteness. D inherits this feature from the head noun that moves into it.[5] In addition, in the CS the head noun is also not specified for the (in)definite feature. Borer refers to this as the salient property of CSN.

(15) *The Salient Property of CSN*
The N-head of CSN is base-generated without ±definite specification.

It follows that in the CS the head noun will not be able to provide its DP with the definite specification that it must have. This task is carried out by the genitive noun (which Borer treats as a complement, contra Ritter and Siloni, who treat it as a Spec of NP). The genitive noun (after merging with its extended head Num) ultimately incorporates into the Num head of the DP projection that contains the N head of the CS. Ignoring irrelevant details, the outcome of this syntactic incorporation is as in (16); N_1 is the head of the CS, and N_2 is the genitive noun.

(16)

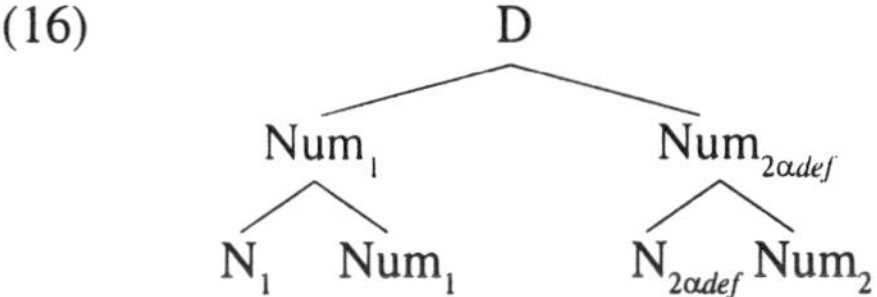

In this representation, N_2 is lexically specified for the definite feature. This feature percolates up the tree and becomes a feature of D and then percolates down to N_1. Consequently, N_1, the head of the CS, ends up specified for the definite feature.

(17)

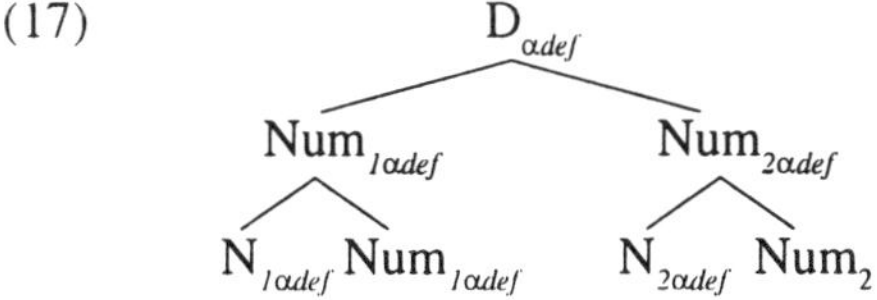

The feature *def* just acquired by the head of the CS percolates down to the other members of the chains of N_1 and Num_1.

I will adopt the important insight of Borer (1996) that the absence of the (in)definiteness marker on the head of the CS must be correlated with the merger of its members. As indicated, this insight is not captured by any of the other analyses of the CS that I am aware of. However, I will depart from Borer in two respects. First, I will argue that the merger of the members of the CS does not take place in the syntax but postsyntactically. Second, I will attribute the absence of the (in)definiteness marker to a morphological process that merges members of the CS, which in turn allows one member to spell-out the features of the other.

I will first take up the issue of where merger takes place and then turn to the complementary distribution between the marker of (in)definiteness and the genitive NP.

9.2   Merger of the Members of the Construct State

Once we accept that the members of the CS form a morphological unit, the question that arises is whether it is generated as a single unit in the syntax (lexical merger) or formed by syntactic incorporation (syntactic merger) or by postsyntactic morphological merger.

9.2.1   Against Lexical Merger

There is strong evidence that the merger in question is not lexical as originally argued in Borer (1988). Four arguments will be given to prove this conclusion. The first two arguments are essentially the Arabic equivalent of the Hebrew data in Borer (1988).

First, one fundamental property of the CS is that it is not an anaphoric island.
Both members of the CS can enter into various syntactic relations. For example, both
can be modified by a relative clause, as illustrated by the following examples from
Moroccan Arabic.

(18) a.   ktab l-wəld lli   kan   hna
          book the-boy who be.past.3ms here
          'the book of the boy who was here'

     b.   ktab l-wəld   lli   ʕṭi-t-ək
          book the-boy that give.past-1s-you
          'the book of the boy which I gave you'

Moreover, the first member of the CS can bind a reflexive (19), which is outside the
CS.

(19) ʕəm nadya ta-y-bɣi   rasu
     uncle Nadia asp-3m-like himself
     'Nadia's uncle like himself'

The second member can be a Negative Polarity Item (20) licensed by a negative outside the CS.

(20) ma-qri-t   ktab ħətta wafiəd
     neg-read.past-1s book any   one
     'I didn't read anyone's book.'

In addition, a quantificational member of the CS can have wide scope over the other
member as argued in Aoun (1996). Thus, in the sentence in (21) from Lebanese Arabic the quantificational genitive NP *waladeen* (boys) can have wide scope with the
intended meaning that there were two pictures, one for each boy.

(21) šef-t   ṣuurit waladeen (men hal-wleed)
     see.past-1s picture boy.d   (of   these-the-boys)
     'I saw a picture of two (of these) boys.'

Assuming that wide scope is captured by raising the quantificational genitive NP
waladeen to a position where it can c-command the indefinite noun *ṣuurit*, this raising is possible only if the QP is not merged with the noun *Suurit* by LF. All these
syntactic relations require that the CS complex be syntactically transparent.[6]

Second, the second member can be a conjunct (Siloni 1997: 53). Again, this is
usually not the case with genuine lexical compounds in Arabic.

(22) ʔižtimaaʕu l-mudiir-i   wa l-kaatib-i   SA
     meeting   the-director-gen and the-secretary-gen
     'the meeting of the director and the secretary'

Notice that (22) cannot involve coordination of CSs with gapping of the first member in the second conjunct (N+NP and N$_{gap}$+NP) given that the first member of the CS is a collective predicate.

Third, two nominals in an ECM (Exceptional Case Marking) relation can form a CS complex (Fassi Fehri 1993: 220; Siloni 1997: 41).

(23) ðannu   r-ražuli   ðakiyy-an xaṭaʔun   SA
     believing-nom the-man-gen clever-acc error-nom
     'Believing that the man is clever is an error.'

The members of the CS in (23) belong to different clauses and presumably do not enter into a thematic relation. This is not usually the case with lexical merger (such as compounding).

The same argument can be made on the basis of data from sentences headed by deverbal nouns. As is well known, in most languages these nominals internally display verbal properties, as evidenced by the fact that they can assign accusative Case and can be modified by VP adverbs, while externally they behave like nouns in that they can get Case assigned to nouns and take genitive arguments (see Fassi Fehri 1993; Hazout 1995; Borer 1996; Siloni 1997; and Yoon 1997). The following Standard Arabic example from Fassi Fehri (1993: 240) illustrates these properties.

(24) ʔaqlaqa-nii   ntiqaad-u   r-ražul-i   bi-stimraarin   hada
     annoy.past.3ms-me criticizing-nom the-man-gen with-persistence-gen this
     l-mašruuʕ-a
     the-project-acc
     'The man's criticizing the project annoyed me.'

Notice that the deverbal noun *ntiqaad-u* carries nominative Case and its subject carries genitive Case. These are clearly nominal property. However, *ntiqaad-u* is modified by a PP adverb and its internal argument *l-mašruu-ʕa* carries accusative Case. These are properties usually associated with verbs. Interestingly, the gerundive nominal and its external argument (the genitive NP) in (24) are in the CS. Moreover, it can be shown that only the deverbal noun can carry the marker of definiteness. To show this I need to make a brief digression about the syntax of nonfinite complements in Arabic.

In Arabic, nonfinite complements can occur in two forms: (1) as complement clauses headed by the complementizer *ʔan* and the non-finite form of the verb (the so-called imperfective), and (2) as complement clauses headed by a deverbal noun, which must carry the definite article.

(25) a.   ʔu-riidu ʔan ʔa-ðhab-a ʔilaa l-masrafi-i   SA
          1s-want to 1s-go-subj to   the-theater-gen
          'I want to go to the theater.'

     b.   ʔu-riidu ð-ðahaab-a   ʔilaa l-masrafi-i
          1s-want the-going-acc to   the-theater-gen
          'I like to go to the theater.'

In (25b), the deverbal noun takes a PP complement. In this context, absence of the definite article is ruled out.

(26) *ʔu-riidu ðahaab-a   ʔilaa l-masrafi-i
     1s-want going-acc to   the-theater-gen

Interestingly, when the complement is an NP the deverbal noun cannot take the definite article (27c); only the genitive subject can do so, as illustrated in (27b).

(27) a.   ʔu-riidu ʔan ʔa-drus-a   š-šiʕr-a
           1s-want to   1s-study-subj the-poetry-acc
           'I want to study poetry'

      b.   ʔu-riidu diraasat-a   š-šiʕr-i
           1s-want studying-acc the-poetry-gen
           'I like to study poetry'

      c. * ʔu-riidu d-diraasat-a   š-šiʕr-i
           1s-want the-studying-acc the-poetry-gen

These facts show clearly that the head of the nonfinite complement and its subject are in the CS.

I will assume with Hazout (1990, 1995), Fassi Fehri (1993), and Borer (1994) that deverbal nouns, particularly action process nominals, have an internal VP dominated by a DP. Most of the analyses assume a structure where a DP dominates a VP.

(28) $[_{DP}$ Nom $[_{VP}$ V]]

The deverbal noun is derived by raising the verb and adjoining it to a nominal morpheme (Hazout 1995: 366).[7]

(29) $[_{DP}$ Nom+V$_i$ $[_{VP}$ t$_i$]]

What is important for the present analysis is that the deverbal noun can be in the CS, as shown here. The fact that it can do so suggests that the CS must be formed subsequent to syntactic verb movement to Nom.[8]

Fourth, the combinatorial principles that govern CS merger are not the same as the principles that regulate lexical merger (compounding, for example). The units affected by this type of merger allow recursion, which lexical compounds in Semitic do not.

(30) kitaab-u   muʕallim-i ʔibn-i   l-mudiir-i   SA
      book-nom teacher-gen son-gen the-director-gen
      'the book of the teacher of the director's son'

In this respect, the CS in (30) sharply contrasts with genuine cases of lexical CS compounds in Arabic and Hebrew, which can consist of two members at most.

(31) bit   l-ma   MA
      room the-water
      'toilet'

To summarize, there is strong evidence that the CS in (1) does not pattern with lexically formed compounds, in the sense that the CS enters the syntax effectively as a single head (even if morphologically complex). All members of the CS are syntactically transparent, a property that does not hold of lexical compounds. Moreover, membership in the CS can involve conjuncts, NPs that are not thematically related (in ECM relation), and more than two members. All these properties suggest that we are not dealing with a lexical word formation process. Finally, unlike the situation with genuine lexical cases of CS clusters, all other instances of the CS dealt with in this book are semantically compositional, in the sense that the meaning of the whole CS complex can be computed from the meanings of its members (Borer 1988).

9.2.2   Against Syntactic Merger

Another alternative to explore is syntactic merger—that is, to allow the members of the CS to enter syntactic derivation as independent elements and then merging them by a process of movement. This alternative can avoid all the problems discussed in the previous section. The transparency of the CS follows because movement leaves traces, which are syntactic entities (copies) that can presumably enter into most of the syntactic relations that their merged antecedent can enter into.[9] Moreover, the fact that conjuncts and ECM subjects can be members of CS may in principle follow as well as long as syntactic conditions on movement and merger are met. Finally, the fact that the CS can contain more than two members may not be a problem; syntax does allow for merger between more than two head positions, (say V, T, and C) in a successive cyclic movement and adjunction fashion, with each step deriving a complex head.

Despite the advantages of syntactic merger, we cannot adopt it for the following reasons. We have seen earlier that the second member can be a conjunct (32a) and can be followed by another CS complex (32b).

(32) a.   ʔižtimaaʕu l-mudiir-i   wa l-kaatib-i   SA
           meeting   the-director-gen and the-secretary-gen
           'the meeting of the director and the secretary'

      b.   ktab ʕəmm l-wəld
           book uncle the-boy
           'the book of the boy's uncle'

These examples clearly show that the merger in question is not syntactic since it violates structure preservation; a maximal projection, as big as a coordinated NP or another CS complex, can merge with a head.

(33)

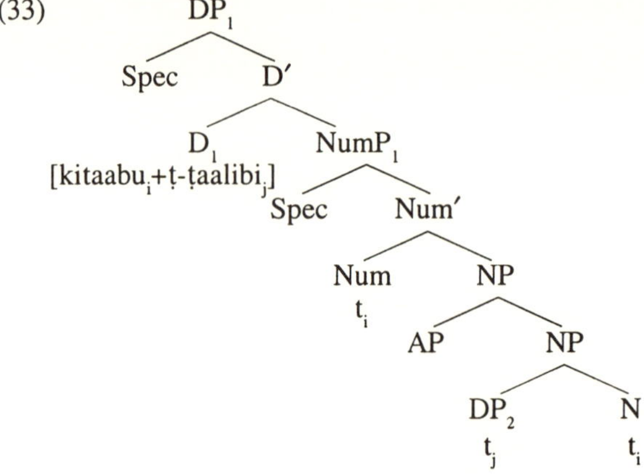

In addition, there is a strong argument from Moroccan Arabic that merger in CS may not be syntactic. As discussed in chapter 5, negation in Moroccan Arabic consists of two elements, *ma* and *š*. In most Arabic dialects, only verbs (and in some dialects only tensed verbs) can take *ma* as a prefix and *š* as suffix. However, as pointed out in chapter 5, in Moroccan Arabic nonverbal predicates can also do so.

(34) a. Ɂana ma-muʕəllim-š   MA
         I   neg-teacher-neg
         'I am not a teacher.'

    b. Ɂana ma-mriḍ-š
         I   neg-ill-neg
         'I am not ill.'

    c. Nadia ma-hna-š
         Nadia neg-here-neg
         'Nadia is not here.'

Focusing on (34a) for the present purposes, this can be accounted for by allowing the head of this predicate to raise to the negative projection as illustrated here (ignoring other functional heads such as TP).

(35)

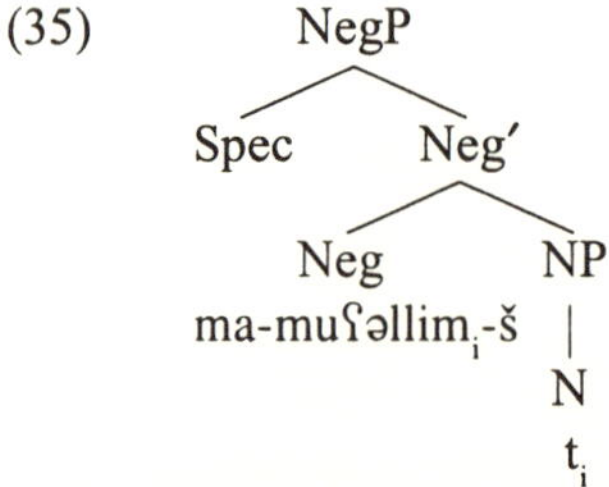

Interestingly, there are limitations on this movement. In particular, if the nominal predicate is within the CS, merger between negation and the nominal predicate cannot take place.[10]

(36)* ma-ktab-š   l-wəld
      neg-book-neg the-boy

The ungrammaticality of (36) can be attributed to the now familiar ban on extraction out of NPs in Arabic illustrated in (37).

(37)

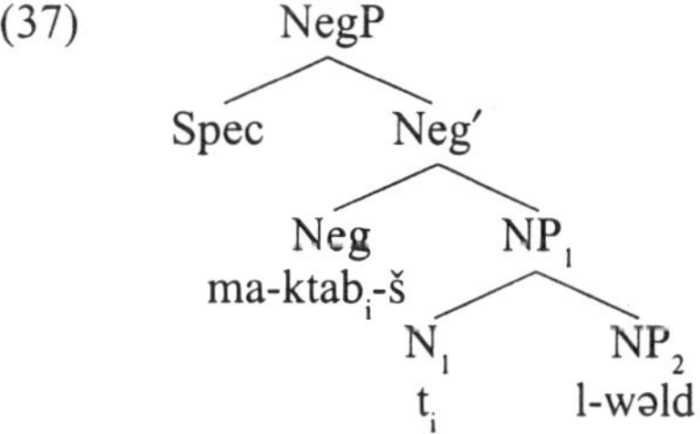

Alternatively, (36) can be equally accounted for if we assume that the two members of the CS merge presyntactically or in the syntax, in which case the ungrammaticality can be attributed to a violation of lexical integrity (movement breaking up what is essentially a single word in the syntax). But this solution cannot extend to the following example (putting aside the problems with lexical merger discussed previously).

(38)* ma-ktab   l-wəld-š
      neg-book the-boy-neg

If the two members of the CS are not merged in the syntax, (38) is ill-formed since it involves movement of a maximal projection to a head, which violates structure preservation, as illustrated in (39).

(39)

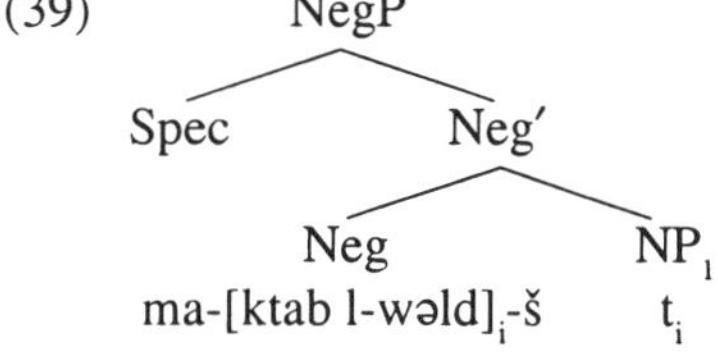

Since movement to negation takes place in the syntax (chapter 5), any postsyntactic merger of the two members of the CS cannot feed syntactic movement. However, if the two members merge in the syntax or enter the syntactic numeration as a single unit, (38) cannot be ruled out since under such an analysis the two members form a single unit, which should undergo syntactic head movement on a par with (34). In other words, the putative syntactic merger should be able to feed further syntactic head movement.

(40)

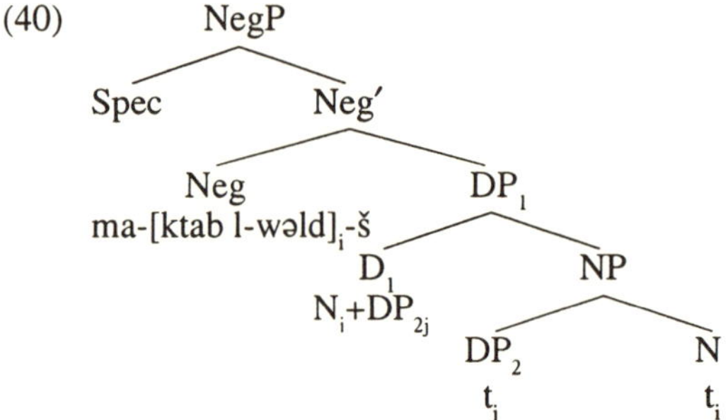

Notice that the ill-formedness of (38) cannot be attributed to the heaviness of the complex that moves to negation. As shown in chapter 5, a complex made up of a verb and the motion predicate can merge with the head of NegP.

(41) a. ma-ɣadi-š   yə-mši   MA
          neg-will-neg 3-go
          'He will not go.'

      b. ma-ɣadi-yə-mši-š
          neg-will-3-go-neg
          'He will not go.'

The verbal complex in (41b) is as heavy as the nominal complex that makes up the CS in (38).

To sum up, in this section I have argued that the members of the CS do not merge in the syntax by the familiar process of head movement (incorporation). Two main reasons make that alternative not viable. First, the merger in question involves a head and a maximal projection, which, if syntactic, would entail a violation of structure preservation. Second, the CS complex does not behave as a single unit in the syntax. In particular, it does not undergo head movement and merges with negation on a par with lexical heads.

9.3   Members of the Construct State Merge Postsyntactically

I would like to argue the members of the CS merge post-syntactically. Assuming postsyntactic merger provides us with a way to account for all the properties of the CS listed in (3) without any of the problems of the lexical or syntactic analysis. The transparency of the CS follows from the fact that all members are independent in the syntax. Moreover, as a morphological process the merger is not sensitive to syntactic conditions on movement. It is subject to morphological conditions only such as that the two elements be adjacent (essentially rebracketing under adjacency).[11] Finally, since the merger is in PF, it does not obey the same restrictions that lexical merger must obey. For example, merger can be with an NP that is not a co-argument.

More importantly, allowing this merger to apply in the morphology where the terminal elements of the syntactic phrase marker are spelled-out explains (3c). Merger with a member that is (in)definite amounts to spelling-out this feature on the other member. Spelling-out (in)definiteness by a morpheme becomes redundant. Thus, the merger of the members of the CS precludes spelling-out the (in)definiteness feature by an independent morpheme on the first member.[12]

(42)   N[±Def]

     /\\
N   NP[±Def]/Determiner

9.4   Merger vs. Percolation

This analysis essentially follows the insight of Borer (1988, 1996). However, instead of assuming that the first member is not specified for (in)definiteness and thus must acquire it by percolation after merger that feeds LF, I am adopting a minimalist/ lexicalist position—namely, that all members of the CS are generated with their (in)definiteness features. Three problems seem to challenge a percolation-based syntactic analysis. First, we have seen that the merger of the two members of the CS violates syntactic conditions (locality and structure preservation). Second, if percolation is the reason that only one member carries the marker of (in)definiteness, it is not clear why all adjectives that modify members of the CS must carry that marker.

(43) qaraʔ-tu   kitaab-a ṭ-ṭaalib-i   l-žadiid-i   ṭ-ṭawiil-a   SA
     read.past-1s book-acc the-student-gen the-new-gen the-long-acc
     'I read the new student's long book.'

Given that both adjectives are within the DP projection, it is surprising that the marker of (in)definiteness percolates down only to the other nominal member of the CS and not to the adjectives contained within the NP.

(44)* qaraʔ-tu   kitaab-a ṭ-ṭaalib-i   žadiid-i   ṭawiil-a   SA
      read.past-1s book-acc the-student-gen the-new-gen the-long-acc

The only way to account for the facts is to restrict percolation to the members of the CS. However, in that case the analysis is not different from the present one— namely, that it is the fact that the nouns are in the CS that explains why only one marker of (in)definiteness is necessary when the morphosyntactic features are spelled-out. Third, percolation does not require merger. All that percolation requires is that the recipient of the relevant feature is not specified for the opposite value of that feature. Thus, the correlation between merger and the distribution of the (in)definiteness does not follow from the percolation analysis.

The alternative analysis is natural if the morphological distribution of the (in)definiteness markers obtains in the same component where the two elements merge. We have argued that both members do not form a unit (word) in the syntax but in the morphology. Since the (in)definiteness feature is interpretable it follows that both are generated with the definiteness feature, which is present throughout the syntactic derivation.

(45)

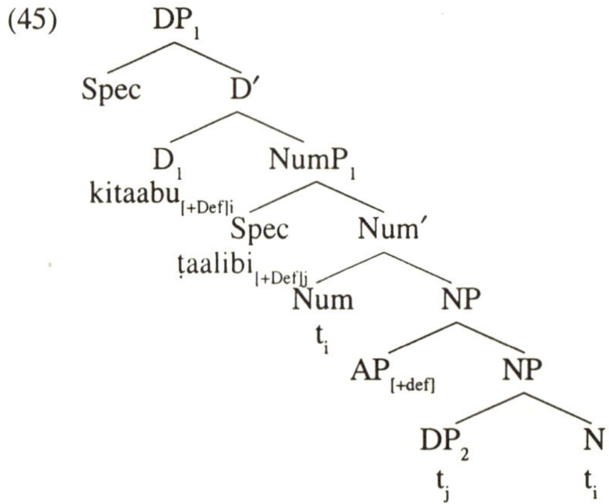

In this representation, both members of the CS and their adjectives are specified for the (in)definiteness feature. In the morphology or at the component where morphosyntactic features are spelled-out, the two members merge. Consequently, spelling out the (in)definiteness feature on the rightmost member virtually turns it into a morphological marker of (in)definiteness, which in turns allows it to spell-out the (in)definiteness feature of the members that merge with it. Therefore, how the feature is spelled-out in the morphology obviously has no consequence for the LF interpretation of the element in question. With respect to adjectives, since they do not merge (are not in the CS) the only way to spell-out their (in)definiteness feature is by a morphological affix.

Finally, one nice consequence of the present analysis is that it is consistent with the fact that merger of the members of the CS is phonologically conditioned. This fact obtains in Moroccan Arabic, where all singular nouns can occur in the CS, but plural NPs formed by the suffixation of the vowel *-a* cannot do so.

(46) a.   nəžžaar   l-ħuma   MA
          carpenter the-neighborhood
          'The neighborhood's carpenter'

     b. * nəžžaar-a   l-ħuma
          carpenter-p the-neighborhood

This phonological restriction on the merger of the members of the CS is expected if the merger in question takes place in the morphology where sensitivity to phonological properties can be adequately articulated.

Therefore, it is safe to conclude that the merger of the two members of the CS does not take place in the syntax or a component that feeds syntax. The members of the CS merge in the morphology (or whatever component constrains the spell-out of morphosyntactic features). Moreover, there is no upper bound on the membership in the CS since merger can be recursive. Thus, the fact that only the last member of CS in (30) carries the definite article follows if the merger proceeds from right to left with the third member merger with second member and the whole complex specified for the definiteness feature (thanks to the third member) merging with the first member and endowing it with the definiteness feature.

(47)   [kitaab-u [muʕallimi ṭ-ṭaalib-i]]

If the preceding analysis is correct, PF is not just the component where the terminal elements of the syntactic phrase marker are spelled-out. It seems to involve bracketing that is morphologically motivated to spell-out morpho-syntactic features and movement processes that are not motivated by feature checking (Aoun and Benmamoun 1998; Zubizarreta 1999). This analysis is consistent with the minimalist view that lexical items in the syntactic derivation/representation are fully specified for their features. In particular, no features can be added or deleted in the course of the syntactic derivation. Thus, any apparent mismatch must be due to the demands of the other components or interfaces. In the context of CS, the absence of the (in)indefiniteness marker on all but the last member of the CS does not imply absence of the (in)definiteness feature at any point in the syntactic derivation. In other words, absence of the morpheme does not entail absence of the feature for the simple reason that there are alternative ways to spell-out features.

9.5   Conclusion

In this chapter, I have provided arguments to account for an important asymmetry that arises in the context of the N+NP sequence. I have shown that the absence of the (in)definiteness marker on the head noun can be accounted for if we assume that the members of the CS sequence merge postsyntactically, which amounts to spelling-out the relevant features on the noun.

This analysis claims that a noun carrying an (in)definiteness feature can spell-out that feature on another noun. In other words, in the CS the (in)definiteness morpheme seems to be in competition with a noun that carries the same feature. This analysis is more natural if embedded within a theory where the syntactic phrase marker contains only semantic and morpho-syntactic features (Halle and Marantz 1993 and Beard 1995, among others). In particular, it does not contain phonological features. At the component where the morphosyntactic features are spelled-out, the language may resort to various options. In the CS, it affixes an (in)definiteness marker and merges it with other elements, effectively, turning the overtly marked noun itself into a maker of (in)definiteness. This situation is by no means restricted to the CS, we have seen in the previous chapter that the agreement asymmetries in Standard Arabic can be accounted for in a similar fashion.

Notes

Chapter 1

1. Throughout the book, when I use the term *Arabic* without specific reference to a particular dialect, the implication is that the facts and generalizations in question hold in all the dialects under study.

2. The term *merge* refers strictly to the morphological combination of elements (Marantz 1988). It is not intended in the broad sense of Chomsky, where Merge is a structure-building operation.

3. Notice that number must be present on both the auxiliary verb and the main verb. Thus, the obligatory presence of number cannot be due to the fact that the subject is null and must be retrieved from the inflection on the verb. The inflection on the main verb in (20b) should be sufficient to retrieve the subject.

4. In Moroccan Arabic, the definite article *l* assimilates to *z*.

5. I will assume that the EPP (Extended Projection Principle) feature is [+D]. Probably the most appropriate feature is [Nom(inal)], which ranges over NP and DPs (Chomsky 1995). The label, however, is not crucial. The main assumption, as far as this book is concerned, is that there seems to be a property of functional categories that requires that they be paired with nominal elements such as NPs.

Chapter 2

1. Since the focus is on morphosyntax, I will not deal in detail with the semantics of the various tenses/aspects in Arabic. Nothing in this chapter or in the subsequent chapters hinges on the exact label of a particular temporal or aspectual category or its interpretation. For a detailed analysis of the semantics of tense in an Arabic dialect, the reader is referred to Eisele's (1988) important dissertation where an analysis of Egyptian Arabic (the dialect of Cairo) is provided. His in-depth semantic analysis to a large extent carries over to Standard Arabic and Moroccan Arabic. See also McCarus (1976), Moutaouakil (1987: 21–52), Caubet (1991), Fassi Fehri (1993), and Bahloul (1994), among many others.

2. The syntax of agreement is dealt with in sufficient detail in chapter 8.

3. The table in (1) is for purely descriptive purposes. It is not intended to reflect an exhaustive analysis of the nature of the agreement morphology. As the reader can easily see some affixes in tables (1) can be further decomposed into smaller morphemes each carrying number and person, with gender specified on either the number or the person morpheme. An in-depth analysis of the distribution of features and affixes in Arabic and other Afro-asiatic languages is provided in Noyer (1992).

4. A fourth mood is the energetic (roughly emphasis), which involves the suffixation of *na* to the imperfective. The energetic is clearly not related to tense or modality and therefore is not relevant to the present discussion.

5. Egyptian Arabic here refers to the dialect of Cairo. The dialect of the Saˤid (Khalafallah 1969) follows the pattern of the dialects of the Maghreb (Algeria, Libya, Mauritania, Morocco, and Tunisia): one prefix for first person (*na*) and a suffix for number (*u*).

6. Eisele (1988: 6-41) and Bahloul (1994: 31–48) provide detailed reviews of the various positions on this issue.

7. Within the Arabic grammatical tradition, the negative *laysa* is considered a verb. The main reason for that stems from the fact that *laysa* agrees with the subject, unlike the other negative particles (Moutaouakil 1987: 78). See chapter 6 for a detailed analysis of this and other negatives in Standard Arabic.

8. See Travis (1979: 3), Fassi Fehri (1993: 76–85), and Bahloul (1994: 34–36), where it is assumed that the vocalic melody carries tense/aspect and voice. I will agree that the vocalic melody carries voice but not tense or aspect.

9. In my view this was one of the important claims of the autosegmental analyses of Arabic—namely, that the various tiers constitute grammatical elements.

10. I will ignore the so-called mood endings in the imperfective since they are not relevant to this discussion.

11. What looks like short full vowels in Moroccan Arabic are underlyingly long vowels. However, I will continue to transcribe them as short vowels.

12. As far as I can tell, this conclusion is valid for all the modern dialects.

13. Benmamoun (1992: 221). See also Ouhalla (1993) and Shlonsky (1997: 96–97), where it is argued that the imperfective in Arabic does not carry tense.

14. A similar point is made in Fassi Fehri (1993: 84). This echoes Palmer (1986: 22), who points out that "moods of the familiar languages (or the subjunctive at least) have a whole variety of semantic functions, and that the choice between them is determined grammatically more than by modal meanings."

15. For example, in Greek, according to Palmer (1986, 22), the subjunctive form of the verb is used in negative imperatives.

16. Apparently, in some classical dialects of Arabic the jussive was also possible after ʔan (Hassan 1973, vol.4: 294).

17. See Eisele (1988) and Fassi Fehri (1993) for reichenbachian analyses of tense in Cairene Arabic and Standard Arabic respetively.

18. See Testen (1994) for a study of the evolution of the subjunctive. His assertion (page 165) that "the subjunctive . . . is . . . arguably a semantically vacuous reflection of the morphology of verbs in a specific type of subordinate clause" accords with the view in the text.

19. Benmamoun (1992), following a well-established analysis within traditional Arabic grammar, suggests that the mood markers are morphological reflexes of these syntactic dependencies. They are akin to Case markers in the context of NPs, which also reflect a grammatical relation between a head and an NP. Traditional Arabic grammarians classify the mood endings under the same label as the Case markers on NPs, namely, ʔi9raab (Hassan 1973, Vol. 4: 277–440; Fleisch 1979: 134). Fassi Fehri, (1993: 163–164) also assumes a Case role for the mood inflections.

20. Bahloul (1994: 59) reports that statistically *sa* is far more frequent than *sawfa* (*sa* occurs in 94 percent of the sample while *sawfa* occurs in only 6 percent).

21. Dahl (1985: 108) classifies Tunisian Arabic as a language that lacks the category Fut. Tunisian Arabic is fairly similar to Moroccan Arabic as far as the tense system is concerned.

22. Motion or movement predicates are a well-known source (among others) from which future morphemes evolve (Bybee, Perkins, and Pagliuca 1994: 266–270). At this point, it seems that the prospective markers in Moroccan Arabic and Egyptian Arabic have not yet attained the full exclusive status of future morphemes.

23. There is good evidence that the imperative is derived from the indicative form of the imperfective. See Brame (1970) and Benmamoun (1996). This provides further independent

evidence that the imperfective does not carry any temporal or aspectual morphology. It is simply the default form of the verb, which is also the input to word formation.

Chapter 3

1. The situation in English is more complicated since lexical verbs do not raise to tense overtly. Various proposals have been advanced. Chomsky (1995), on the one hand, suggests that the [V] feature of the main verb raises covertly to check the [+V] feature of tense. Roberts (1998), on the other hand, proposes that the [V] feature of verb raises overtly while the lower verbal copy get spelled-out. Bobaljik (1994), in turn, revives Chomsky's (1957) analysis and argues that the merger of tense and the verb does not involve movement. Rather, it obtains under adjacency when T and VP are adjacent (excluding adverbs, which are not relevant to syntactic adjacency).

2. It is also possible that there may be a functional projection that is not specified for any of the two categorial features. The functional projection in question would be specified for its interpretable features only. Since interpretable features do not need to force movement at any point in the derivation (Chomsky 1995) we expect absence of movement in a language with such functional projection. This presents an empirical question that I will leave open.

3. See Bakir (1980), Jelinek (1981), Fassi Fehri (1982), Eid (1983), Mouchaweh (1986), Moutaouakil (1989), Fassi Fehri (1993), and Bahloul (1994). The same issue arises in Hebrew, see Berman and Grosu (1976), Doron (1986), Rapapport (1987), Heggie (1988), and Shlonsky (1997).

4. All these positions were coherent with the assumptions current at the time.

5. See Progovac (1994) and the references cited there.

6. Shlonsky (1997) also explores the possibility of a null copula in the context of nonverbal and benoni predicates in Hebrew. For different reasons, he concludes that there may be no null copula in Arabic (1997: 102). The arguments I present corroborate this conclusion.

7. See Moutaouakil (1987: 68-76) for conceptual arguments against the copula deletion hypothesis and an alternative within the functional grammar of Simon Dick that posits a copula only when it is overt. In this respect, the analysis I argue for agrees in spirit with Moutaouakil's account.

8. Of course, one could argue that the putative null copula may or may not merge with the nonverbal predicate. On the one hand, if it merges with the nonverbal predicate the whole complex merges with negation. On the other hand, if it does not merge with the nonverbal predicate, it can only merge with negation. Needless to say, that this is an ad-hoc assumption that does not follow from any morpho-phonological property of the null copula. All it does is make the copula invisible as far as minimality effects are concerned. The simplest assumption is that it is not there.

9. In a way, a stage-level predicate has the interpretation of an individual level predicate when it refers to the moment of speech.

10. Conversely, it is not clear why the putative copula deletion rule applies only in the present tense.

11. In Hebrew, an optional pronominal copula can occur with nonverbal predicates (see the references cited in note 3).

(i)   ha-yeled hu student
       the-boy he student
       'The boy is a student.'

In Arabic, this option is not available (Eid 1991: 40).

(ii)* Omar huwa zariif
      Omar he   nice

The pronominal is possible only when the predicate is definite.

(iii) Omar huwa l-mudir
     Omar he   the-director
     'Omar is the director.'

For detailed recent analyses of the pronoun copula see Ouhalla (1997) and Shlonsky (1998).

12. At this point, I will assume that the features of functional categories are privative; i.e., they are specified for positive values only. I don't see any empirical consequences that follow from assuming that they can be negatively specified for some features.

13. It may turn out that this classification of tense is universal. That is, the present tense could be universally [+D] only and the past and other tenses universally [+V, +D]. That would require a different analysis of Do-support such as the one given in Grimshaw (1997). I will leave this issue open.

Chapter 4

1. In Moroccan Arabic, all verbs must merge with negation. However, this has nothing to do with tense, for nonverbal predicates in this language, as opposed to their counterparts in Egyptian Arabic, also merge with negation. See chapter 5 for an in-depth analysis of the contrast between Egyptian Arabic and Moroccan Arabic.

2. In chapter 6, I will elaborate on this analysis by arguing that *laysa* is a variant of *laa*. Both carry agreement, which is spelled-out differently.

3. The same situation obtains in Hebrew. The negative *ʕeyn* patterns with *laysa* in that it occurs in present tense contexts only (Shlonsky 1997: 64). By contrast, *lo* occurs in both present tense and past tense contexts (Shlonsky 1997: 12–14) very much like the Standard Arabic *laa*.

4. Both verbs (in the past and the present) express an eternal property when used in these contexts.

5. This analysis of the *n* could explain the focus interpretation of independent pronouns in Arabic (see chapter 8).

Chapter 5

1. In these dialects, it seems that the absence of *ma* in these contexts is not obligatory. This could signal a process whereby *š* is becoming the main marker of negation.

2. See also Halila (1992).

3. See Hirschbühler and Labelle (1994) for arguments that *pas* is not in the Spec of a projection headed by *ne*.

4. Notice that this analysis can only be maintained under the assumption that LF movement to the Spec of NegP exists. As shown in Benmamoun (1997), this assumption is questionable. These elements seem to be licensed in their surface position by spell-out. This is consistent with Chomsky's (1995) theory that interpretable features do not force abstract movement. Moreover, even if *š* were to occupy the Spec of NegP it does not follow automatically that abstract movement of Negative elements to the Spec of VP precludes the presence of *š* overtly for the same reason that the supposed movement of the associate to matrix subject position in expletive argument chains (i) does not preclude the presence of the expletive.

(i) There is a student in the room

See Ouhalla (forthcoming) for an alternative analysis of the complementary distribution between NPIs and *š*.

5. See Benmamoun (1997).

6. The problem for the analysis that locates *š* in Spec becomes more serious if the

imperfective verb in present tense sentences does not move to tense in Egyptian Arabic. Under such a scenario, it is not clear how *š* ends up as enclitic.

7. See, for example, Youssi (1992) and Caubet (1993).

8. The issue of the internal structure of Wh-quantifiers is taken up in Tsai (1994).

9. Another plausible alternative is provided by Ouhalla (forthcoming) who argues that *š* is a variable bound by a quantificational element such as negation, a question morpheme, or an existential operator.

10. For descriptive purposes I will continue to gloss *š* as Neg.

11. It is not important if it turns out that what I characterized as a pronominal in (28) is an agreement morpheme.

12. The transcriptions and gloss are mine.

13. Matar considers *b* part of the negative complex.

14. Apparently, not all prepositions can merge with negation (Jelinek 1983: 75, Eisele 1988: 187). However, the significant point remains that even the prepositions that can merge with negation can only do so when they carry the clitic as illustrated in (44).

15. By Egyptian Arabic I intend to refer to the dialect of Cairo. The dialect of Saʕidi described in Khalafallah (1969: 100–102) allows for merger of negation and nonverbal predicates (the gloss is not provided in the original):

(i)   liktaab   ma-žadiid-šey
      the book neg-new-neg
      'The book is not new.'

16. The idea that predicate adjectives and nouns can check the [+D] feature of negation is one more plausible argument for characterizing the relevant feature as [Nom] or even as [N] rather than [D]. If it turns out that only elements that carry a [+D] feature can check/be paired with a [+D] feature on a functional category, the merger between negation and nonverbal predicates must, then, be due to other reasons, probably simply morphological.

17. In Moroccan Arabic, when the Wh-operator is genitive, within an NP or PP, it is realized as *mən*. When it is not embedded within an NP or PP, it is realized as *škun*.

Chapter 6

1. Other negatives such as *lammaa*, an emphatic variant of *maa*, will be ignored. It is virtually extinct in the modern variety of Standard Arabic. However, the behavior of this negative does not challenge any aspects of the analysis.

2. See Shlonsky (1997: 104) for an alternative analysis that locates the negative projection above TP.

3. Lasnik (1995) suggests a similar analysis for the contrast between French and English with respect to verb movement. He suggests that in French the tense inflection is generated directly in T, while in English it is generated on the verb.

4. With respect to the dialects where tense is always realized on the verb, we could also allow tense to be generated independently of the verb. The fact that tense is not realized on negation could simply be due to the inability of negation to host temporal inflection. Thus, the verb inflects for tense in the context of *ma-š* because the latter is not a potential morphological host.

5. Unlike MA, SA does not allow nonverbal predicates to merge with *laa*. Apparent cases of merger are most probably instances of constituent negation.

6. See Grimshaw (1997) for an Optimality Theoretic account of this problem. Under her system sentences with Do-support can compete with those without Do-support.

7. See also Bresnan (1996) and Sells (1996), where it is shown that words and phrases can compete. Crudely put, in instances where a single lexical item can fulfill the role of a phrase,

the language opts for the single lexical item (assuming the constraint ranking in the language allows that).

8. The issue is moot if it turns out that this is constituent negation. In that case, presumably negation is generated directly on the constituent.

9. I have opted for an analysis whereby *maa* is located between TP and VP for two reasons: First, to minimize the syntactic difference between *maa* and *laa* to the Spec vs. head status; and second, to explain the evolution of negation in the modern dialects from Standard Arabic. Most of the dialects I am aware of use *maa*, which as I have shown in chapter 5 is in a projection between TP and VP. This could be explained if we assume that the dialects have opted for the simple negative which has no tensed variants.

10. Traditionally, it is claimed that *lamma*+V is the negation of *qad*+V, while *maa*+V is just a negation of a verb or negation of *la-qad*+V (see Larcher 1994). However, in modern Standard Arabic, where *lammaa* is not used, *maa* could have taken over the function of *lammaa* and should probably better be equated with *qad*+V. The main point is that there are interpretive differences between *laa/lam*+V and *maa*+V, which in turn implies that there is no competition between the two (in other words, they have different LFs). I should also mention that Bahloul (1994, 168) in his frequency study of these negatives in newspaper articles found out that *maa* seems to be less frequent than the negatives we looked at previously.

11. There is another variant *qad* used in the future that conveys probablity.

(i) qad   ya-habu
     possible 3m-go
     'He might go.'

Chapter 7

1. I should stress that nothing hinges on the exact label of the projection that contains the Imp feature. What is crucial for the present analysis is that there is an Imp feature that must merge with verb and that the projection that contains Imp is higher than sentential negation in English and Arabic.

2. In this section, I limit the discussion to second person imperatives, where most languages are more likely to show distinct forms for positive imperatives (Brame 1970).

3. As pointed out earlier, when absence of person agreement yields an initial consonant cluster rules of glottal prosthesis and vowel insertion apply (Brame 1970)

4. The "jussive" label has been traditionally used with the negative imperative and the imperfective form in the context of the negative past tense *lam*. If the various mood labels distinguish verbs according to their endings, I see no reason that the same label cannot be given to positive imperatives.

5. In positive imperatives, the second person plural may require a different verbal paradigm (see Zanuttini 1997).

6. Kayne (1992) argues that there is a covert modal in Italian infinitival negative imperatives. The presence of the modal accounts for the infinitive form of the verb (infinitives occur in the context of modals) and clitic climbing in negative imperatives (the clitic adjoins to the modal).

7. This conclusion is supported by the fact that in Arabic and Hebrew (Ritter 1995) the third person pronoun is related to the demonstrative pronoun.

8. This analysis depends crucially on whether the distribution of anaphors requires a subject in the syntactic representation.

(i) t-həlla f-rasək
     2-care in-yourself
     'Take care of yourself.'

If it does, then the inability of the subject of imperatives to check the [+D] feature must be due to some other factor. I will leave this issue open.

9. How does this analysis of Arabic imperatives extend to imperatives in other languages, particularly of the Romance family? One possibility is that the verbs in negative imperatives carry a [+D] feature. This seems to be the case of infinitives that display nominal properties. As such, they can fulfill the same function that person agreement fulfils in Arabic— namely, checking the [+D] feature of the head of sentential negation. What these forms are contributing to negative imperative sentences is just the formal [+D] feature. In this respect, they pattern with the verb *do* when it is inserted to check [+V] features in the context of sentential negation and the deictic locative pronoun *there* when it is inserted in existential sentences to check the [+D] feature of tense (Chomsky 1995). In all these instances, the elements in question have been stripped of their interpretable features. The only features that are visible to the syntactic derivation/representation are the categorial features.

Chapter 8

1. See Shlonsky and Roberts (1996) for an analysis in terms of the weak/strong dichotomy.

2. One alternative is to assume that singular agreement is weak and plural is strong. This incorrectly predicts that a singular subject cannot occur in the preverbal position.

3. See Mohammad (1989) and Fassi Fehri (1993) for discussions of the expletive and its role in agreement.

4. See Fassi Fehri (1993) for an incorporation analysis of the complementary distribution between full agreement and the lexical postverbal subject. I should note that, on the one hand, the incorporation account is problematic only under the assumption that the incorporated pronominal consists of person, number, and gender features. This is what all the advocates of the incorporation analysis assume. On the other hand, if it turns out that the pronominal consists only of the number (and gender) feature, then incorporation could be a viable alternative provided it can contend with the facts in (20) and (22).

5. I argued in chapter 4 that historically the agreement features evolved from incorporated pronominals. This allowed us to account for the placement of the person affix as a prefix or suffix depending on tense and verb movement. In Standard Arabic, it is clear that the person feature is an agreement morpheme.

6. The facts in (22) are problematic for both incorporation analyses and accounts that posit two independent agreement paradigms, one weak and one strong. For the incorporation account one must recognize that the resumptive pronoun strategy is obligatory in all Wh-constructions in Arabic involving subject extraction, a questionable assumption (see Shlonsky 1992). For the two-paradigm analysis one must introduce some stipulation that would have the effect of requiring the strong paradigm in the context of wh-traces.

7. Most previous analyses of the agreement asymmetry in Standard Arabic have focused mainly on simple sentences with preverbal and postverbal lexical subjects.

8. See, for example, Pollard and Sag (1994).

9. See Shlonsky (1997) for a discussion of subject positions in Arabic.

10. This view seems to be consistent with the theory that agreement does not head an independent syntactic projection (Iatridou 1990, Benmamoun 1992, 1993, Chomsky 1995).

11. See Börjars et al. (1996) for a detailed discussion of this subject.

12. Pronominals are, of course, specified for the person feature. However, overt independent pronouns in Arabic are not arguments, as mentioned earlier. Therefore, it is not possible to test how they interact with agreement on the verb.

13. Imperatives lack the person prefix, but they are certainly easy to identify as verbs because their morphology is different from that of nominals. For example, in Standard Arabic,

the deletion of the person prefix in imperatives leads to initial consonant clusters which in turn forces glottal prosthesis (see chapter 2). This situation does not arise with nouns.

14. Are all cases of complementary distribution between agreement and lexical NPs reducible to PF merger? The facts from Irish (McCloskey and Hale 1984; McCloskey 1986) suggest a negative answer. For example, in Irish there is full agreement in the context of Wh-traces, while a morphological merger analysis predicts exactly the opposite. However, a careful look at Irish (and Celtic languages in general) shows that its agreement system is radically different from that of Standard Arabic. First, as far as I know there is no partial agreement in the VSO order. Second, the agreement features are always realized by a single morpheme (no separate affixes for the different features). All these properties may indicate that the agreement features in Irish are realizations of the pronominal subject (which gets incorporated). The fact that there is no partial agreement follows because there is no agreement in the first place. Likewise, Wh-variables, as arguments, are expected to pattern with overt lexical subjects in not requiring agreement inflection.

15. Another plausible alternative to merger is percolation of the number feature from the postverbal subject to the verb. The percolated number feature would then preclude the number suffix on the verb. One advantage of percolation is that it does not require strict adjacency. The two are not incompatible in the present context since they can both adequately address the generalization in (28) in morphological terms rather than syntactic terms. Also, both merger and percolation must prevent the preverbal subject from being in complementary distribution with the number affix. For present purposes I will stick to the merger analysis, for reasons that will become obvious in section 8.7.

16. See also McCloskey (1986) for an analysis of agreement and coordination in Irish.

17. I leave many irrelevant issues aside, such as whether the coordination in question involves higher functional projections and whether the second verb is a gap or a trace of across-the-board head movement. See Aoun, Benmamoun and Sportiche (1994, forthcoming) and Aoun and Benmamoun (1999) for discussions of these issues.

18. The absence of the vowel suffixes that carry number and gender is clearly not phonologically motivated, for these same affixes do not get syncopated when affixed to verbs followed by the lexical subject.

    (i)   zad-**u**   lə-wlad
            advanced-p the-children
            'The children went forward.'

19. A less complicated alternative would consist of saying that spell-out by merger would involve breaking up the nonproximate demonstrative, a process that is probably not allowed. This is a viable alternative but is not consistent with the analysis we provided for Standard Arabic where the realization of number by an affix attaches it directly to the stem, while spell-out by merger can tolerate intervening elements.

20. This is the main reason that I did not opt for percolation as the mechanism at work in partial verb subject agreement in Standard Arabic. There is no reason that percolation should be sensitive to whether the demonstrative carries the nonproximate suffix. In other words, peripherality should not be a factor as far as percolation is concerned. Nevertheless, it is still plausible that percolation is at work in verb subject agreement and merger is at work in demonstrative noun agreement. I will leave this issue open.

Chapter 9

1. Moroccan Arabic, like all modern Arabic dialects, does not have any overt morphological markers of Case.

2. In most modern dialects, there is no overt morphological marker for indefinite nouns.

3. See also Aoun (1978), where the distribution of this marker in the CS is discussed.

4. As to how the surface location of the adjective is derived, I refer the reader to Ritter (1991), Borer (1994), and Siloni (1997), who assume that adjectives are left adjoined to NP, though the machinery that derives the surface order may be different.

5. Actually, it is the extended projection of N, Num, that moves into D. However, this detail is not crucial for the discussion. The crucial point is that ultimately it is the feature of N that determines the definite specification of D.

6. Borer (1996) provides data from Hebrew that show that Negative Polarity Items and quantificational genitive NPs with wide scope readings are not allowed. Borer takes these facts to argue that the formation of CS in Hebrew takes place in the syntax, because the formation of the CS precludes the members of the CS from being involved in subsequent syntactic processes that involve movement. By the same reasoning, the Arabic facts indicate that the formation of the CS takes place in a post-syntactic component. As pointed out by Joseph Aoun (personal communication), it may turn out the formation of the CS can take place at various components, in the syntax in Hebrew and postsyntactically in Arabic.

7. The representation in (28) presents only the basic aspects of the structure that are relevant to the present discussion. For details see Hazout (1990, 1995), Fassi Fehri (1993) and Borer (1994). For a different view see Bresnan (1997) and Siloni (1997).

8. It is tempting to capitalize on this generalization and argue that the merger in the CS is itself one way to satisfy the Case relation between the genitive and the head noun (Siloni 1998) on a par with noun incorporation (Baker 1988). However, one major difference between noun incorporation and CS merger is that all members of the CS surface with their Case markers. This suggests that the merger may not be for Case purposes, given that it does not preclude the presence of Case morphemes.

9. However, there are relations that require reference to the overt element rather than the trace/copy. For example, NPIs seem to require to be licensed where they are spelled-out (Benmamoun 1997) rather than in the position of their trace. Consider the asymmetry between fronted PPs that contain NPIs and their counterparts in situ.

(i)   ma-tlaqit   mʕa ʕəmm ħətta wafiəd
       neg-met.1s-neg with uncle any   one
       'I didn't meet anyone's uncle.'
(ii)* mʕa ʕəmm ħətta wafiəd ma-tlaqi-t
       with uncle any   one   neg-meet.past-1s

Under an analysis where the transparency of the CS is due to the presence of traces, one must make a special provision that in this particular instance it is the overt element that is relevant.

10. Khalafallah (1969, 101) cites one example from Saʕidi Egyptian Arabic where negation seems to merge with the first member of the CS (the gloss is mine; it is not provided in the original)

(i)   irraažel ma-nazir-ši   lmidrasi
       the-man neg-headmaster-neg the-school
       'The man is not the headmaster.'

It seems that this dialect allows for heads (but probably not XPs) to move out of NPs.

11. As pointed out by Bohas and Al-Qaadirii (1998), some elements can intervene between the members of the CS. This situation, though marked, arises in two contexts: (1) when the first member of the CS is a deverbal noun (ia), and (2) when the intervening element is a parenthetical (ib).

(i)   a. tarku   yawman nafsi-ka . . .
          leaving   one day self-your
          'Leaving yourself . . .'
      b. huwa γulaamu ?in šaa?a llaahu bni ?axiika
          he   boy   if   wills God   son brother-your
          'He is, God willing, the vallet of your brother'

The deverbal noun (ia) patterns with verbs, which allows elements to intervene between it and the subject (chapter 8). This implies that the deverbal noun raises to a position higher than DP, in which case merger is with a copy. With respect to parenthetical elements (ib), which can also break up the CS even when it does not involve deverbal nouns, the situation seems to be similar to the well-known fact that in English where an expletive can break up a word (Aronoff 1976; McCawley 1978; Siegle 1978; McMillan 1980; McCarthy 1982).

(ii)   every-bloody-body

It is plausible that parenthetical elements are inserted postsyntactically at the prosodic edge of the two members of the CS.

12. The definiteness feature is also not spelled-out if the head noun carries a clitic.

(i)   a.   kitaabu-haa   SA
            book-her
            'her book'
      b. * l-kitaabu-haa
            the-book-her

Assuming that the clitic on the noun in (ib) carries definiteness features, the ill-formedness of (ib) follows if we assume that a lexical item cannot be doubly marked for the same feature (Marantz 1988).

Bibliography

Abu-Haidar, F. (1979) *A Study of the Spoken Arabic of Baskinta*. E. J. Brill, Leiden.

Alexiadou, A., and Anagnostopoulou, E. (1999) EPP without Spec, IP. In Adjer, D., Pintzuk, S., Plunkett, B., and Tsoulas, G., eds., *Specifiers: Minimalist Approaches*, pages 93–109. Oxford University Press, Oxford.

Aoun, J. (1978) Structure Interne du Syntagme Nominal en Arabe: l'idafa. *Analyses Theorie*, 2: 1–40.

Aoun, Y. (1981) Parts of Speech: A Case of Redistribution. In *Theory of Markedness in Generative Grammar: Proceedings of the 1979 Glow Conference*, pages 3–23. Pisa.

Aoun, J. (1996) Clitic-Doubled Arguments. Unpublished Manuscript, University of Southern California, Los Angeles.

Aoun, J., and Benmamoun, E. (1998) Minimality, Reconstruction, and PF Movement. *Linguistic Inquiry* 29: 569–597.

Aoun, J., and Benmamoun, E. (1999) Gapping, PG Merger, and Patterns of Partial Agreement. In Lappin, S., and Benmamoun, E. eds., Fragments: Studies in Ellipsis and Gapping, pages 170–187. Oxford University Press, Oxford.

Aoun, J., and Choueiri, L. (1997) Epithets. Unpublished Manuscript, University of Southern California, Los Angeles.

Aoun, J. and Li, Y.-H.A. (1993) Wh in-situ: Syntax or LF. *Linguistic Inquiry* 24.2: 199 238.

Aoun, J., Benmamoun, E., and Sportiche, D. (1994) Agreement and Conjunction in Some Varieties of Arabic. *Linguistic Inquiry* 25: 195–220.

Aoun, J., Benmamoun, E., and Sportiche, D. (Forthcoming) Further Remarks on First Conjunct Agreement. *Linguistic Inquiry* 30.

Aronoff, M. (1976) *Word Formation in Generative Grammar*. MIT Press, Cambridge.

Ayoub, G. (1981) *Structure de la Phrase en Arabe Standard*. Doctoral Thesis, Université de Paris VII, Paris.

Bahloul, M. (1994) *The Syntax and Semantics of Taxis, Aspect, Tense and Modality in Standard Arabic*. Ph.D. Thesis, Cornell University, Ithaca.

Bahloul, M., and Harbert, W. (1993) Agreement Asymmetries in Arabic. In Mead, J., ed., *Proceedings of WCCFL 11*, pages 15–31. CSLI, Stanford.

Baker, M. (1988) *Incorporation: A Theory of Grammatical Function Changing*, University of Chicago Press, Chicago.

Bakir, M. (1980) *Aspects of Clause Structure in Arabic*. Ph.D. Thesis, Indiana University, Bloomington.

Beard, R. (1995) *Lexeme-Morpheme Base Morphology*. State University of New York, Albany.

Benmamoun, E. (1992) *Inflectional and Functional Morphology: Problems of Projection, Representation and Derivation*, Ph.D. Thesis, University of Southern California, Los Angeles.

Benmamoun, E. (1993) The Status of Agreement and the Agreement Projection in Arabic. *Studies in the Linguistic Sciences* 23: 61–71. University of Illinois at Urbana-Champaign, Urbana.

Benmamoun, E. (1996) The Derivation of the Imperative in Arabic. In Eid, M., ed., *Perspectives on Arabic Linguistics IX*, pages 151–164. John Benjamins, Amsterdam.

Benmamoun, E. (1997) Licensing of Negative Polarity in Moroccan Arabic. *Natural Language and Linguistic Theory* 15: 263–287.

Berman, E., and Grosu, A. (1976) Aspects of the Copula in Modern Hebrew. In Cole, P., ed., *Studies in Modern Hebrew Syntax and Semantics*, pages 265-285. North Holland, Amsterdam.

Beukema, F., and Coopmans, P. (1989) A Government-Binding Perspective on the Imperative in English. *Linguistics*, 25: 417–436.

Bobaljik, J. (1994) What Does Adjacency Do? *MITWPL* 22: 1–31.

Bohas, G., and Al-Qaadirii, A. (1998) Des Faits, Des Grammariens et Des Linguistes. *Arabica* XLV: 297-319.

Borer, H. (1984) Parametric Syntax. Foris, Dordrecht.

Borer, H. (1986) I-Subjects. *Linguistic Inquiry* 17: 375–416.

Borer, H. (1988) On the Morphological Parallelism between Compounds and Constructs. In Booij, G. and van Marle, J., eds., *Yearbook of Morphology*, pages 45–65. Foris, Dordrecht.

Borer, Hagit. (1996) The Construct in Review. In Lecarme, J., Lowenstamm, J., and Shlonsky, U., eds., *Studies In Afroasiatic Grammar*, pages 30–61. Hollands Academic Graphics, The Hague.

Borg, A., and Azzopardi-Alexander, M. (1997) *Maltese*. Routledge, London.

Börjars, K., Vincent, N., and Chapman, C. (1996) Paradigms, periphrases and pronominal inflection: a feature-based account. Booij, G. and van Marle, J., eds., *Yearbook of Morphology*, pages 155–180. Kluwer, Dordrecht.

Bouchard, D. (1995) *The Semantics of Syntax: A Minimalist Approach to Grammar*. University of Chicago Press, Chicago.

Brame, M. (1970) *Arabic Phonology: Implications for Phonological Theory and Historical Semitic*. Ph.D. Thesis, MIT, Cambridge.

Bresnan, J. (1996) Optimal Syntax: Notes on Projection, Heads and Optimality. Unpublished Manuscript, Stanford University, Stanford.

Bresnan, J. (1997) Mixed Categories as Head Sharing Constructions. Unpublished Manuscript, Stanford University, Stanford.

Brockelmann, C. (1910) *Linguistique Sémitique*. Translated from German by Marçais, W. and Cohen, M. Librairie Paul Geuthner, Paris.

Bybee, J., Perkins, R., and Pagliuca, W. (1994) *The Evolution of Grammar.* University of Chicago Press, Chicago.

Camacho, J. (1997) *The Syntax of NP Coordination*. Ph.D. Thesis, University of Southern California, Los Angeles.

Carstairs-McCarthy, A. (1987) *Allomorphy in Infexion*. Croom Helm, London.

Caubet, D. (1991) The Active Participle as a Means to Renew the Aspectual System: A Comparative Study in Several Dialects of Arabic. In Kaye, A. S., ed., *Semitic Studies,* pages 207–224. Otto Harrassowitz, Wiesbaden.

Caubet, D. (1993) *L'Arabe Marocain*. Éditions Peeters, Paris.

Caubet, D. (1996) La Négation en Arabe Maghrébin. In Chaker, S., and Caubet, C., eds., *La Négation en Berbére eten Arabe Maghrébin*, pages 79–97. L'Harmattan, Paris.

Chomsky, N. (1957) *Syntactic Structures*. Mouton, The Hague.

Chomsky, N. (1964) *Current Issues in Linguistic Theory*. Mouton, The Hague.

Chomsky, N. (1991) Some Notes on the Economy of Derivation and Representation. In Freidin, R., ed., *Principles and Parameters in Comparative Grammar*, pages 417–454. MIT Press, Cambridge.

Chomsky, N. (1995) *The Minimalist Program*. MIT Press, Cambridge.

Cinque, G. (1999) *Adverbs and Functional Heads: A Cross-Linguistic Perspective*. Oxford University Press, Oxford.

Comrie, B. (1976) *Tense*. Cambridge University Press, Cambridge.

Cowell, M. (1964) *A Reference Grammar of Syrian Arabic*. Georgetown University Press, Georgetown.

Dahl, Ö. (1985) *Tense and Aspect Systems*. Blackwell, Oxford.

Déchaine, R.-M. (1993) *Predicates across Categories*. Ph.D thesis. University of Massachusetts, Amherst.

Doron, E. (1986) The Pronominal "Copula" as Agreement Clitic. In Borer, H., ed., *Syntax of Pronominal Clitics*, pages 313–332. Academic Press, New York.

Doron, E. (1996) The Predicate in Arabic. In Lecarme, J., Lowenstamm, J., and Shlonksy, U, eds., *Studies in Afroasiatic Grammar*, pages 77–87. Holland Academic Graphics, Leiden.

Eid, M. (1983) The Copula Function of Pronouns. *Lingua* 59: 197-207.

Eid, M. (1991) Verbless Sentences in Arabic and Hebrew. In Comrie, B., and Eid, M., eds., *Perspectives on Arabic Linguistics III*, pages 31–61. John Benjamins, Amsterdam.

Eisele, J. (1988) *The Syntax and Semantics of Tense, Aspect, and Time Reference in Cairene Arabic*. Ph.D. thesis, University of Chicago.

Emonds, J. (1978) The Verbal Comple of V'-V in French. *Linguistic Inquiry* 9: 151–175.

Ennaji, M. (1993) AGR and Clitics: The Morphology-Syntax Interface. Unpublished Manuscript, Faculte des Lettres, Fez.

Fassi Fehri, A. (1982) *Linguistique Arabe: Forme et Interpretation*. Publications de la Faculté des Lettres et Sciences Humaines, Rabat.

Fassi Fehri, A. (1988) Agreement in Arabic, Binding and Coherence. In Barlow, M., and Ferguson, C., eds., *Agreement in Natural Language: Approaches, Theories, Description*, pages 107–158. CSLI, Stanford.

Fassi Fehri, A. (1993) *Issues in the Structure of Arabic Clauses and Words*. Kluwer, Dordrecht.

Ferguson, C. (1983) God Wishes in Syrian Arabic. *Midsteranean Language Review* 1: 65–83.

Fleisch, H. (1979) *Traité de Philologie Arabe*. Librairie Orientale, Beirut.

Gamal-Eldin, S. (1967) *A Syntactic Study of Egyptian Colloquial Arabic*. Mouton, The Hague.

Gary, J. O., and Gamal-Eldin, S. (1982) *Cairene Egyptian Colloquial Arabic*. North Holland, Amsterdam.

Gray, L. H. (1934) *Introduction to Comparative Semitic Linguistics*. Philo Press, Amsterdam.

Grimshaw, J. (1997) Projections, Heads, and Optimality. *Linguistic Inquiry* 28: 373–422.

Haegeman, L. (1995) *The Syntax of Negation*. Cambridge University Press, Cambridge.

Hale, K. (1990) Some Remarks on Agreement and Incorporation. Unpublished Manuscript, MIT, Cambridge.

Halila, H. (1992) *Subject Specifity Effects in Tunisian Arabic*. Ph.D. Thesis, University of Southern California, Los Angeles.

Halle, M., and Marantz, A. (1993) Distributed Morphology. In Hale, K., and Keyser, S., eds., *The View from Building 20*, pages 111–176. MIT Press, Cambridge.

Harris, J. (1997) There Is No Imperative Paradigm in Spanish. In Martínez-Gil, F. and Morales-Front, A., eds., *Phonology and Morphology of the Major Iberian Languages*, pages 537–557, Georgetown University Press, Washington, D.C.

Hassan, A. (1973) *Al-NaHw Al-Waafii*. Dar Al Maarif, Cairo.

Hazout, I. (1990) *Verbal Nouns: Theta Theoretic Studies in Hebrew and Arabic*. Ph.D. Thesis, University of Massachusetts, Amherst.

Hazout, I. (1995) Action Nominalizations and the Lexicalist Hypothesis. *Natural Language and Linguistic Theory* 13: 355-404.

Heggie. L. (1988) *The Syntax of Copular Structures.* Ph.D. Thesis, University of Southern California, Los Angeles.

Hirschbühler, P., and Labelle, M. (1994) Changes in Verb Position in French Negative Infinitival Clauses. *Language Variation and Change* 6: 149–178.

Holes, C. (1990) *Gulf Arabic.* Routledge, London.

Iaaich, J. (1996) La Négation en Hassaniyya. In Chaker, S., and Caubet, D. eds., *La Négation en Berbére et en Arabe Maghrébin,* pages 163–176. L'Harmattan, Paris.

Iatridou, S. (1990) About Agr(P). *Linguistic Inquiry* 21: 551-577.

Jelinek, E. (1981) *On Defining Categories: Aux and Predicate in Colloquial Arabic.* Ph.D Thesis, University of Arizona, Tuscon.

Katz, J., and Postal, P. (1964) *An Integrated Theory of Linguistic Descriptions.* MIT Press, Cambridge.

Kayne, R. (1992) Italian Negative Infinitival Imperatives and Clitic Climbing. In Tasmowsky, L., and Zribi-Hertz, A., eds., *Hommages à Nicolas Ruwet,* pages 300–12. Communication and Cognition, Ghent.

Khalafallah, A. (1969) *A Descritptive Grammar of Saiidi Egyptian Colloquial Arabic.* Mouton, The Hague.

Klima, E. (1964) Negation in English. In Fodor, J. A. and Katz, J. J., eds., *The Structure of Language,* pages 246–323. Prentice Hall, Englewood Cliffs, New Jersey.

Krifka, M., Pelletier, F., Carlson, G., ter Meulen, A., Chierchia, G., and Link, G. (1995) Genericity: An Introduction. In Carlson, G., and Pelletier, F., eds., *The Generic Book.,* pages 1-124. University of Chicago Press, Chicago.

Laka, I. (1990) *Negation in Syntax: On the Nature of Functional Categories and Projections.* Ph.D. thesis, MIT, Cambridge.

Larcher, P. (1994) Ma Faala vs Lam Yafal: Une Hypothesèse Pragmatique. *Arabica* 41: 388–415.

Lasnik, H. (1981) Restricting the Theory of Transformations: A Case Study. In Horstein, N., and Lightfoot, D., eds., *Explanations in Linguistics. The Logical Problem of Language Acquisition,* pages 152–173. Longman, London.

Lasnik, H. (1995) Verbal Morphology: *Syntactic Structures* Meets *the Minimalist Program.* In Campos, H., and Kempchinsky, P., eds., *Evolution and Revolution in Linguistic Theory,* pages 251–275. Georgetown University Press, Washington, D.C.

Marantz, A. (1988) Apparent Exceptions to the Projection Principle. In Everaert, M., Huybregts, R., and Trommelen, M., eds., *Morphology and Modularity,* pages 217–232. Foris, Dordrecht.

Matar, A. (1976) *Dhawaahir Naadhira fii lahajaat l-xaliij l-'arabii.* College of Education, Quatar.

Mathews, P. H. (1974) *Morphology.* Cambridge University Press, Cambridge.

McCarthy, J. (1979) *Formal Problems in Semitic Phonology and Morphology.* Ph.D. thesis, MIT, Cambridge.

McCarthy, J. (1981) A Prosodic Theory of Non-concatenative Morphology. *Linguistic Inquiry* 12: 373-418.

McCarthy, J. (1982) Prosodic Structure and Expletive Infixation. *Language* 58: 574–590.

McCarus, E. (1976) A Semantic Analysis of Arabic Verbs. In Orlin, L. L., ed., *Michigan Oriental Studies in honor of George G. Cameron,* pages 3–28. The University of Michigan, Ann Arbor.

McCawley, J. (1978) Where You Can Shove Infixes. In Bell, A, and Hooper, J., eds., *Syllables and Segments,* pages 213-221. North Holland, Amsterdam.

McCloskey, J. (1986) Inflection and Conjunction in Modern Irish. *Natural Language and Linguistic Theory* 4: 245-281.

McCloskey, J. (1996) Subjects and Subject Positions. In Borsley, R. and Roberts, I., eds., *The Syntax of the Celtic Languages*, pages 241–283. Cambridge University Press, Cambridge.

McCloskey, J., and Hale, K. (1984) On the Syntax of Person-Number Inflection in Modern Irish. *Natural Language and Linguistic Theory* 1: 487–534.

McMillan, J. (1980) Infixing and Interposing in English. *American Speech* 55: 163–183.

Mohamed, I., and Ouhalla, J. (1995) Negation and Modality in Early Child Arabic. In Eid, M., ed., *Perspectives on Arabic Linguistics VII*, pages 69–90. John Benjamins, Amsterdam.

Mohammad, M. (1988) On the Parallelism between IP and DP. In Borer, H., ed., *Proceedings of WCCFL VII*, pages 241–254. CSLI, Stanford.

Mohammad, M. (1989) *The Sentence Structure of Arabic*, Ph.D. Thesis, University of Southern California, Los Angeles.

Mohammad, M. (1998) Just How Complex Is the Agreement System in Arabic. Paper presented at the Conference on Semitic Syntax, May 1–3, University of Southern California, Los Angeles.

Moritz, L., and Valois, D (1994). Pied-Piping and Specifier-Head Agreement. *Linguistic Inquiry* 25: 667–707.

Mouchaweh, L. (1986) *De la Syntaxe des Petites Prespositions*. Doctoral thesis, Université de Paris VIII, Paris.

Moutaouakil, A. (1987) *min qaDaayaa r-raabiT fii l-lugha l-'arabiyya.* 'ocaadh, Casablanca.

Moutaouakil, A. (1989) *Pragramatic Functions in a Functional Grammar of Arabic.* Foris, Dordrecht.

Moutaouakil, A. (1993) `l-waDhiifa wa l-binya. 'ocaadh, Casablanca.

Munn, A. (1993) *Topics in the Syntax and Semantics of Coordinate Structures.* Ph. D Thesis, University of Maryland, College Park.

Munn, A. (Forthcoming) First Conjunct Agreement: Against a Clausal Analysis. *Linguistic Inquiry* 30.

Noyer, R. (1992) *Features, Positions and Affixes in Autonomous Morphological Structure.* Ph.D Thesis, MIT. Cambridge.

Ouhalla, J. (1990) Sentential Negation, Relativized Minimality and Aspectual Status of Auxiliaries. *Linguistic Review* 7: 183–231.

Ouhalla, J. (1991) *Functional Categories and Parametric Variation.* Routledge, London.

Ouhalla, J. (1992) Focus in Standard Arabic. *Linguistics in Potsdam* 1: 65-92.

Ouhalla, J. (1993) Negation, Focus and Tense: The Arabic maa and laa. *Rivista di Linguistica* 5: 275–300.

Ouhalla, J. (1994) Verb Movement and Word Order in Arabic. In Lightfoot, D. and Hornstein, N., eds., *Verb Movement,* pages 41–72. Cambridge University Press, Cambridge.

Ouhalla, J. (1997) Remarks on Focus in Standard Arabic. In Eid, M., and Ratcliffe, R., eds., *Perspectives on Arabic Linguistics X*, pages 9–45. John Benjamins, Amsterdam.

Ouhalla, J. (Forthcoming) The Structure and Logical Form of Negative Sentences. *Linguistic Analysis.*

Owens, J. (1984) *A Short Reference Grammar of Eastern Libyan Arabic.* Otto Harrassowitz, Wiesbaden.

Palmer, F. R. (1986) *Mood and Modality.* Cambridge University Press, Cambridge.

Palva, H. (1972) *Studies in the Arabic Dialect of the Semi-Nomadic l-aarma Tribe.* Acta Universitatis Gothorburgensis.

Pollard, C., and Sag, I. (1994) *Head-Driven Phrase Structure Grammar.* University of Chicago Press, Chicago.

Pollock, J.-Y. (1989) Verb Movement, UG and the Structure of IP. *Linguistic Inquiry* 20: 365–424.

Progovac, L. (1994) *Negative and Positive Polarity*. Cambridge University Press, Cambridge.

Rapapport, T. (1987) *Copula, Nominal, and Small Clauses*. Ph.D. Thesis, MIT, Cambridge.

Ritter, E. (1987) NSO Noun Phrases in Modern Hebrew. In McDonough, J., and Plunkett, B., eds., *Proceedings of NELS 17*, pages 521–537. GSLA, Amherst.

Ritter, E. (1991) Two Functional Categories in Noun Phrases: Evidence from Modern Hebrew. *Syntax and Semantics* 25: 37–62

Ritter, E. (1995) On the Syntactic Category of Pronouns and Agreement. *Natural Language and Linguistic Theory* 13: 405–443.

Rivero, M.-L. (1994) Negation, Imperatives and Wackernagel Effects. *Rivista di Linguistica* 6: 39–66.

Rivero, M.-L. (1995) Imperatives, V-movement and logical mood. *Journal of Linguistics* 31: 301–332.

Rivero, M.-L., and Terzi, A. (1995) Imperatives, V-movement and Logical Mood. *Journal of Linguistics* 31: 301–332.

Rizzi, L. (1990) *Relativized Minimality*. MIT Press, Cambridge.

Rizzi, L. (1997) The Fine Structure of the Left Periphery. In Haegeman, L., ed., *Elements of Grammar*, pages 281–337. Kluwer Academic Publishers, Dordrecht.

Roberts, I. (1998) Have/Be Raising, Move F, and Procrastinate. *Linguistic Inquiry* 29: 113–125.

Schmerling, S. (1982) How Imperatives Are Special, and How they Aren't. In Schneider, R., Tuite, K., and Chametzky, R., eds., pages 202–218. CLS, Chicago.

Sells, P. (1996) Optimality and Economy of Expression in Japanese and Korean. Unpublished Manuscript, Stanford University, Stanford.

Shlonsky, U. (1992) Resumptive Pronouns as Last Resort. *Linguistic Inquiry* 23: 443-468.

Shlonsky, U. (1997) *Clause Structure and Word Order in Hebrew and Arabic: An Essay in Comparative Semitic Syntax*. Oxford University Press, Oxford.

Shlonsky, U. (1998) Subject Positions and Copular Constructions. Unpublished Manuscript, University of Geneva, Geneva.

Siegle, D. (1978) *Topics in English Morphology*. Garland, New York.

Siloni, T. (1997) *Noun Phrases and Nominalization: The Syntax of DPs*. Kluwer, Dordrecht.

Simone-Senelle, M.-C. (1996) Negation in Some Arabic Dialects of the Thaamah of the Yemen. In Eid, M., and Parkinson, D., eds., *Perspectives on Arabic Linguistics IX*, pages 206–221. John Benjamins, Amsterdam.

Sportiche, D. (1990) Movement, Agreement and Case. Unpublished Manuscript. UCLA, Los Angeles.

Steel, S. (1981) *An Encyclopedia of AUX: A Study of Cross-Linguistic Equivalence*. MIT Press, Cambridge.

Testen, D. (1994) On the Development of the Arabic Subjunctive. In Eid, M., Cantarino, V., and Walters, K., eds., *Perspectives on Arabic Linguistics VI*, pages 151–166. John Benjamins, Amsterdam.

Travis, A. (1979) *Inflectional Affixation in Transformational Grammar: Evidence from the Arabic Paradigm*. Ph.D. Thesis. University of Puerto Rico.

Tsai, W.-T.D. (1994) Economizing the Theory of A-bar Dependencies. Ph.D. Thesis, MIT, Cambridge.

Vanhove, M. (1996) The Negation maasii in a Yaafi`i Dialect (Yemen). In Eid, M., and Parkinson, D., eds., *Perspectives on Arabic Linguistics IX*, pages 195–206. John Benjamins, Amsterdam.

Watson, J. (1993) *A Syntax of Sanani Arabic*. Otto Harrassowitz, Wiesbaden.

Williams, E. (1994) *Thematic Structure in Syntax*. MIT Press. Cambridge.

Wise, H. (1975) *A Transformational Grammar of Spoken Egyptian Arabic*. Basil Blackwell, Oxford.

Woidich, M. (1968) *Negation und Negative SÄte in Ägyptisch-Arabischen*. Doctoral thesis, Universität zu München.

Wright, W. (1889) *A Grammar of the Arabic Language*. Cambridge University Press (1981) edition, Cambridge.

Yoon, H.- S. J. (1997) The Dissociation between External and Internal Syntax and Its Implications for Morphosyntax Interface. Unpublished Manuscript, University of Illinois, Urbana.

Youssi, A. (1992) *Grammaire et Lexique de L'Arabe Marocain Moderne*. Wallada, Casablanca.

Zanuttini, R. (1997) *Negation and Clause Structure: A Comparative Study of Romance Languages*. Oxford University Press, Oxford.

Zubizarreta, M.-L. (1998) *Prosody, Focus, and Word Order*, MIT Press. Cambridge.

Index